I0625758

Rainshine

♌

A book of dreams, by Jim Jordan

With filigree from Brandis Svendsen
Photographs by Ann McCormick
Drawings by Daniel Young
Cover art by Roger Adams of
Laser Guided Visions and
Oil paintings by
Santiago Ribeiro.

2nd Printing © 2025,
        Oblectation Press.
1st Printing, © 2010,
        Abecediary Press.
Both of Seattle, Washington, USA.

Writing and layout © 2010 Jim Jordan
Filigree © 2008 Brandis Svendsen
Photographs © 2008 Ann McCormick
Drawings © 2008 Daniel Young
Oil paintings © 2010 Santiago Ribeiro
Cover art © 2008 Laser Guided Visions
The above six, worked in conjunction on this book.

Quote on pg. 34 © 1997 Hollywood Pictures
Quote on pg. 48 ©1996 George Clinton, P-Funk
Wisdom and Love pg. 3 © Sri Nisargadatta Maharaj

Library of Congress Control Number: 2010900793
ISBN: 978-1957397023

Some (but not all) names have been changed or
completely invented in order to keep the innocent,
and not so much so, anonymous. Some of the images
in here are vividly real, some are imagined.
    ~ Remember, they are dreams.

Contents

Images

Some Pains I Have Had

Introduction

to the

2nd printing of Rainshine

The year is now 2025, and it has been fifteen years since the first printing of this book. Within this reboot, there are only a few edits in relation to spelling, attribution, and ultimately, this introduction is added to attune a new reader to the book, its context from within a different time, and is based on aligning this opus of my efforts from the past with today's new realities that are so vastly different from the time in which it was first created.

In the late 1990's and the early 2000's, I was regularly involved with productions on stages that featured me reading or singing the contents of this book. When I found myself living in Seattle, working on sculptures and learning about community, I got inspired to put this collection together so that a complete collection of my work could be available. Many people had been buying individual books from me that I made, and I wanted to create a piece that people could really enjoy for their homes. So from 2007, I began making it. Much to my chagrin, in the year 2010, during which this book was released, the American economy was in tatters. I had been living in Asia since 2007, until late 2009, and had missed the visceral experience of the cataclysm of the market shock that was punctuated by the fall of Enron, the housing crisis, and the cratering of the jobs market into which I naïvely meandered from a lovely couple of years in South Korea.

I released Rainshine in that time, imagining that it would transcend the climate and found that my blissful blindness to the reality on the ground was incompatible with a hope for sales.

Gifting, as a principle came to mind. I mean, I sold quite a few to wonderful people. There were openings, settings with people walking by for me to share them. I sold one to a famous musician here, a CEO of festival arts there, a few friends who were still well enough off to afford the book for being insulated by their own realities, a few folks who passed by the places I set up in festivals or at runway shows where I was promoting it… But ultimately, I gave away many of these books to people who wished to have them but couldn't afford them, and decided to not go beyond the first run at that time even though I had sold thousands of books, mostly chapbooks up to that point, containing exactly the contents of this book, but in a less organized layout. Instead, I edged towards getting regular work and found it incredibly difficult due to the economic climate of the time. I left America again, to a territory that I could count on for good pay and a healthy environment for production of arts and life. I left in 2010 for Vietnam.

Over the next ten years, I moved again to South Korea and eventually China, where I stayed for most of my recent time away. This re-release of *Rainshine* is in concert with my return to the United States, where I intend to stay for a respectable duration.

My new poetry is not in this book, but will be present in the upcoming book that is based on my time in China, currently with a working title of *Takin' the Long Road*. My favorite that you can look forward to is one about a dreamscape where physics laws are inverted! Built for my Chinese students in British curriculum courses, I went about educating them in a way that hopefully was more fun than what other vocabulary teachers might have offered. We had a good time and learned a bunch too. That book too, will be released on Oblectation Press in the near future. It will be more of a travelogue with occasional poetry rather than how this book is designed.

I hope this copy of *Rainshine* in your hand will be enjoyed. It is from a piece of time in my life during which I actively employed the power of poetry for social change, to relate emotions, to help keep ideas alive in the world. Since then, I've been distant from the world of poetic presentation in the cafes and theaters that it was otherwise homed in, in the past. My hope is that other people, like you, will find the energy within these pages that lived — Look for surprises like within the closing chapter, with its poetics and short stories, with its fiction about a labor strike and non-fiction about social advocates, as a poignant segment that holds a lot of heart for me. I hope that you take time there, intentionally, to allow yourself to be inspired, along with any of the other emotions you may experience for taking time with *Rainshine*.

The chapters are thoughtfully created so that you can shift from one mood to another. Do that! Don't let one mode (like the pain laid down in chapter four) own your experience for too long. Flip to other sections if you feel in a rut. Maybe mark what you've read, and your thoughts on the contents page. On the other hand, you can allow yourself the pleasure of staying in one mode if you like, as well…

And do us all a favor and hear these out loud. If you don't use your own voice, which you may like to do, take the time to imagine a person speaking, singing, or shouting these words. That cadence of human, spoken-voice is important. It is not a novel you hold in your hand today, but a collection of Poetry, Short Stories, and Things That Used To Be Songs.

Welcome to *Rainshine*~ May it take you places.

Jim Jordan AKA Jimmer Shine

01/01/2025

Introduction

to the

1ˢᵗ printing

Sitting in Yeosu, Korea to write this introduction, I'm realizing that this is the only portion of this book to've specifically been written while I've stayed here in Korea. I've spent two full years here focused on the creation of Rainshine, focusing on the format and visual structure. My mind's purely been in creation mode from materials at hand, rather than looking around for inspiration. Thoughts from this ever-so intrepid experience will be shared in other literary environments. But yeah, two years...

This book contains writings that are poems, short stories, things that used to be songs, and other assorted thoughts from a period of time stretching over 15 years. Mostly poetic, it is quite topically and structurally diverse. As such, I realized that while organizing the pieces into sets to break them down, if just a bit, that I found four main ideas and three separate "other" sections really kind of made themselves present. They are the 7 chapters.

"What Was" being an "other" column that is designed around ideas of what I have witnessed, either personally, or spiritually that I consider somehow connected to time. "Images," being the more esoteric of the three, containing poems and comments that are statements or linguistic paintings sort of, as if giving a snapshot of a feeling. And "Freestanding Poems," which acts as a container for pieces that could be, or have been, given venue alone – they are pieces that can stand on their own, as it were – in an aesthetic format well beyond the context of this hand-held tome of inspirations – I do hope they inspire you.

So the four named chapters of "Love," "Some Pains I Have Had," "The Music of Life," and "Surreal," stand otherwise as *chambers of sensation*, if you will. They are fairly focused chapters, and so, will not often deviate from their named theme. So if, while reading, a flavor has become too strong, for having read too much of the pain or the bliss – then turn the page by a grip. This is not a novel! Open at random and go to the beginning of the piece you've opened to, in order to have a fresh reading. Then, either read on from there or close the book and do it again. Also, if you want to read within a particular mood, you can reach for it.

That's not to say that I haven't given thought to how each inclusion flows into the next. On the contrary, I have spent many hundreds, if not thousands, of hours considering how the poems, stories, and words-otherwise, meet the pieces that they are collected with, and I've spent many hours creating what I believe to be a cohesive stream, from what were completely disconnected beforehand. It would be useful to consider background music while you're reading for a lot of the pieces within "The Music of Life," and a few others that you will notice are set up with a clear rhythm designed. As they were written to music, reading them plain, simply sounds kind of funny sometimes. You'll figure it out.

I think it would be fitting to give a quick thanks to the artists who have shared their work with me for Rainshine here. More is shared at the end of the book, in the Acknowledgements pages at the end of the book. Without the filigree from Brandis, the drawings from Daniel, the photographs from Ann, the reproductions of the oil and canvas work of Santiago, the assistance in Photoshop by 백정임, as well as the cover art design, subtitle, and lenticular cover production from Raja of Laser Guided Visions, I would not have completed this book in its current form. Their contributions were elemental and very simply, allowed this book to be born into reality.

Sometimes, while sitting still, I write. When I was young, the only understanding I had of writing was artistic (thanks Mom!). Formal styling came rather late for me. I started writing young, so *all* of what I wrote was art. It's all I knew and understood at the time. Teachers and friends started asking for my work in bulk before I graduated high school – this collection is a continuation of that theme.

In creating *Rainshine*, I have tried to create the kindest container for words I have put down that I can. "I'm trying to build a really cool noun," is something that I've said more than a few times these last few years in the process. I hope that you enjoy the format here. Blake inspired me, but I can't draw worth bones. The contributions from the others really let it be.

While I've created this for people around me, I've noticed I don't have a "target audience." Pieces in here go in every direction – sweet pieces for grandparents – angry rants – psychedelic meditations – historical fiction and non-fiction. The base is simply too wide for "Oh, I'm aiming for the 18-25 crowd," or "Just the hippies please," or "Oh, it's a kid's book."

No, this book is aimed at the psychographic of "People who want to own a tome of written English created as art." So I hope that the emergence of *Rainshine* will be that for you.

Sept. 22, 2009

Jim Jordan

Questions

I can't figure out what my poetry is for. Can it change people and the way things are? Is everything the way it's supposed to be or can we be instrumental? OK, there it is. To be instrumental. But to what tones? Tones of hope? Tones of profound realization? Tones of the path taken on the way to a profound realization? How to manifest this? Do I start with a list of issues that need to be spoken to? What level of inspiration should...

This book is dedicated to all the people who don't quite get poetry yet. I sure as anything don't. It is also dedicated to all the people who live within the aesthetic ~ and simply don't desire escape. I sure don't. This book is dedicated to all the people who are lovers or know pain. May you be cosmic or plain, medicated or sane, this book is for you. You inspired it.

People Want to be Entertained!!

Laughter is good for the digestion.
~Nietzsche

Freestanding Poems

The Mightiest Weapon

I've heard the pen is mightier than the sword.
Yet all a pen's good for is relating word for word,
What someone thought of, that no one has seen before.
Poured out in an order,
One by one,
Conceiving next year's lore.

An idea, a thought, a meditation.
An absolvement, a writ, or a realization.
The pen, conceivably, could move the highest mountain.
It's been known to topple civilizations.

In the past, words are what have ended oppressive rules.
In the future, my intention is to use it as a tool.
The pen is what makes it possible
For a position to be heard.

They were wrong
When they said
That the pen was any different…

The pen is a hugely powerful sword.

2

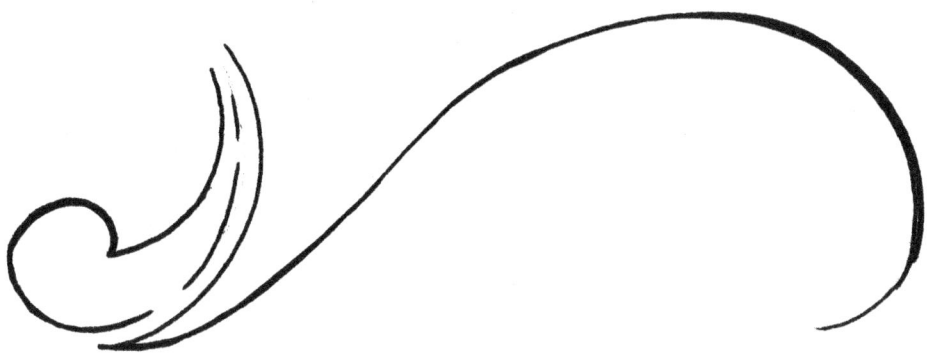

Wisdom and Love

When I realize that I am nothing,
That is Wisdom.
When I realize that I am everything,
That is Love;
And between these two,
My life moves.

An echo of Sri Nisargadatta Maharaj

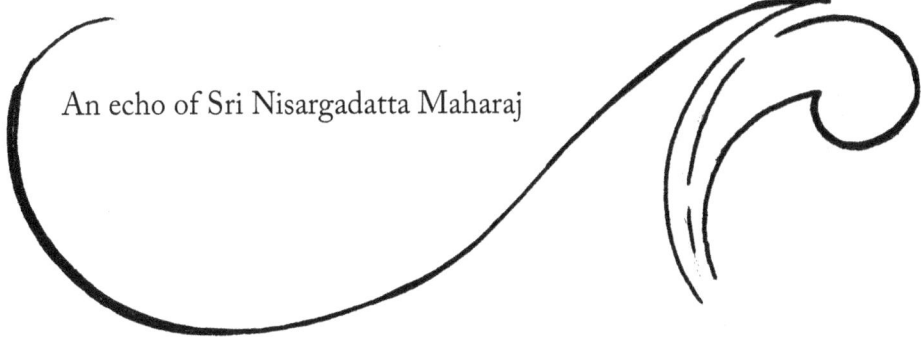

A Poem with No Name...

Our resistance to the wind
Made us grin
So many years ago.
But yo, so many miles
Have past since last time
Your rhyme came my way;
And all I can say
As I sway in the breeze
With broken knees,
Holdin' on for my life, is
I've meditated on a
More fluid world,
All curled
Up in a ball
With y'all.

A planet, I hear it's
Called.

There are all these lovely
Languages, many customs;
Often, people interact.

Acting is of a stage,
And a sage of the humans once said that
"All the world's a stage
And we are all but actors,"
Meaning: We interact while living.

Funny how things
Seem pro-
Found.

4

A Pause for Lauren

All the profundities in the world can't give the pleasure of knowing that you're loved.

There are only so many profound thoughts that can help someone. Sometimes I'm sure that there are just not enough Buddhists. There seem to be way to many people that enjoy the act of the kill. There are simply too many people that seem to be secure by hating and by excluding others… I guess they're just paranoid, that they don't know how to love and trust. I know that I'm that way sometimes, I just think that there are some people that need to foster up.

I wish I knew how to be nicer. There seem to be too many people that are simply not profound. Too many people that are comfortable doing things that hurt the world. I haven't been able to buy a steak for years. I haven't been able to go to a fast food joint for years. I haven't been able to drink a coke in days. There are so many things that mean so much.

5

I wish I knew how to cry. My cousin Lauren is no longer among the living, and I don't think that she wanted it any other way. I almost cried for her, I screamed a few times. The eyes did get wet, they itched, I scratched. Just didn't have the depth of pain that was needed for them to fall. I know that she hated being alive. I know that she felt better on the way out. It hurts to know that she had that much pain. But she did.

She was loved. I loved her. She was a beautiful person. She was an incredible baker in homes and professional kitchens. She was an incredible artist. She was so down with the groove of cool swoops and colors. She was a visual artist. It was far out what she could do. I miss her…

Gotta pause sometimes.

Surfin' the Buddha

Many days float lightly,
So many others weigh a ton.
Sometimes we find love nightly,
Sometimes what we find is just fun.

I've seen days where I slip up;
Me and my pride can fall flat on my back.
Other days everything slides perfect,
Where not a single thing's lacked.

I figure the balance
Is what it's all about.
I'm just "Surfin' the Buddha."
That's the name of my route,

Because I dig the semi-spiritual,
And what just plain makes sense.
But still, I'm okay with knowing that
Things'll be weird at times.
Yo,
'Cause though I try hard,
I know I'm here –
Just by chance.

6

No Roads Lead Home

Home can not be understood by many today.
Home is a place that can be found through Way;
A way or path like Taoism, Christianity, Buddhism,
Artistry, or Corporate Living offer to give.

All ways and paths are like roads,
And when traveled, new sights and experiences
Will occur.
So home is always changing, because we come from a
New, greater past.
Home is a concept that will truly, always last.

So you see,
Roads don't lead home;
Because home is at the head of the road in the
First place.

Home really leads the road.

7

Poetry Changes with the Earth

It seems that the nature of poetry changes with the Earth.
Today, I can write:

I sit in a strip mall
Coffee shop
And watch the trees
Turn colors;
Up there, where
The water tower stands.

When, years ago, someone wouldn't have been able to mention the strip malls or even the water tower – it would've been just the trees. We'd have seen something more like:

Ah, the changing
And rearranging of the
Emotions of the trees,
As they say, "Please look at me!
I'll be different soon."

It's funny, I think, how personification of the trees only happened in the second piece. Though I wrote them both, I gave more emotion and spirituality in the piece I called possible from older times.

Representatively, I see this as showing a kind of basic or formatic revolution within the world of spiritual concepts as of late. This poetic or spiritual revolution is directly connected to the dozens of other revolutions that have occurred within the realm of humanity through the last 250-300 years.

Revolution shows that someone feels revolted, and as such revolts, causing the stated revolution. This revolution is incurred by the revoltee from a revolter, who in turn revolts the said revoltee. Therefore the initial revolutionary is revolted by a revolting revolutionary reality, may it be physically human, commercial, industrial, spiritual, etc. – causing the revolution, resulting in yet another revolution, which then in turn, revolts somebody, making them feel like they need to revolt. It's a cycle due to their deposed disposition.

And so, just as with Earth and Humanity; Poetry changes in revolutionary bounds, naturally.

9

Poetry is still, as it always has been, linguistic expression. Its form though, is what changes. Form, on account of the changing environment must alter, in order to contain the new reality.

An Invitation

Come all ye people
Black, white, male, female;
Come to my world,
Where unity prevails.

10

Where we do not look
At your sex, creed or color;
We don't even ask
'Bout your father or mother.

Come all ye Buddhist,
Catholics, Zen, Muslims, or Jews;
Come to my world
Where we all start anew.

We will leave this world,
So mean and so cruel –
To such a wonderful place,
Where love shall rule.

This world we now live in
Was not made for us.
We must go to a place
Where we can love and trust.

I think of this place
So far, far, away
Where honesty and love
Will reign all night and day.

All this fighting and hatred,
I cannot live with;
I tell of this place –
People say it's a myth.

I cannot believe
What they say to be true.
All we need is the strength,
And that strength comes from you.

11

For B-Tree

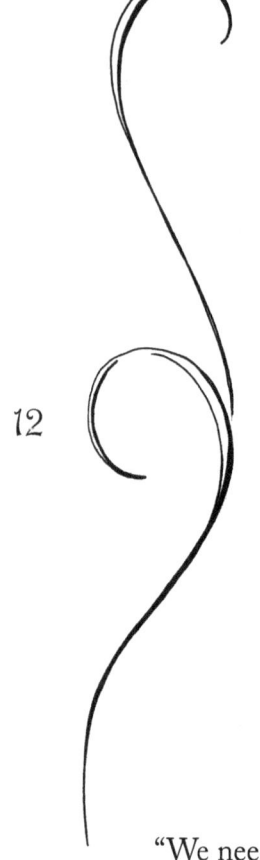

To disassociate my brain
From rushing forward all insane,
I squeeze my thoughts.
And it seems I've fought so
Goddamn much,
I'm getting out of touch.

I wanna paint the
White house paisley,
And have sex out on the grass
On a summer day.

I wanna drive downtown
With a good conscience.
Oil is seeping to far
Into our way.

We simply need to
Refigure what it is we say,
And how it is we play.

"We need to live simply, such that others may simply live..."

That statement has such serious meaning.

We need to argue less
About how we stress,
So that we don't have to guess
If we'll make it as a species,
Or if we'll kill ourselves
Someday.

What can one man say today?
I might say "Kenaf."
You may laugh,
But, yea, kenaf.

It's a reed, not like a good book,
But like a big bush.
We can make our paper of the future from it,
See VisionPaper.com, they're already doing it.

As closure, I just want to say:
I spoke to a friend 'bout poetic suicide.
I guess I really just wanna glide
Through all the natural elements I see.
Because you ask me, I wanna
Build.
Build, move, build and grow!

Forgive me B-Tree for borrowing your great phrase,
But in my haze, I'm the only you that's here.

You're away, out East
Fighting a war that's
So near, we can hear
From the distance, the bombs
In your mind.
I hope that they dissolve towards
Your peace man.

Move, Build, Grow!!

13

continued –>

So we can sew
Our dreamed illusions.
Too many confusions
That I see, just don't plain need to be.

*   *   *

So we can jam!!

Because the scam
Is to seek evolution.
We don't have to revolt for solution.
We can make it beautiful,
If we would exercise
More than our eyes.

Makes me think about
Where we've gone.

Makes me think about
What we've thrown,

And whether we've grown,
Or if we've sewn seeds of weeds
In the reeds.

Makes me wonder 'bout all the trees.
And about how it is we seize on
What it is to move, build and grow.
Wow.

14

There's so much pain.
But it, is
To dissolve itself,
And that is its purpose.
Pain allows for focus,
Pain provides the chaos,
Pain will be loss, and yet found.
It will be healed by sound,
And kill, yet hopefully, smoothly,
And not so rough. – Makin' it tough
To dissolve itself – or solve itself,
As in unity's pain, to believe we're sane.

Makes a head refrain.
Complain all you want,
But punt all concepts
To see where they go –>
So they may grow
Hopefully.

15

Memorable

16

Constructive ontological consideration

Pens, I use a lot of them because I notice they dry up,
Or end up stolen or lost...
I have one from twelve years back.
I'd like to think that out of my success at great,
Short relationships,
I'd like to be with someone who wouldn't leave town.
"Aw debt!" has been in my thoughts since before I knew Sophia.
As I pen that name, I remember who and what I owe.

Time

In February, I'm Black.
In March, shakin' off ice crystals to Spring.
In April, I'm a poet,
Though I know I should be always.
In May, I'm getting a little older.
In June, I hope I'm sunnin' somewhere.
I don't like the word "July."
August reminds me of a real good person.
September may be somewhere new.
October's Ma's birthday.
Now I'm Great-full-living –
Told Gran-mama she got a promotion.

De 'J

17

Is Socrates Guilty?

Socrates was as guilty as the sky is blue.
That is what I'm here to tell you.
Did he corrupt the youth of the day?
You bet he did.
He had what the old folks didn't dig,
And that was reason.

He would go out and talk about
His theories on the seasons,
While bashing the old folks about!

He knew how to speak like he was singing a song.
He felt that, someday, they'd come along
On his reasoning trip he was on.

They called him a philosopher
Because he loved wisdom more than anything else.
What he was doing, was trying to do
Was get some answers to questions he'd asked his self.

If he couldn't find an answer there,
He would go and ask someone else
That he held in some type of high regard.
He was driven one time to ask an oracle
A burning question that had lingered on his mind
For some time.

It said that he was the wisest.
He couldn't believe it.
What was up with his mind?

Why did it seem like he was the first
To ask questions that the answers to
Might not be just what the questioned parties
Involved wanted to hear above all?
Is what he did right?

Is there another question we might want to ask ourselves?
"Could he have done more?"
After all, he found a lot of problems with society,
But all he did was talk about them.
There was no other action than that.
He succeeded in getting his point across so much so,
He was immortalized in the pages that fill our books.

He was guilty all right,
But it's a guilt that within, we all should dabble.
Otherwise, we could be rightly considered rabble.

So next time you sit down to a bong hit, a cold beer,
Or a pizza that you're splitting with friends,
Remember to reflect, and consider
All that has to do with amends.

The Cowboy

A long, long, time ago,
A cowboy opened up shop.
He went down to the hotel
To begin to sell his crop.

The officer on duty
Informed him of his rights,
Took him downtown,
And put under lights,

The stuff he was growin',
And then he was shown
The room he would
Spend many nights...

Wondering 'bout lost days,
What he could've been doin',
With the time he missed out on,
With the life he's now ruined.

This cowboy they say
Is now living abroad,
With a Costa Rican housewife
Whose company makes her seem kinda odd.

To those who don't know this cowboy
From the days of long ago,
He's really a pleasant fella,
Just misunderstood.

Two Friends Are a Thing

Two friends are so good
      For itself, yea.
Telling each other their goodness
      For each other.
Like a brother, or a sister, only works.

Dag.

Two friends are good for each other.
      Hearin' the goods, well,
Gives confidence.

Confidence is a motivational force
      That is able to be so positive
That its sight alone is
      Enough to cheer someone else.

Sometimes it takes
Someone else to see
The goods in another person.

Yea, see, when a person
Gets down
Or something like that,
They need to hear
What they've got goin' for em —
They might forget.

      Yea,
Friends are good stuff.

It's a crazy,
Mixed up,
Phucked up, world.

When I look around,
I wonder just how it got
So twirled.

But then I remember
The voter turnout,
That day in November.

How did it happen this way?
People boycott the vote
Sayin' how little it matters.
Now our constitution's in tatters.

We got a world of war lookin' at us
Through binoculars
At the remnants of Nixon/Ford
And Ronald Reagan's regime.

How did it happen this way?
What can anyone say?
It's such a lovely world;

It's gonna have some explosions
That for a while, are gonna seem absurd.

But as the Love Flag flies,
The anger will die.
We've just got to sigh
A few extra times,
So that the chimes
Of Goodspace can echo.

The
Echo of
Goodspace

22

Friendship

All sorts of people come across our planet. All sorts of people come across the way and path we choose. If we meet someone that we enjoy traveling with in our life's flow, we should let that person know that they are enjoyed. We should try and make that person feel like a part of the plan. There are too many distractions in the world, too much stimuli.

Sharing time together is a refuge from the storm. That person is a remembrance of our own mortality, of our own finiteness, in a way that looks back at us with probing questions and soothing touches, such that we are forced to questions ourselves, and be comfortable with that at the same time.

23

We are accidents of nature, or fated with unknown quests. Either way, honest companions are helpful. To be able to share a feeling with someone that will share one back, keeps a feeling alive, helps it survive. To have one alone without a receiver, almost wastes it it can seem.

I have to wonder if there's a lesson in the notion that a professional killer can say that when killing, he can see in a person's eyes whether or not the person who is about to die has known love in their life; that those who have, emit a look of peace; and those who have not, show fear at that ultimate time.

I wonder how a minister can administer last rights to a dying congregation of hospice patients on a regular basis. Such selflessness and balance in one's self… I think it's courage; grace under pressure. I wonder if Dr. Seuss was adept at diffusing latent turmoil naturally, or if he had help.

To be fearless when death smiles a welcome. To be kind when pain is near. To be hopeful when times are good and bad, and never disdaining a good tear. To be honest when lies would be welcome. For kidding around during idol time. For making up new stories. This is what a friendship is about.

Perseverance

For Aunt Tommie

So I was thinking, as I was blinking,
Strutting on through some stuff.
Though it was tough, so really rough,
I rolled the sluff, and just kept on going.

And so I went on.
See I was bent on,
This certain gentle thing –

Just to bring
A frame of mind,
That will not mind
Taking the path it takes; to get where's I
Was supposed to be, in my perceptual state of mind –

And as I find myself here thinking such,
I remember the clutch;
The where I get,
Is a point in the path itself.

And as this is seen, I think a fresh clean scene
With a larger screen for wider consideration
Brings abilities for continuation more to a head.

Perseverance was what was impressed upon me from my
Grandparents' generation.

So I have optimism,
For the known, internal, light.

On Thinking Differently

In order for one to have thought individually,
One must have decided to question…
Question what it is to be doing the things
That we do, and do well.

Occasionally, our findings are not
What would be seen as pleasant;
They are gross.
We somehow feel the need to revolt.

Remember what revolution is…

25

It is rapid evolution, it is to evolve once again.
With new information, we are forced to think differently than
We had in the past.

Every new byte of information
Pushes us towards being an info-nation.
We rapidly grow intellectually,
Yet succumb to degradation continually.
The general knowledge of the populous at large
Has multiplied in the last hundred years
Dramatically.

Often-times, the knowledge distorts, warps,
Or alters a person for the worse.
People sometimes don't know what to do
With the knowledge they contain,
And literally, go crazy.

Those of us that do make it through
The gauntlet of knowledge spewing entities,
Must attempt to change the world for the better.

If I Should Die

If I should die
And you are around,
Put a joint behind my ear.

26

Because if there's one thing
That I want in the afterlife,
It ain't gonna be a cold beer.

Everything that someone
Can sing, comes from the soul.
Even Rock and Roll,
In these days in the haze –

We're grazing on the amazing –

The fazing out of symptomaticization…
Democratization is a fantasy for
Everyone that I ever met.

The things we do forget…
We definitely later regret.

Grazing on the Amazing

27

Infusion –

I wish I could lesson confusion.

The shot — The agent bent the concept dramatically.

Fanatically, I give notions
Of intel-potions for the
Motions of our thoughts,
So maybe I will have brought
A bit of change to what I see to be strange.

The king's warriors are
Now more numerous than ever.
I think I've found what might be the right lever
For changing these things.
Ooo, the random springs
Of activity – nonpassivity
As resistance force. Ooo,
What is the FORCE?

Letter to a Boomer

As children, you yelled "Revolution!"
You got what you asked for.
Now as adults, you have your world,
But your children are now ravaged by war.

What you said years ago,
Scared your parents by the masses.
What in essence, you told them,
Was for them to kiss your asses.

28

As children of your generation,
We don't appreciate it much,
That you're singing the same tune
To those who are in your clutch.

Please try to remember
That you brought us here,
And don't ever forget
How much a child needs an ear.

For we are not all crazy,
We just don't know what to do.
You tell us to follow your principles,
When rejecting them is what is taught by you.

All I can say,
Is that we're hurting inside.
Your war-torn babies
Are about out of pride.

This, as you know,
Is what makes our country so great,
But there is something that is leading us
And it's teaching us to hate.

"Who is it," I wonder,
"That's leading our kids today?"
By definition, a leader,
Is one who shows the way.

29

Up to this point,
This has been your job.
Now stop for a moment,
And look around at this mob,

Of children you have raised
With "Revolution!" as your cry.
Now you've won your war,
But you haven't stopped yelling.
All I can do is ask "Why?"

But, as a favor to your children,
I do have a request;
That you listen to your children,
And give the yelling a rest.

Gary the Squirrel

Gary a kind, little squirrel,
Was a hard working man.
He worked in the daytime,
And ran on foraged bran.

At the beginning of the summer, once every year,
He got one day free
To do with as he pleased.
This year, he went to the sea.

A picnic was his plan,
For his day of R & R.
It happened this way every year,
His friends would come from afar.

But this year his R.S.V.P.'s were nil.
Not a one of his friends wrote back.
He wondered how it could be,
He thought to himself "Maybe it's me."
Then out of the forest
Came a CRACK!

A gunshot was heard,
By Gary the Squirrel.
He then saw quite plainly,
He was the last creature in the whole wide world

Left to run around free,
With the wind and the trees and the sky.
Gary then shuddered at the realization
That he too, soon would die.

Gary sat and cried, for quite a while,
Down by the beach, for he was all alone.
He'd lived quite a life, this Gary we call a squirrel;
He had lived just long enough to see his world turn to stone.

30

The world's forests are being stripped clean,
By a particular creature called "Man."
When asked of the reason behind this destruction
The answer is "Just because we can."

Well, I don't believe that ability transcends privileges.
I don't see in nature where else that is true.
We are the only known creatures that destroy just for fun!
This destruction must stop.
But the beginning of the end, must be initiated by you.

...

Then Gary went on home,
On that frigid, fateful day;
And he noticed a bit more plainly
His passings along the way.
He noticed that there were no birds
Soaring in the mid-summer breeze.
The gasses now polluting the air
Were enough to make a man wheeze.

And with no clean air,
We can have no clean dirt.
The rain from the sky,
Instead of helping, now hurts.
And with no clean dirt,
We can have no clean water,
For the runoff
Runs off from the hills.

And without the water,
Where are we left?
And what about those,
To which this is all theft?
Those like Gary and me,
Who are creatures of the Earth.
For we are in need of a homeostatic environment,
And have been ever since birth.

What's in a Name?

Life seems like a magician's whim
Each time I turn around
And say to someone "Jim."

They would've asked: "What's your name?"
It's such a truly simple frame.

But all the same,
Since it's not Tim, or Tom, or Bob;
The bomb seems to've been dropped,
And lopped was a dread of a head;
No longer dead,
Alive again.
No more pain.

Like an opium -
Wanna Utop~AM again.
Ain't gonna pretend.
It seems I've found a new friend
Who can honestly, truly, mend
Oh, what I want to send!

I want to make the whole world brighter.
I want to be a fighter.
I wanna be tighter
Than any living rapper.
I wanna be a toe tapper, and a writer.

Could it be lighter?
Could it be brighter?
"What kinda lightning is needed?"
I pleaded one time, in rhyme, in the summertime.
And I'm still tryin' to be flyin', even though I have no wings.
So I'll keep bein' the one who sings on any bus.

I think it's us that brought me here –   33
What is dear to me is to be free
And help others be that way –

Who can bring a new day but God?
So that's odd to some,
Let them thumb from place to place
Lookin' for the days
That they'll be happy, and see what they can find
While on the Earth.

Like a rebirth,
One thing that is truly tragic,
Is unrealized magic.

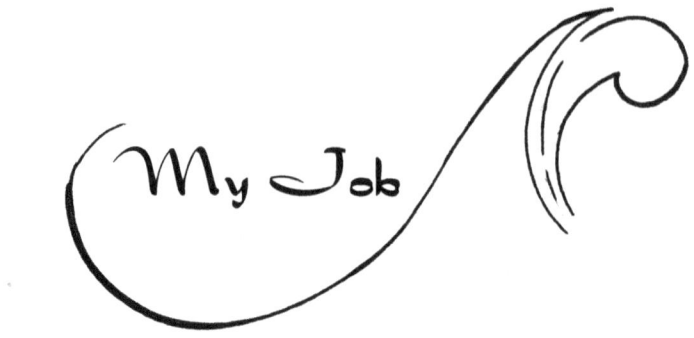

34

"I wasn't raised in a loving environment.
It's not an excuse, it's a reason.
My soul was empty,
It's my job to fill it."

From: GrossPointBlank. –Martin.

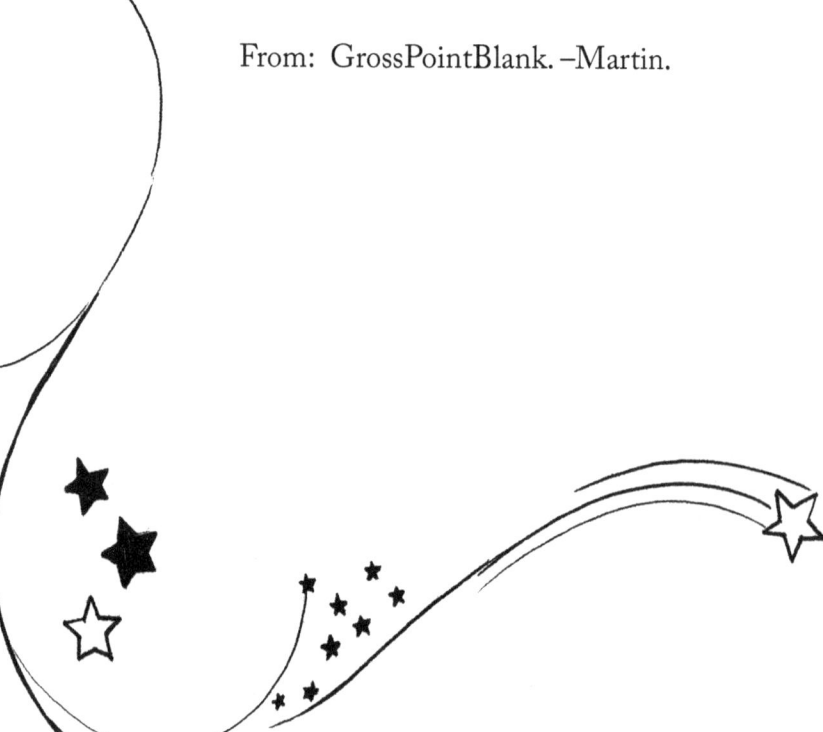

...Trying to answer the question.

...Trying to question the answer.

...Trying to find the answer
    To the question implied.

...Trying to find who lied,
    And still answer the question.

...Trying to answer the tried,
    And know all the questions.

...Trying to answer the question implied.

35

...Trying to be one
    Who simply went and tried.

...To question the answer implied.

...Trying to question the answer implied!

...Trying to answer the question
            – Implied.

Got to Keep Trying...

Memo on Jews by a Virtuous Catholic Soul

Twinkling of the stars
Illuminated the eve,
Of which thousands of the persecuted
Prepared there for their leave

Of the homeland, which was
The most pleasant of lands,
'Till the horsed men came 'round,
And with them the sands:

36

Those that would blow
Right into the hearts,
Of those which had followed
One of the most powerful of starts

Of thought and creation.
I hear of them quite well.
But regardless of the fact
That they started us out,
We tell them their place is in Hell.

She Found You to be a Rapist

I like her style. I like her grace.
I like how she punched you,
Right smack in your face.
You'll be castrated and berated,
Because you don't understand lace.

You're bleeding badly.
For that, I'm laughing madly,
Until I see a trace
Of a tear, rolling down
Her tender, glowing cheek.

37

You punishment is to subdue,
So we don't have to see you again.
Now my attention is focused on her.
We're trying to learn how to live life again.

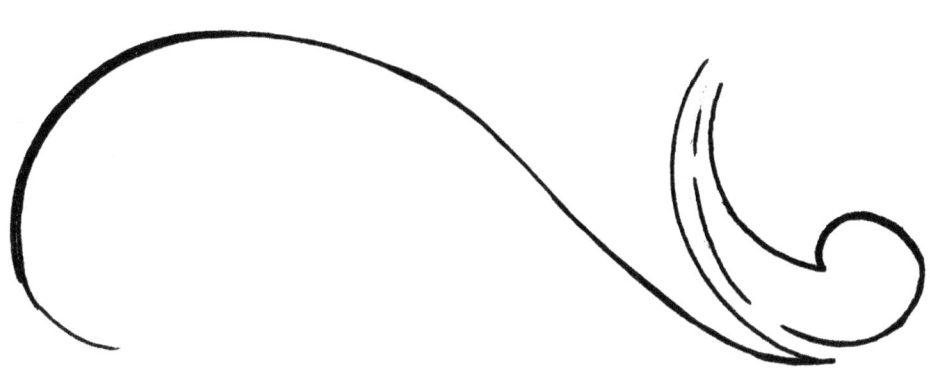

On a Leaf

Floating down a stream
I dream...

The heat is beating down.
The water beckons me to drink, but I cannot.
The stench is the heated aroma of decay,
And I dream of release.

As I journey through the current
I experience turbulence.
I realize my mortality.
I anticipate the next section of rapids.

Yes, they will bring more toil,
More trouble, and pain.
But each time, it hurts a little less.
With my dream, I even feel safe.

My dream, as it takes me away,
Acts as a shelter as I drift.
I dream of where I am going to,
Though I know not what I'll see.

I dream of a painless journey
Into an abyss of no melee.
I dream myself into another level of consciousness.
I dream myself until I'm free.

Free of the rocks, stray branches,
And anything else I should meet.
I dream myself near oblivious,
Yet still I can not retreat.

The water still rushes swiftly,
And I am tossed to and fro in the stream.

I ache; there's no one to help me.
I pain, and nobody cares.
I'm lonely with no one beside me.
I scream and nobody hears.
With no end in sight,
I think that I might
Envelop myself in my dream.

39

Hackysacking

The sun beats warmly on our backs.
The girls are all watching from the shade.
With a hackysack and a downtown to play in,
I believe I've got my summer made.

The intensity usually rises when KC is around,
He's said to be the best hackysacker to be found.

Ah, here comes Burnout,
With his ebony, flowing mane.
He gets a bad rap for the name that he bares
Because the fact remains

That when you need to know something,
You know just who to ask.
I respect him for keeping his head on straight.
He's really got a grueling task,

One that takes commitment and courage.
You wouldn't believe how much grass he smokes,
Yet he continues to retain his composure
Through a hail of incoming tokes.

My turn. Bam! "Rainbow!"
Oh, what a beautiful sport!
"Let's take a break for a joint now guys."
This'll probably be short.

It's hard to stop playing once you get started.
An addiction to the game can get bad.
That's what, they say, happened to KC.
'Cause when KC can't play, he gets mad.

I just keep on taking it
In my typical moderate style.
I'll even sit down and say I'm beat
Just so I can watch for a while.

40

THE eSSeNCe OF perpleXtioN.

...

LOVE

The hedgehog plays in the sun

ON A RAINY DAY

Dripping rainbows,

olive Green ... Seas!

You're a Dove

I say,
    I say,
        I say,
        Here we are,
                Livin' on this star
                        Of a planet.

Can it really be
        That you have set me
             Into a groove,
                Where I want to move
                    Myself off a shelf, into
            Activity known as "your creature"?
Double feature…

Would you feature me
        In your world?

        I know you're swirled
            In your existence.
                Please don't meet me with resistance.
            What I'm asking of you is, "please be a friend."
            I believe we can mend
                Tares of our wares that
                    We carry with us.
                      Yes,
              \(:^)*
Join me on my myth bus tonight…
        It'll be all right,   Come on!
            It's time for the dawn.
            We got to be gone.
        The night is over.
            The light is clover,

42

'N you got four leaves on you.
I believe that it's true
That I got lucky to find you;
En I'll stand behind you
Whenever you need,
Even in front of you, if you want me to.
I'll be there for you.
See that I'm speaking truth.   There ain't no sleuth
That's gonna find nothin'   But a little love button
Cuttin' through my shirt.   It doesn't even hurt.
It kinda feels good.
I guess it should.   En it kinda could
Be the best thing in the world,
So swirled;
See me as your brother.
There ain' no other I see in the same light as you.

When the sky's so blue,
I wanna see you   smile,
Like it's been a while
Since ya felt that good.

See, this bird loves to love,
And you're a dove to me.

43

Love

44

Roses have thorns,
And trees have trunks.
With love we all mourn,
Makin' us all look like punks.

Love is filled with grandeur,
Happiness and joy.
Love will toss you in an ocean,
Like a child with a toy.

Love can be as beautiful
As flowers in the sun.
Love can be wonderful,
With it, you can have fun.

Your Trace

You loved me and shoved me for just as well.
I can tell that you are really love incarnate,

And in spirit.

I can hear it when I'm thousands of miles away,
And these days your trace has shown me

45

That no longer must I groan –
I dig that.

Uncharted and Wild

I reach to you, yearning;
    Fill me up with energy.

    I reach to you,
        Yearning.

    Fill me up with Energy.

I feel the fire burning,
The spark is alive inside of me.
    The wind begins to blow,
    And I know
        That you are near.

I hear the whisper in my ear.
The message comes so clear

        To that spot inside
    That does not know
Of noise and clutter and thought.

    The angel, the child,
    Uncharted and wild,
    You're mystically styled.

May you emanate for eons.

46

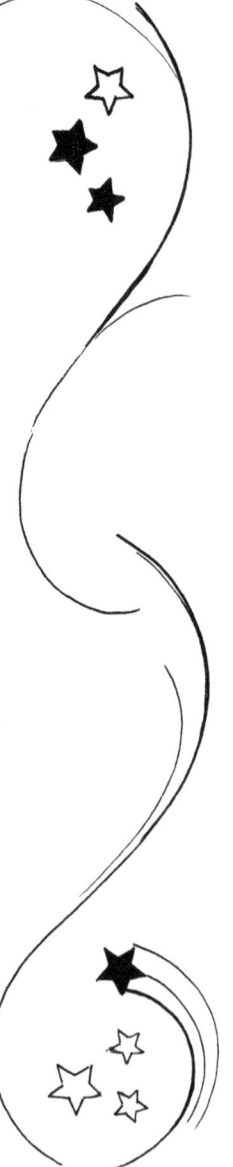

A Little Gift

A little gift
Can lift a heart
So much it can start
To radiate.

Radiation can be good.

This, you can now see.
An' baby, just maybe,
One day it'll be

That every anybody

Can walk around with me
Or you,
And not have to feel blue
For how they are treated.

Oh, the street, it
Has too many stories
That are way too gory.

I want to feel like I live in a time
That rhyme or love can
Actually make a difference.

I guess I'll get to maybe see
After the gift I have goes free.

What would you let be?

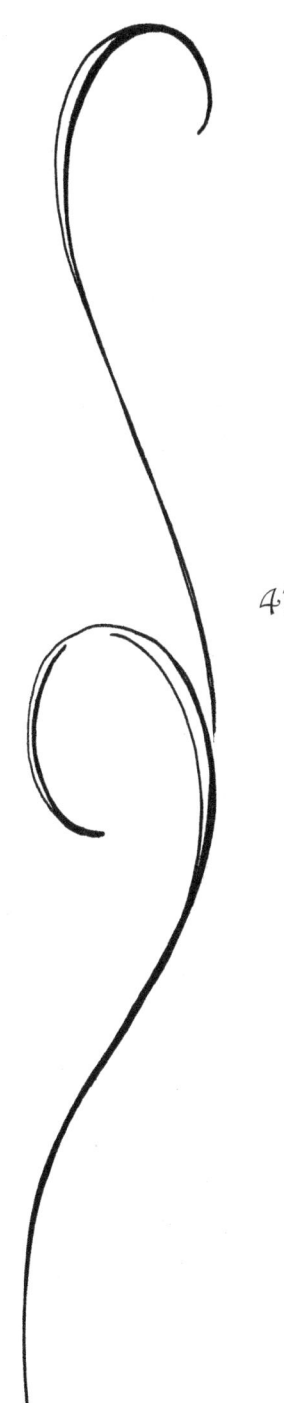

47

Inspired by a Ruby

The things I see, feel, and imagine;
They are the fault of you.
Thank you.

There are fresh ripples of
Truth-serum-like moments
That roll from me when I'm with you
That you welcome, with a smile and your hand.
So thank you.

I know that showing up,
Professing of a patina'd love for you was unexpected,
But your acceptance of it, and me,
Has been a delight.

There are many things to figure out.
I'm glad that one of the things
Being considered,

Is an "Us," as a one.

From, Jim

"Any percent of you, is as good as the whole pie.
Any fraction of love, brings dividends of interest."
— George Clinton

48

Duets

Sung together,
Shining.

The streetlight
Shone down,
Lighting up the
Corner.

A look up.
The whole sky lit,
Just a little.
The stars,
A sung guitar cry,,,

The sound
Elopes with the
Night;
Gone.
Might show up
Again.

A reminder
Of days past.
Wrapped in a new
Night –
Clear.
Seeing all
That clouded.
All that is there.
All over – newness.

49

The Light in the Breath of a Dancer

She walks up to the floor to look out to see how it's
Dancing before going in.

She's with Mya, who's smile's so discreet that the cunning
Can be confused.

They walk
As though floating, through the hall.

Mya turns around at the entrance
To breathe.

The fragrant light warms her
From her sinuses to her soul.

And to silently sit here...
Catchin' eyes with'em all,
Yet still
So
Singular.

Ocean

People come, and people go;
And then, I'm reminded
Of the ocean.

The sea breeze,
The light sways of the trees,
The sand between the toes,
The way the wind, it blows
As it approaches
From the salty waters.
These are the things that please
The daughters.

A tease
Is a poem
About a place.

The grace that it flows in
Is like cool water, flowing in the
Middle of a bright day's
Sunshine, as it
Glows from above.

It takes you to the space that we all know and love.
It's the beauty of
The ocean that, for me, soothes
Like lotion and
Acts like a potion that
Makes me feel love.

Perfectly Whelmed

Can a person be perfectly-whelmed?
It's not overwhelmed, not underwhelmed,
But just right.
Where there is just enough density to keep a heavy boat
Floating correctly,
And just enough lightness
To keep things fresh.

Because I am right there.

52

I feel perfectly whelmed, and perfectly pleased,
Perfectly excited, and perfectly seized
In the midst ∼ of the moment.

It's what I can't deny even if I try.
There's a situation brewing, right in front of my eyes
That is making me see the glory
Of what it is that I
Have been trying to connect to,
But somehow kept on missing.

But at this point, I'm just blissing,
Because the lips I have been kissing
Are on a fabulous young lady
Who is numbing my blues away.

I'm surprisingly pleased,
The way that she's breezed
Into my experience.

Poem

Sometimes during beautiful poetry,
    Bob Marley shows up to say
    That people can be cool sometimes.
A black and white cat named Mel,
    After Mel Torme – the fave from Night Court –
    Is sometimes the answer,
When I ask everywhere and everything
    For something, just something,
    To ease the pain.
Other times, I'll find a book that
    Takes me away to a
    New dimension, a new plateau;
A new world that I'd never considered.
                  I like that.
    Sometimes Jim Carroll will show up to
    Say "You can get away with it."
Or, absurdity will save the day.
    Humanity and existence have to
    Many levels to count, to many
To even fathom considering them all.
    The trick is to realize where
    You are when you're there.

53

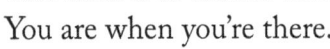

When We Were a Gift

We gave ourselves to each other,
Each of us differently.
Each of us pulled back,
Differently.

We totally enjoyed each other's time
When we were together,
But when,
But when we would let go,   (Oh no!)
Our minds would spin,
Only to be balanced when
We would come together again.

It was confusing, and abusing,
What we were doing to ourselves,
While we were away.

Our symmetry was plain and clear
When we could stand there, face to ear;
We understood each other.
We could help each other groove.

54

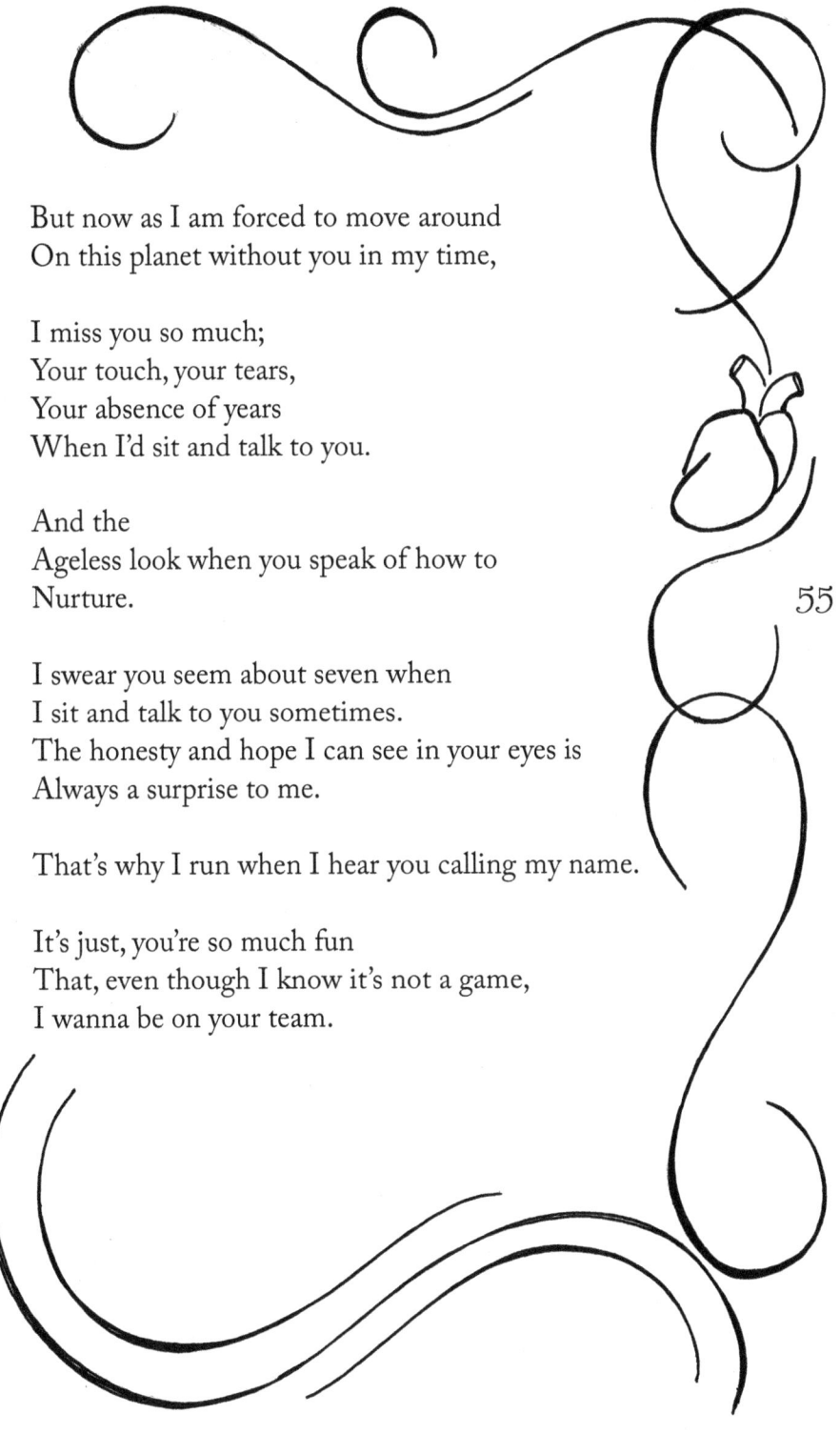

But now as I am forced to move around
On this planet without you in my time,

I miss you so much;
Your touch, your tears,
Your absence of years
When I'd sit and talk to you.

And the
Ageless look when you speak of how to
Nurture.

I swear you seem about seven when
I sit and talk to you sometimes.
The honesty and hope I can see in your eyes is
Always a surprise to me.

That's why I run when I hear you calling my name.

It's just, you're so much fun
That, even though I know it's not a game,
I wanna be on your team.

You Fractilized in my Mind!

When I look – you're who I find,
When I'm looking for
Who I'd enjoy cooking for…

For sure, you're not mine,
But we decided that that's fine already.
I keep lookin' at you
And I want'a
Touch you as I have………

I live tangled up in blue, and then there's you,
Messin' with my head so cool,
The way that'cha do.
But I do wish I could touch
You one more time.

'Cause there's no rhyme
That can match
The feeling of your lips
When they rest on mine;
Or just how fine it feels,
And kind,
When you squeeze
My muscles all fine.

57

And like a card that's been played,
There are some things that you said
That I remember I okayed.

Now, dead is how I feel.
'Cause I just can't deal another hand,
When these things land.

'Cause I want'a
Take a stand,
That I wish your hand
Would fall into mine again.

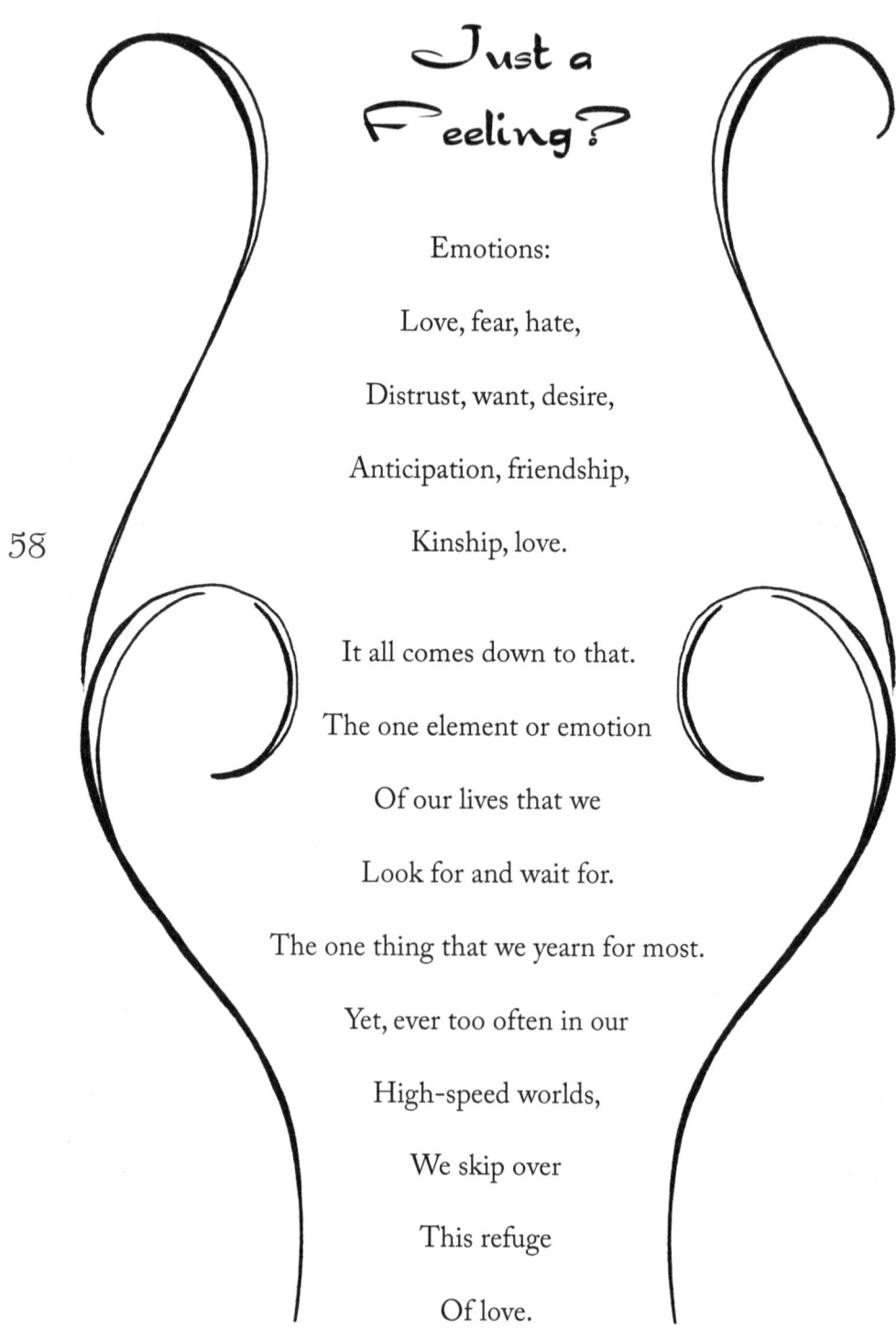

Just a Feeling?

Emotions:

Love, fear, hate,

Distrust, want, desire,

Anticipation, friendship,

Kinship, love.

It all comes down to that.

The one element or emotion

Of our lives that we

Look for and wait for.

The one thing that we yearn for most.

Yet, ever too often in our

High-speed worlds,

We skip over

This refuge

Of love.

58

Thoughts on a Question

"Why should we love others?"
Is a question asked today.
If not us, then who?
I mean, love really is the way

To have happiness and peace
Within the personal soul.
Love is an emotion
Which we can't control.

So, if we were not to love
Each other as we do,
It's that we'd be suppressing
What it is that gives a clue

To the fact that we are human,
And not some high-tech robot.
Love is an emotion
That really hits the spot.

It's beautiful –
So why not revere it?
It brings warmth,
So why should one conceal it?

Love makes a person real.

This world we live in
Forgets that too much.
It's a tragedy that someone can genuinely ask
"Why should we love others?

My question is "Why not?"

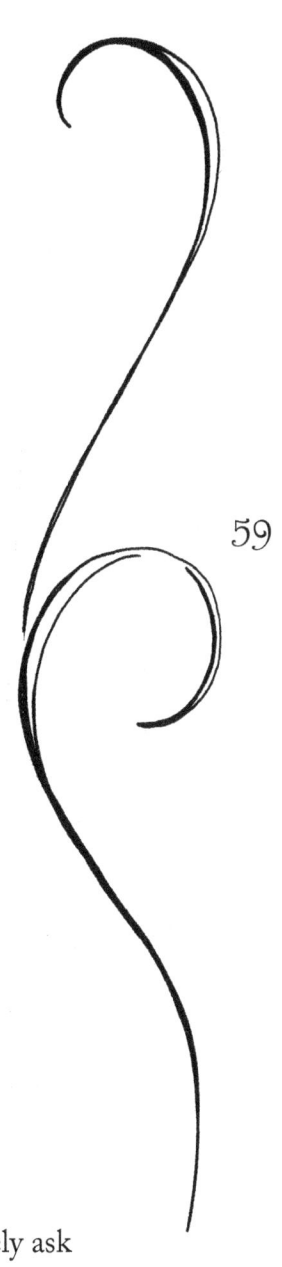

59

Star Light, Star Bright

Star light, star bright,
Who was it that I was with last night?

Her face was bold and handsome.
Her touch was soft and warm.
Now my heart has lost all its flutters,
It's grown into a swarm

Of reelings, for not knowing
Who it was, that was there.
But I know as your brightness will continue to shine,
That it's a good feeling I'm left here to bare.

60

Time Will Occur

So you say that you are young,
As you near the age of twenty.
Well, I sure retain your thoughts,
As they feed my mind aplenty.
Now,
I dream of your dreams,

And what may be there within.
Many pictures in my mind
Become the thoughts that make me grin
In times of meditation,
Created by held-back thought;
Piercing my soul,
Enveloping naught;
Nestled close to my most dear intentions;
Treasured as a jewel in my mind.

61

Admiring you in your pulled back way,
My words can hardly find
Even a touch of what I wish we could share.
Today is but a moment
And I'll be patient, I'll dare.
Regarding holding out,
And waiting for you in your time.
Everything I now feel,
Is hoping to be subtly sublime.

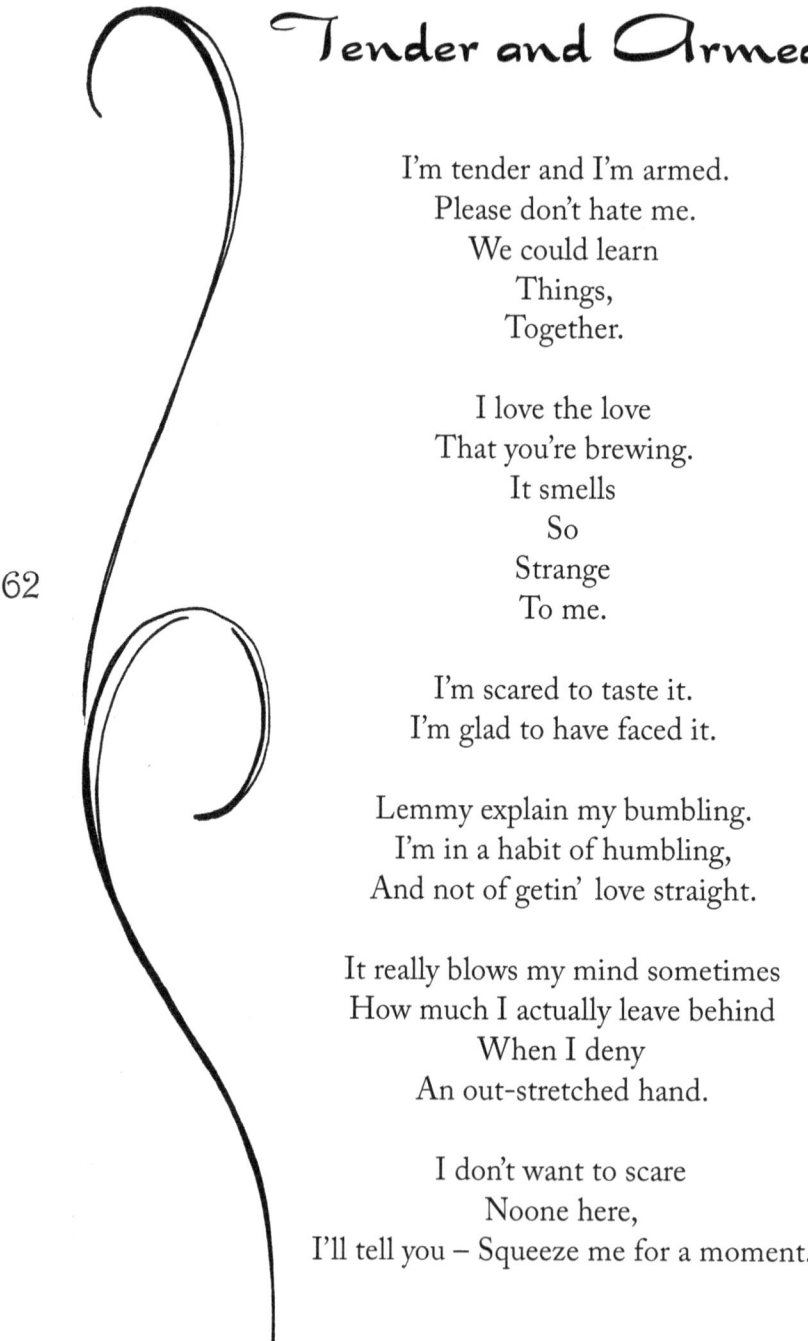

Tender and Armed

I'm tender and I'm armed.
Please don't hate me.
We could learn
Things,
Together.

I love the love
That you're brewing.
It smells
So
Strange
To me.

I'm scared to taste it.
I'm glad to have faced it.

Lemmy explain my bumbling.
I'm in a habit of humbling,
And not of getin' love straight.

It really blows my mind sometimes
How much I actually leave behind
When I deny
An out-stretched hand.

I don't want to scare
Noone here,
I'll tell you – Squeeze me for a moment.

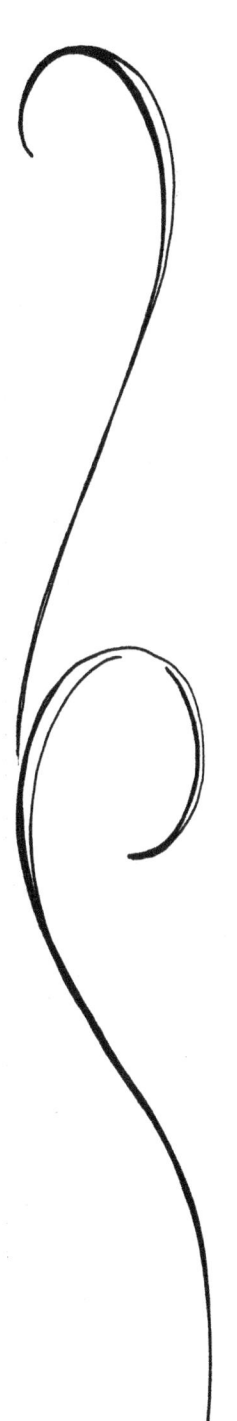
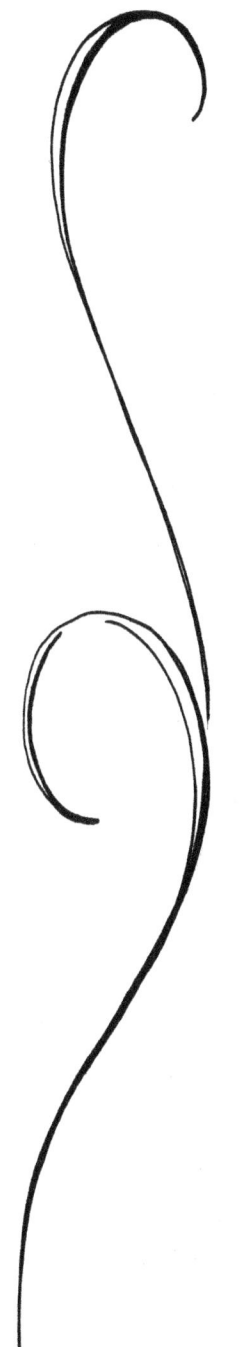

So near,
You
See me,
Turning;

For I was lost not long ago.

You just recently saved me.

So now I'm new,
Looking at you.

63

You really do
Look good to me,
To the point that I'm a little bit
Scared.

All the freedom you offer
Is so
Wild!

Am I no longer a child
Even when I've really
Just been born?

I've been torn
For so long.

You sang me the honor song,
And I don't want it to go wrong.

Days of Haze

Untouchable by your phrase.
May it be a faze.
Leave me in this haze

For days.

....

And so I stays around...
What it is I found
Floating through my mind
Were definitely wined, dined
And fully full thoughts.

64

Lined up,
Maybe you'll pick my head from others.
Brothers across the world
Could fall for you.

My call to you is
Not out of vain.

The pain I would feel
If you would peel me off your world...

You told me that you just wouldn't do that,
And I believe you,
Completely.

And you've got to see
That you could be
An element in a beautiful seen year.
I call you dear, I call you babe.
It's all because I'd call you lover;
And so I hover right here,

And I might near giving you these rhymes
Of simple love,
Though good sense keeps me away.

"Away goes [my] heart
To a no-longer-stranger."
Is a song's line, playing in the air.
It's a song about someone who looks
At someone and thinks to herself
About how the two could be together in
Future times.
It's a beautiful song.
It talks
Of curiosity;
A curiosity of whether they
Value each other equally.
It's an incredibly sweet thought to me;
About these two who see each other.
View,
Scope,
Perception;
All that jargon meaning
How we look,
Is always breathing in fluctuation,
With an ethereal —
                    Wide-view possible,
                              At least.

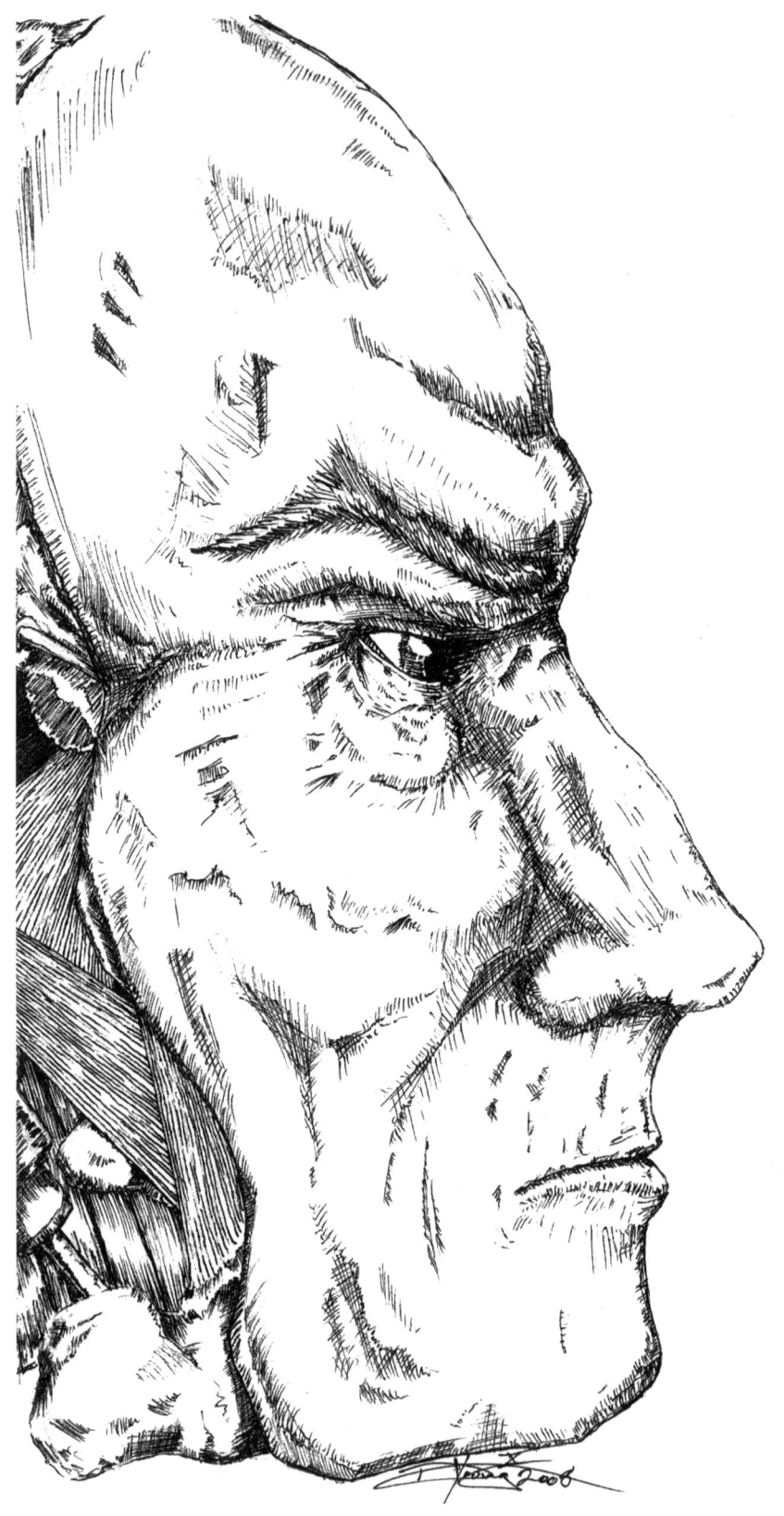

A Cynic's Meditation

Wundrin' in the grass
Why people don't want
Love anymore.

I wunder if they don't
Know what it is.
Yea, I'm totally confused.
It's like my brain's abused.

I just can't figure out
Why people doubt
That love is the answer
Today.

But what can anybody really say?
It's just one day upon the play.

The question is:
"Do ya wunna listen?"

I Dreamt

I'd like to see the friend that called tonight.
Her body was right… Ah, but the night tonight.

I thought I'd been left for dust by God,
      But it was just the rest.
I thought I was having good or bad times,
      But then, they were really the best!
I guessed wrong
      That everyone would like rhymes
         But
        Then I got the nod.
      A beautiful woman said sometimes
There can be too many rhymes -> love
Love though… With love
The sky opens up.
It's so alive.
It even seems like
Satan and God are a team.
A Dream?
They hang out together
All the time
Why,
Why do I rhyme?

68

A Little Gift

A little gift
Can lift a heart
So much it can start
To radiate.

Radiation can be good.

This, you can now see.
An' baby, just maybe,
One day it'll be

That every anybody

Can walk around with me
Or you,
And not have to feel blue
For how they are treated.

Oh, the street, it
Has too many stories
That are way too gory.

I want to feel like I live in a time
That rhyme or love can
Actually make a difference.

I guess I'll get to maybe see
After the gift I have goes free.

What would you let be?

69

Tonal Variation

Tonal variation, oh tonal variation,
Why do you suck sometimes?
I'll be in a rhythm,
Things'll be going well;
Then with one slight contortion,
You throw everything to hell.

I'm weaving sweetness with someone lovely,
And you show up as bold as a bomb.
Though with a subtleness and slinkyness,
You arrive like "Good morning," over breakfast with mom.

You've worked with me,
Not against me, before;
While talking to the young lady,
Whom I currently adore;

And you called in a friend,
Like you were on a mission;
You had my phone call cut short,
You interfered with my transmission!

Now she's upset with me,
And it's all your damn fault!
Had you not straight side-swiped my ass,
I'd be as happy as a bathing Foucault.

70

I've Got to Listen Some More

The guitar's playing sweetly,
And the imagination rolls.
An echo of warm wind in the rhythm,
Or the melody. Who can tell?
I roll my mind to love songs that I've sung,
And the blues that I'll find
Next time I find myself on a stage.
I know it's time to turn the page,
But I just plain ol' keep on livin'
Like the one I'm on's just fine.

I don't want to change the notions of how I live.
I feel comfortable being aloof
And staying strange.
That way I won't rearrange
What I find to be equilibrium,
When I find myself playing
The same old heart games.
Got to stop.
Got to end it before it begins.
'Cause as I know, nobody wins at those
Games anyway.
I've lost so many times.
The rhymes attest to them all.
I got to listen some more.

Be Free

Hey girl, why you so hung up on me?
I'm not as great as I seem.
I wonder what you see.
I wonder if what you see is a dream.

You seem to want me so badly,
Oh madly!
Oh girl, what do you see in me?
What drives you crazy
Like I see you today?

72

You want a way to live?
What can I give to you?
What do you want from me?
I can't see.

You can try and make me.
Be free.

I want to know.
You need to show me.

You seem to be in love.
Oh, sweet little dove,
I know that I helped you be
This way,

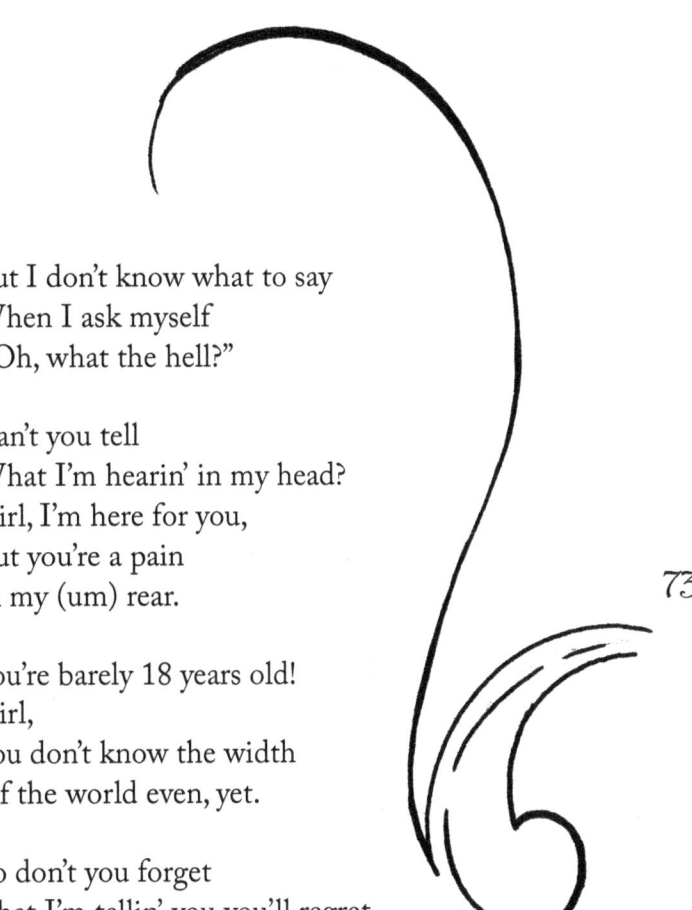

But I don't know what to say
When I ask myself
"Oh, what the hell?"

Can't you tell
What I'm hearin' in my head?
Girl, I'm here for you,
But you're a pain
In my (um) rear.

You're barely 18 years old!
Girl,
You don't know the width
Of the world even, yet.

So don't you forget
That I'm tellin' you you'll regret
If you fret
On silly old me.

Be free.
You gotta see
That you gotta be
Looking around.

There are too many things
You haven't found
That are profound.

73

Musician, Step Up.

When I livin' thought,
About what has been the regular route
Of our men... I think I can
Maybe help, if I let yelps get
Somewhat heard;

Spreading the word of what the fuck is real.
The deal gets changed
When life is rearranged;
A bit deranged,
But the world is just so nutz anyway.

Underneath each fray is a reason.
It's got everything and nothing
To do with all the seasons.
The pleasin's got to keep on.
We're trying for the dawn
Of an era.

Righteous action for us...
To dig livin' –

74

Is it a given
That we groove when we move,
Or does it take thinking?
What chu know?

We've gotta let glow
What we do today!

75

Whether we realize it or not;
We got to give a shot of love.
It comes from above.
All the volumes of love;
Evolving like a glove on somebody's hand.
Our land that we criss 'n cross,
Is in need of our care.
Let's give our share.

The Meaningful Grin

A bond 'tween two souls
Can be formed with a kiss.
It's the time which can show
Whether one's hit or has missed.

The caress of the lips
Can be the most powerful sensation,
Ever to be known
With the power of elation.

A sensuous smile
Gone away for a time,
But not to be missed,
For 'tis composing a great rhyme.

Not consisting of words,
But merely of thoughts,
'Tween two people's spirits,
Those which had been brought,

To light, by the fire,
Burning down deep within,
The minds of the beholders
Of the meaningful grin.

76

The Rose

I awoke to the sound
Of a knock on my door.
I can't remember
If I'd yelled at a postman before.

I don't think I will, ever again,
For this one, delivered a rose.
He told me "Sign here."
His wish, I indulged.
I didn't think of my wearing no clothes.

I spun right around
And slammed the door shut.
I wondered who'd sent it,
Who'd taken their time to produce such a cut?

I think I know! No, it couldn't be her,
She's gone out of town for the week.
Yes, *her* she's the one! Oh, how can I be sure?
I'm starting to feel quite weak.

How should I choose which one I should ask?
I'm sure some will surely be mad.
But of those that stay,
I kind of expect in some way,
Future roses won't be quite as sad.

77

To Beach that Dance

Ya know, I heard that the poet needs his pain, but I find that *this* guy who keeps getting called a poet has good times because of it. Sure, there have been some really crappy times, and I've gone through some truly distorting times on the depressing level, but these days as of late have been so kind that I sometimes don't know what to do but give thanks to Jah, or the sky, or the fact that I stuck my fingers in light sockets when I was young after licking them for the feeling the shock would give me.

Every now and then, I'll blame my strange abilities on head injuries I got when I fell off a car. I claim to have a mutated brain. I'm not sure how real that is, but it works for a laugh. I don't know how to write about something that happened last night other than to just straight write it.

I was at a show at a place in town that I work the door at, and I saw someone who I've been in love with for about three months. The cool thing about this love affair is that she's loved me too during that time. Well see, I also saw her last weekend at a festival put on by High Times and we danced together again, and I told her that I wanted to spawn. The next thing I knew she was in a meditative turtle-like state. It was kind of weird, so I felt like she was having a lot of consideration on the idea, so what I did was I decided I should write her a letter.

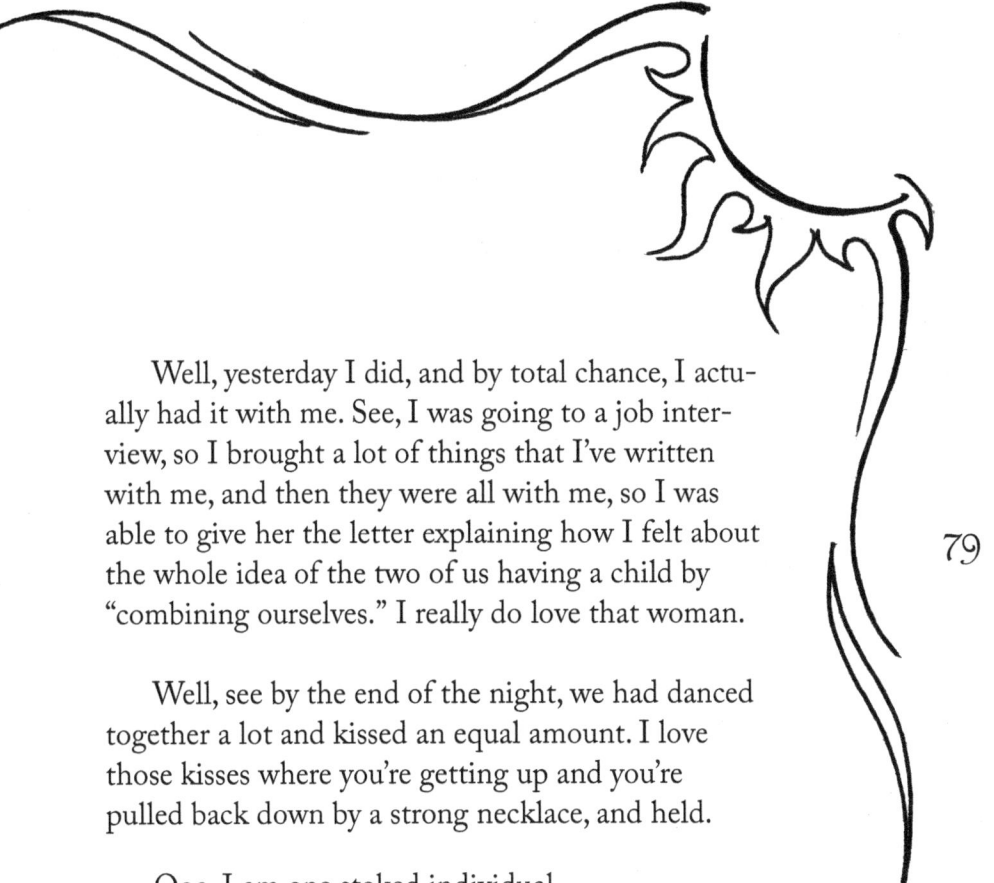

Well, yesterday I did, and by total chance, I actually had it with me. See, I was going to a job interview, so I brought a lot of things that I've written with me, and then they were all with me, so I was able to give her the letter explaining how I felt about the whole idea of the two of us having a child by "combining ourselves." I really do love that woman.

Well, see by the end of the night, we had danced together a lot and kissed an equal amount. I love those kisses where you're getting up and you're pulled back down by a strong necklace, and held.

Ooo, I am one stoked individual.

She introduced me to the most successful gypsies I've ever seen in action – age of myself – strikingly enjoyable crew to've been jamming with. We had this dance thing at the end of the show that shook the whole place – I'd love to beach that dance.

Armageddon

Armageddon seems to be on the way.
I kinda play it for either way.
I figure just maybe,
It ain't gonna happen that way.
Does it matter any fuckin' way?
One day, every one dies.
All lies are non-existent at that point.
So smoke a joint to enjoy living.
What are we leaving to future generations?
We need to change our ways.
Too many days we keep on walkin' weird ways.
We need to refigure what it is that we do.
Oo oo oo, I feel you
In your pain, here in the rain, where
We must regain the plane of existence
With least resistance.
And with persistence, we just might make it.
I'd stake it on my life.
The fuckin' strife don't mean a thing
If we don't learn from it.
Don't be a pointless use of flesh,
Come, and mesh, with love.

Daughter, So Beautiful

(I blame the Beatles)

My Daughter, So Beautiful,

You're in my head,
De'vine.
You remind me of a song
I know.
See, there's
This one choice line
That keeps echoing
Inside my thoughts.
I know the words just fine.

"Sont des mots qui vont très bien ensemble,
Très bien ensemble…"

My daughter, you're so beautiful.
I don't understand
Why you've kept me
Near you. I'm an ordinary
Regular old guy.
My, my, my
I love you, I love you, I love you.

I hope you understand that it's a most important thing to me,
To hold your hand.

Daughter De'vine has
Webbed its roots across you
And become, one with you.

Remembrances

I wonder how you are,
As we see clothes that are not weaved,
Time that has not passed,
Time that has.

I wonder how you are,
With leggings tight around your calves,
The color purple nestled in your soul.

Remembrances of good art,
And good timing,

And mute souls.

82

It's Not Even Noon

I really miss
 Your kiss.
I really miss
 Seeing your face.

Just a trace of your smile
In the letter that you sent.

Straight up, I am bent
 On seeing you soon.
I need to fly to the moon.

It's not even noon,
And I've got my mind on you,
Like I always do.

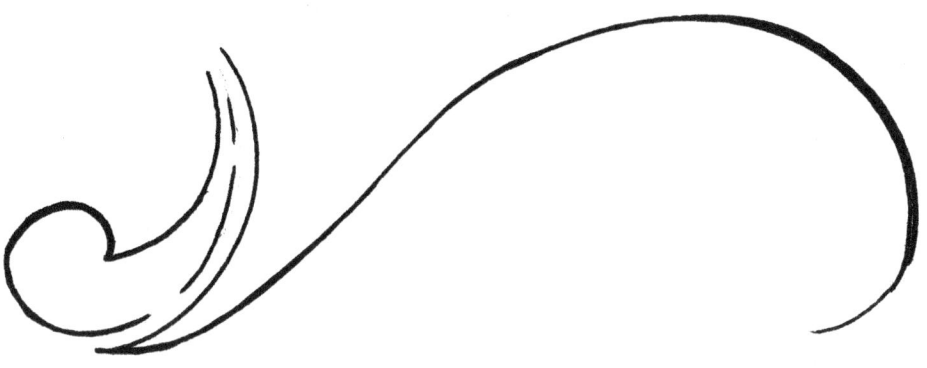

4 Sophia

Radio's on the fritz,
One thing's I got's is cherry pits.

So I'm sittin', drinkin',
Thinking 'bout what I'll do
When I'm chefin' en paintin'
En writin' for you.
You ain't wrote back.
Or have you?
I ain't been on e-mail for a while.

You keep me honest.
Even though I may be lying to myself,
About you.
I'm in Las Vegas,
Land of temptation,
So I drink whisky 'N coke,
And eat cherries.
No joke, I can't seem to bet
More than a nickel per hand,
'Cause I'm waitin' for employment
And I got to waste time.
I gave up on writin' letters
That I just knew couldn't rhyme,
Because it hurts me to lose someone
As beautiful as you.
And I know that my chances are slim,
But I know that if I try and stay true,

I'll see you coming at my soul,
Or maybe my name just isn't Jim.

I might be stupid for thinking
About you so much.
You were just far too beautiful
For me to forget.
You make me question my whole life,
And what I'm here for.
I don't think that my thoughts
Are something that I'll regret.

'Kause you're pure, and
I don't have
Much of that in my life.
Maybe I did go
Just a bit far
Asking you to be my wife.
But you are gorgeous and slender,
And brilliant minded too.

85

And I don't think that I'll
Ever find someone again like you,
If I kept searching and looking
Until doomsday approached.

I could be wrong though.
Please tell me if my thoughts have encroached
On your life to the point where you're
Uncomfortable.
Because I would
Disappear like a gas for your peace.

Got a Wick?

I still hope that you join me
For a good time on December the 3rd.
I hope that you're looking forward to it.
If not, then I give you my word:

You won't hear again from my rhyming tail.
You obviously won't want me around.
But I swear as I sit here,
You'll miss a flight with a phoenix
Who is currently sitting still on the ground.

We all love to have random good times,
And we all love to know how to plan.
Sometimes we get somewhere
Because we've built up into it.
Other times, we just do what we can.

All these events are extra
    To the one thing,
        That's the desire.
    That, I hope, still burns.

JJ

I Wonder

I wonder if U2 will ever find what they were looking for.
I wonder if they knew what it was.
— Could it have been Winnie the Pooh style contentment?
The Tao?
A friend?
They never seem to've found it.
Hmm.
It's a sad song.

Robert Plant would have told'em to get cool.
He'd've schooled 'em on the need for love;
A whole lot of it.
He knows learnin', good times, depth, love, lots of love;
A whole lot of it.
He knew that love was a filler of voids.
He knew that love helped a person be more – better complete.
That's a man who loved.
Love…

Love is like friendship;
Lots of telling good qualities,
Appreciating diversity within,
Enjoying the richness of a person.
–A Single Human–
Sovereign, yet loving.
Kindness, caring, caressing is sometimes in effect,
Because human contact is important to all.
Love is one of the best concepts
Within the realm of humanity.

87

Lotus

I think of you
And how much I have always loved you.
You went to Bali,
And I never was able to hold you again.

You were like ice cream;
So delicious, and so quickly gone.
I could never
Find your flavor again.

You are an angel to me.
Holding my soul inside
A perfect female form.

Please wrap yourself around me again;
I want to be whole and one with you again.

You got to let me send
My loving feelings to you.
I need you for inspiration,
My love is true.

If you were only here,
I'd kiss you again
And you would understand then
Just what a lotus you are to me.

Love Lives Within

The guy you're with has an assault
Rifle with an attached bayonet,
But the way you looked at me,
I just can't forget.

You seem like someone that love lives within.
I love that you can bring beauty to sin.

89

There are so many things I want to see you near.
There are so many places
I want us both to steer.

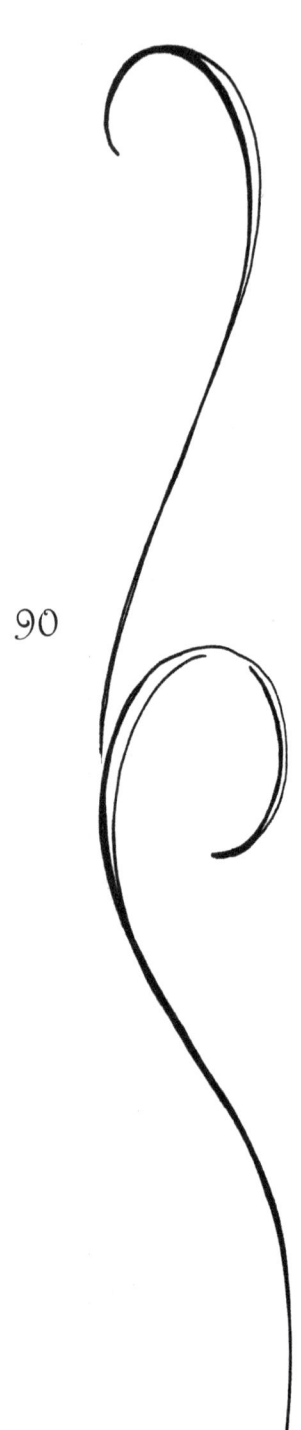

Mary Mary

Mary Mary, quite contrary,
Bustin' my brain cells about;
You made my life plain smile girl.
En now you're gonna get out
Of the country for a while.
Well, I'll miss you,
And I'll kiss you as I dream.
But I'll make it seem
Like you weren't gone.
We've got to keep on,
'Cause all this
Has been bliss to me.
The way you kiss me
Taps my soul to your veins.

Mary, oh Mary,
Not guarded or wary,
Filled with intrigue and drive,
You've been a bliss to know,
To see how you strive,
How you go for your goals,
Knowing you've got a clarity of
Mind that can't be faked,
Finding comfort in knowing that
It's often better to be different
From everyone else.

90

Kinda Just Dig the Soul

I dig the cat for the sake
And the quake of love,
Kinda just dig the soul.

I love you as it is.
Could do a list,
But I ain't got time.
It'd take my life.
Okay, I'll do it.
But cha gotta let me brew it,
And it goes along in stages.
You know the ages have left a lot of
Sticky resin around.

The sound
Of love and its yang there…

But we got now and
What we can do until we're
Through being here,
Which is as loud as the beautiful
As the rain as it shines,
Coming to cleanse as only it can.

It can make me slip.
It can make me trip.
Just take it from the hip,
And give it right back.
That's how it stays pure.
Of that I'm sure.

Somewhere Near Something New

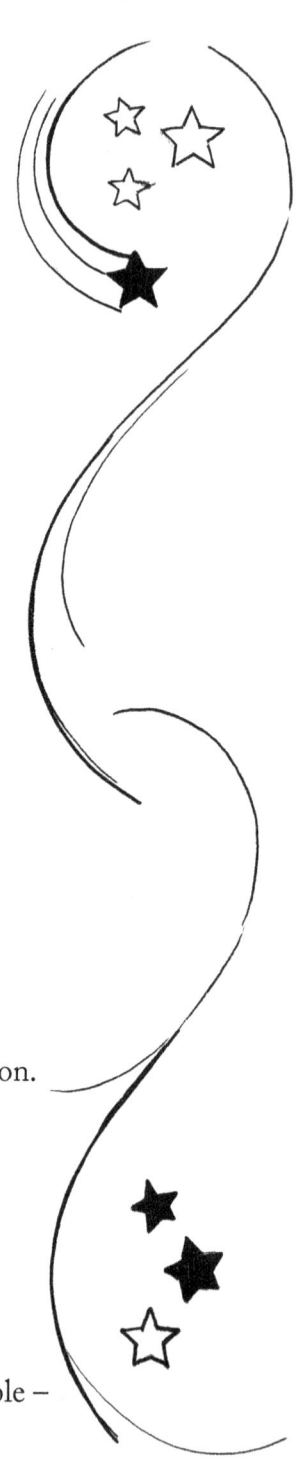

I'm here, somewhere near something new.
From here I can see you. You're beautiful.
Ooo, so fruitful,
You know
I like a dike as much as anyone.
Just for fun, I like to ramble.
See, I'm here on a scramble.
I just scrammed from a city,
Mmm, so far away.
I just got to say
That you seem like a cool way to travel.
I ain't gonna judge,
But I ain't gonna budge.
You're the most beautiful thing I have
Seen in this beautiful scene.

I like to live serene.
That's why I say I ain' gonna be mean.
Just let me clean my spirit while I'm here.
It seems like you might question and fear,
But don't shed a tear, not this year.
I'm here tryin' to spread positivity,
Not bring no nativity to the clear.
I just want a friend.
I'm tryin' to mend what I hold dear.
I always steer 'cept when I am lookin' for direction.
I sometimes need a correction.
Ooo, I can get that from a connection.
I am coasting, toasting my beer,
I'm roasting the boasting this year.
I'm trying to run from coast to coast.
It's been the slowest route,
Tryin' this silly type of shout.
No reason to pout, I remember people like a steeple –
Like it were my religion.

My derision makes me a little bit altered.
Some say I faltered, but who are any of us anyway?
I know all that I can say,
Would make anybody feel
Like they are real, 'n that is my job.
Hopefully I won't be hit by the mob.
I don't like to be robbed. But then, does anyone?

I juss want to have fun,
Shed a little bit of sun in this rainy atmosphere.
"What's it like to be near a flame?" some will ask.
It's not like it's a task to warm in the sunshine.
It feels fine.
It's like drinkin' some wine in a Riviera setting.
One thing I'm not wanting to be forgetting
Is your personal preference
To each setting that I bring to your mind.
I wonder, do you mind
That I feel that it is my job
To find what is beautiful in this world,
And one of my finds has been you?
I'm speakin' as true as I can imagine.
What do you imagine for you while you're here, so near me?
Don't fear me, I know I might have come on strong.
I hope it didn't sound at all wrong.
It's just that I believe that I think in song.
So very, very long, I have felt this way.
There's nothing that I can do to sway
That it has been my way of life.

Someday, somewhere, I might just call for a wife,
But at this point,
A joint has married me to the rhymes.
These are hard times to go through,
Or are they easier than we even understand?
I been through the land and

93

continued –>

Nothin' but sand is our base.
But look at my face as I sing for you,
I don't have a ring for you,
Just an offer of company.

I saw a guy who looked like a lump,
And he didn't know how to get off his couch.
I simply said "Ouch!" for the sake of humanity.
For the sake of the same people, I am here.

Would you let me be near you on a regular basis?
Your face is like ecstasy to me.
You got to see, I also spied your soul,
So pure, that you're like a vision to me.

I'm stuck in rock and roll.
My soul doesn't have a clue who I meet.
Sometimes the rhymes just come through to you
'Cause you deserved'em for bein' so beautiful.
I can't believe that I got so lucky to've met you.

I could go on for days,
The haze that fell in front of my eyes…
The guys, the lies that you have seen…

I'm none'a them. I am Jim.
Someone new you met.
Hopefully you won't have the occasion to forget me,
Or regret me.

Sometimes

Sometimes I need to be away
To think about what it is I'll say,
So that I don't mislead or misspeak,
Or not speak at all.

I drive real fast with my mind,
Because I hope to eventually find,
A person whom I can enthrall,

With my silliness, my seriousness,
My issues and delights,
My politics, my poetry,
True Zen, for the sake of the heights.
        And while I know
I should temper my speed,

I still get dreamy quickly,
And I don't quite know how to brake.
But you'll notice I'm honest,
A good listener, and really can't fake
My intentions.
And I'm content to not lead.

I have an unusual path to walk right now,
And I know that I don't need to rush,
So I meander towards a massage
Because I know 'twould be obtuse to gush,

Since I really know you nary but a tidbit,
And you may not even know my whole name
But we had quite a moment and I live to write so,
Here, have a poem. I hope you don't think that it's lame.

95

Beautiful Flower

Beautiful flower,
Your smell is a pungent bliss of harmonies.
Your delicate petals
Are as colorful as a flock of butterflies.

Your ability to transcend
Matches or surpasses all elements
And entitical forces.

Do not fear my hand as it nears you.
I don't wish to pluck you from your ground.
I will only caress you in admiration.

You leaves are wide –
How they've fed you so.

Your roots,
Somehow, at sometime,
Found a strain of aquification
That was so unique;
It has helped produce a magnificence
That is so rare a quality that,
In my experience,
Is so often looked over,
Yet is so clearly apparent when 'tis being searched for.

It's an attribution that
My sub-consciousness was in charge of looking for.

Upon recognition of your qualities,
Love for you occurred.

Devotion

And so I slept.
I was sleepy.
My last thoughts, always

Are with her.
I sleep, and dream of
More to do.

97

Breakfast was swift and nutritious.
Everything is possible now.

Tomorrow's dreams may have substance,
Only today will determine that.
Got to say it's started well, rather
Early. And I'm not sure what I'll meet

Throughout the day.
Here in Babylon,
Even the subtleties count.
Realization of dreams is

Determined by the ability to
Rationalize the scope of
Everything being dealt with
Around the situation of life,
Metaphorically, and solidly.

Elephant Shoes

Gritty Unity U.

So intricate
And incensed,
Smelling so surprisingly fine.

Who are you dear?
Why are you here?
I thought that it was going to
Be a fine day.
Now, I feel extra good.

Who are you?
What do you want me to do?
I wanta serve you.
I wanta swerve you,
Into a grin.
Am I coming in
Clear?

Dear, what year do you
Want me to smile?
I'm so confused, so
I'll just stand around for a while.
I might make some sound.
Hopefully you won't frown.

What is this town going to do
In our near future?
Do ya dear, suture what ya see?

Elephant Shoes

I May Stay

You came across my world,
You made me twirl
My concepts around.

I thought that I'd
Get out'a town.
But now,
You seem like a dream;
And so, I won't go.

99

She wrapped her arms around her breast
Like an ocean wave upon its crest.
One wondered how to do the best,
When nothing else was like the rest.

She felt like she was lonely.
I told her she was only gonna cry –
She wasn't gonna die.

Traced Dove

She'd spent so much time with her lover.
She didn't know how to hover
By herself.

I put on a shelf the love I had for her that day,
'N when I went my way,
I felt she loved me too.

Oo, how beautiful she was.
She gave me a buzz just looking at her.
I ain't here to flatter.

I felt that I just had to have her.
Is that wrong? My song already said
She'd somethin' else in her head.

What I dreaded is that she didn't want me at all.
I ain't tall, I can't give her money.
But ooo, I would lick her like honey.

It's like I yearn for a burn to
Earn a taste of –
Don't wanna waste love.

Like a traced dove on construction paper,
I can't forget that silhouette
I saw, that made me drop my jaw.

The Pillow of You

I hugged the pillow of you,
      Though you were only 3 feet away.
I hugged the pillow of you,
      Because it was you to me that day.

You'd laid your head on that pillow
For the nine hours previous.
I loved that pillow because
It kept you comfortable – not grievous.
It also smelled like you.
You laughed when you saw me
      Hug your pillow.
I couldn't help it.
It was love.

101

I Got Five Minutes

I got five minutes, a hankering for debauchery,
And a song that makes me smile is
Coming in my ear.

There's gonna be changes soon.
George Bush is being accused of war crimes,
And I may stay here another year.

The song is over. Someone's pitching a product,
And now the headache wanders back into
The day.

New moment, new song, new feeling,
And I'm reeling in the warmth of the
Springtime.
What can anybody really say?

I just hope I make it through again.
I've experienced so much pain.

I hope I make it through,
Because there's you.

Love Construction

Me, I got dreams.
I want to always have happy female companionship.
Want people to enjoy me being around,
Want to hear my sound,
And think it fine when I'm chilled.
'Till I'm killed, I'll be on this path.

The path is love construction.

103

Pointless Love

I wonder why I miss you so.
I really wish I'd never met you sometimes.
Baby, you gave me purpose again.
I was flailing in the wind before I found you leanin' on a pole.
You wrecked my pointlessness,
Now my mind's open again.
I wonder how you did it babe.
You made me true.
I tried not to fall in love with you.
I thought that there was something wrong with love.
Love explained that that wasn't true.
You haven't called or written in days.
You've taken a vacation from our haze.
I understand, and I don't mind.
Sometimes, I look and I find
That I shouldn't think about you either.
I'd have more time, but then I think I wouldn't have you,
And I think I'm insane for thinking blind.
I realize that your eyes make me more than fine,
They make me think about every thought I ever had pure,
Like you're some cure to me bein' without a point.

104

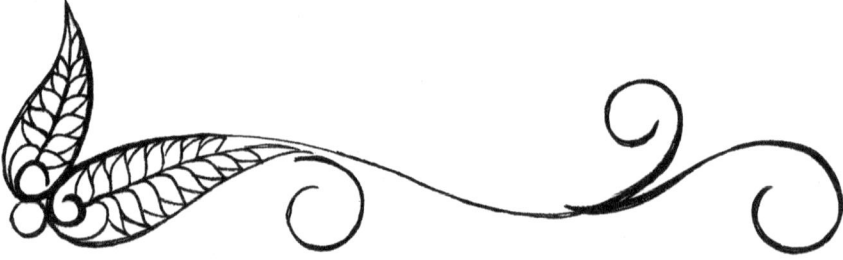

Pyramidal Distinction

Your scent is as intoxicating
As the finest smokable plants.
I just imagined smoking you someday.
The effect would be addictive –

You're in a class all your own.
(Pyramidal distinction does that sometimes.)

I know this,
Soaring through the air I saw you from.

Damn, you were clear to me.

I kept on looking at you.
I was like bumpin' into shit left and right.
–The term I used was "gaga"–
How 'bout comin' somewhere with me?
We'll walk right next to each other.
What a sight we'll be!

105

Om in Stride

All of Womandom receives my love.
It's driving me quickly now.
The speed limits have been removed,
And all that I think's "Wow."

My God is all of Womandom –
The Way of All is with the High Priestess,
And she's always had my love.

...I love how you love every place, and
Maybe you'll come back to mine.

106

I'm,
Thinking
About being approached, myself.
So much unassurity is in my mind even though
It totally fits around.

Lately it seems that I must now let go of
The religion that I was with.
They told me not to love the Earth.
I think that they're uncouth.

I kin dig on grooving
With other cats, I think.
But I have no desire to.
So I'll Om instead,
In stride.

To Hover

Heavin's given me love,
    A leavened bread for a dove
    That I know I will grow.
And I will hopefully be able to show
That I am the man, for the girl I love.

I must'ave gotten my share from above.
    I know I love her.
        I want to be her lover.
        I want to hover in her life
            For the rest of mine.
    She's finer than any girl
    I've ever known.
So to her, a throne!
    I done wanna be alone.

107

Sexual Creature

108

Yes, I'm a sexual creature,
It's one of my features.
I hope that you still respect me all right.
It's true that in the middle of the night
I might get a bit heated and frisky,
And it might even be risky
To do the things that I think about.
So if we choose to drive the pleasure route,
Let's pull out a condom.
Our world has dawned'em.
They really are a nice safety tool.
And when used as a rule,
They'll protect any fool,
And even lengthen the time of actual bliss.
And so give me a kiss.
'Cause I'm a sexual man.
And hopefully I won't have to have sex with my hand.

Lust Self Consumes

The fact that you still feel like smiling at me
In all your groovyness,
Whether you do those things that we talk and think about,
Isn't what matters.
As long as love is alive between us.

109

I'm givin' you so much of myself,
I hope you don't throw it away.
We can play our games,
And feed the flames of feelings we've got.
But I'll tell you the truth,
I'm doing all'a this for us.

Our lusts will self-consume,
As we resume
Our personal freedom,
In all.

A Gift

I present to you my heart and soul
When this Christmas Eve turns dawn.
I present to you my heart and soul
To ensure our friendship goes on.

I know we have had our times and our troubles,
Our arguments and fights.
But I know that it's true,
That you'll stay with me through
All of these forthcoming nights.

You've been there for me, whenever I've needed
A hand or maybe a hug.
And so, maybe now,
If I can figure out how,
I can return this favor with love.

I think if you let me, I can do this well,
For I think I've grown up inside.
I don't ask you to leave him,
It's true you may need him,
But within you I wish to confide,

Every such feeling, idea, or emotion
That happens to come to mind.
And if you do the same,
I believe we'll remain
Better friends than either of us could find.

And so,

I present to you my heart and my soul,
With which you may do with as you please.
But remember, be careful,
Of each I've got one.
But to you, I have handed the keys.

111

Moss' Bloom

As in the forest,
We are here,
Living to grow.

See, with you near,
The forest's shelter is clear.

The fog that came
And left a tear,
It now feeds moss
That's growing, this year,
A love,
That's blooming,
For you, my dear.

When I Think of You

When I think of you,
My dreams have tears.
Your void is a spur in my heart.

When I think of you,
I dream of delight.
I imagine bliss in coming
Days, weeks and months.

When I think of you,
Serenity is not a dream,
It is a reality;

For you are love.

113

Love Myth and Mystery

So the feeling of love can contradict.
To transcend or to…

"The love of the living / The love of 'God',"
As he smokes his pipe

/is poetry the art of obsession?/

Love is all over the place.

Were the Egyptians "innocent" of love?
~Were the Greeks the first?!
      ^ That claim is phuched up!
              but it's said.
Platonic love –> The sharing of mind.
Yet Plato's loving was…

What of self effacing –> love for the other?
Without self love…
"Agape" –> transcendental love towards above.
St. Jerome said one should not love with passion
       Medieval love –> Rare –> (mostly business contracts)
->Desire –>'n Knight + Lady
          –>cloudiness of Attraction

Freud thought spirit was nil,
          And he puffs again.

Fromm –> "loneliness [sux]"
     –>concern + growth.
        Bahhhhhhh!

J. Lark

115

Q: Why not join the military?

A: (by Jordan Clark) Wanna sit back, drink honey coffee and smoke ganga.

Poised Like a Quatrain

Poised like a quatrain,
Ready to pounce...
I wonder how lust
Became intelligent.

116

Images

118

Denim

I wonder how we've come to this.

I wonder why it seems,

That God has died,

And the world has fried

Every crevice 'cept for blue jeans.

Insinuation –
Quite a station.
Got inspired, even wired by it.
Don't forget to go ahead and try it.

Just keep on livin',
And keep on givin'
Away what you say.

Maybe,
I don't always feel alive.

Yea, I felt dead just yesterday night.
I know I'm alive –
This frikin' jive won't stop comin'
       From me, geez —
This freakin' pen.

-Somewhere along the line
    I thought it was the Zen.

Insinuation ~

119

The Trek's Release

Once along the trek,
There's no turning back.

Once you begin,
There's no looking back.

Don't turn your back on me.
Forever more, be with me.

Go on your journey.
Release. Have no fear.

Release like grease is on your fingers ~
Smooth,
To soothe your mind.

With peaceful thoughts refined,
The confines release peace freely.

120

The Cactus

Along a lonely stretch
Of barren desert highway,
A prickly cactus grows.

But 'tis not the average
Prickly cactus, no;
For this one, he knows.

He knows 'bout the mysteries,
Of where the Old West has gone.
He knows about the sunrise,
Or as it used to be, the dawn;

He knows why it's missing,
He's seen them all go by.
He's seen them in their big dirty trucks.
He really misses the sky;

Or as it used to be that is,
Before the men in trucks came 'round;
And the sky was blue,
And the birds, they flew;
Long before the dawn of the town.

Ahh, the Smile

Smiles have a tendency to make me feel free,
And complete,
As a willow tree,
Blowing in the breeze;
Stationed near a cool, clear pond where,
When it comes time to freeze,
Becomes a rink for the children,
Who will sit on the willow's roots.

They'll join in song
As the days grow long,
Then revel in the snow in their boots.

Smiles cannot be faked,
For a farce can easily be seen through.

Smiles are a feeling,
That let the sun shine through.

122

The Water Flows On

Calm.
It is beautiful in the river today.
The sun is shining.
There is a slight breeze,
And the water flows on.
There is a noticeable current pulling along
The passengers of the raft I'm on.
The morning has opened a whole world of opportunity
As the sun emerges to produce the finest dawn.

There are three birds flying West in the sky,
And I stop to watch them.
They glide on the breeze's crest,
As they dance for me,
Unknowingly.
And the water flows on.

123

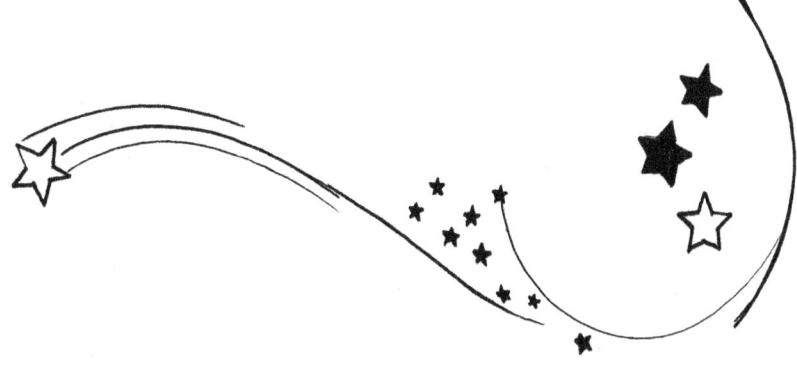

So 9

So I'm thinking about the time that gets spent
On the energy to pay rent.
I wonder about how much really gets done.
I wonder if I should remember the fun.

The lover, she ain't there like I think she should be.
I wonder if it's me, I wonder if I just think too...

124

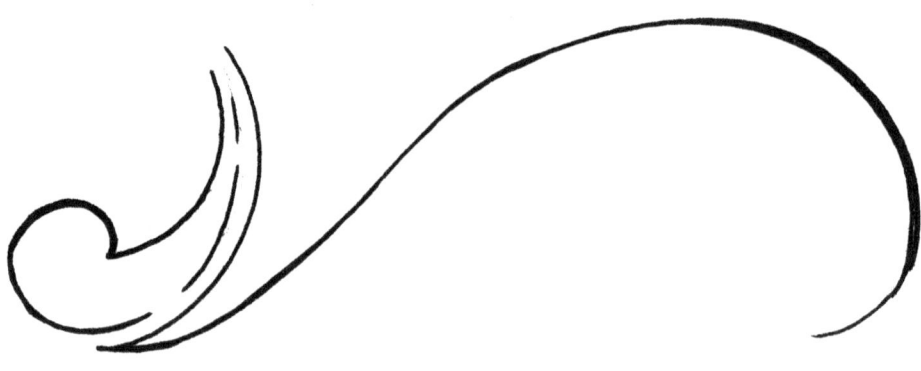

The Beautiful Sight of the Breeze

The cloud formations that I've seen are enough to make me feel like I'll have a life of travel. They've been too beautiful, and bountiful.

Too many starry nights on the trails of America for me to stay away. I need to see them forever. The lever of motivation will always change, but the accomplishments will keep on coming.

125

Beautiful women – we have the most beautiful women in the world, except for the equally beautiful women that truly can be found elsewhere.

I just think that we are luckier than we realize, all the time. We've got such a tremendous stockpile of beauty, that its actual worth is misunderstood on account of the tremendous volume.

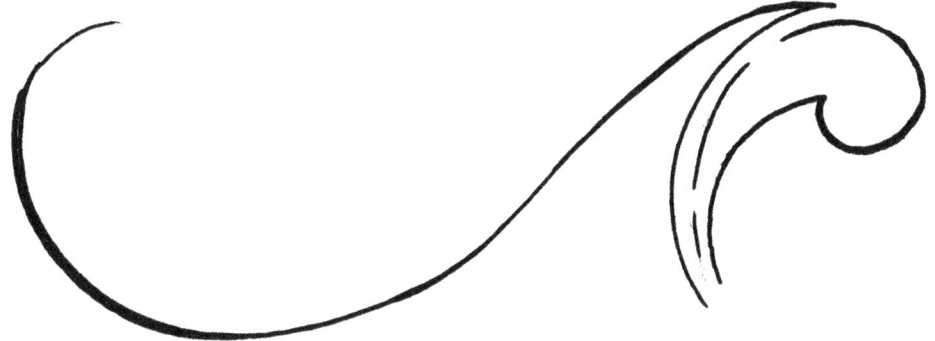

The City at Night

126

The city at night – hums.
Or maybe that's the A.C..
A helicopter flies overhead.
Maybe it's a cop on patrol,
Or maybe somebody's about dead.

I have an interstate
Living outside my window,
Cars like blood cells in a vein
In a constant flow.

My roommate's not here,
He went home
Or something.
I don't care, it's quiet, it's 4:AM.

Autumn

The leaves have fallen,
Now hidden deep beneath the foliage.

The air bites like a frightened animal.

The dew no longer melts in the morning sun.

127

The most beautiful of all sights can be seen,
The loss of all surrounding life.

Existential Apathy

Looking for the reason,
       Finding just way too much.
Figuring that last season
    Was the time to strongly clutch,

The reason, the basis,
The karmically new.
But for some reason, the face is
       Entirely blue.

128

Looking into patterns
    Of paisley, spun and plaid,
For the chaos that's missing.
    Maybe it's really all mad.

'Cause there's a bomb in the hotel
    That used to be fine,
And I'm not hoping much now,
    To have a next line.

I Trace...

And so I give another thought
To what it is before me,
Looking me in the face.
I trace just for a moment,
'Cause I realize
Nothing here can last.

But still I keep along,
And I wonder if I'm strong,
While I know I'm wrong
For doing so.

129

And I wonder a little more just what it's all about.

Well, is it for having a good time?
Or is it for pulling
Along the
Whole dang
Species?

What was it there again?
I have to ask my friend...

Pete, Why?

~For Angel

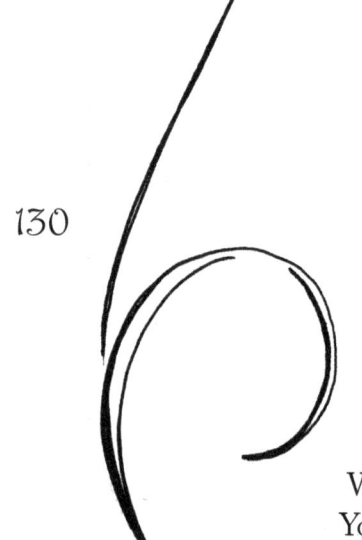

Cleat high into the sky!
Get your footing.
Eat some pudding to feel good,
'Cause when you feel all right,
You know that you might
Remember the light.

It had chased away your fright
So many years ago.
So, maybe now,
It will be what shows the way
When you look around.
And you'll be able to say,
That when you look up into
The gaping wide old air, —
You'll be able to find
Your favorite solace there.

When you let your hair blow wide,
You'll soon forget how you've cried.
You sighed so many times.
I don't feel that the rhymes
Are even necessary any more.

Your cure will be found
When you look around
And try to figure out
What it is that you're about.
What is your route?
Aren't you steerin' anyway?

Find your friends today.
That's all this one can say.

130

Flash the Breath

There are chills, thrills, and
      All sorts of stills
           That make us breathe
     Cool, slowly, and
               Meditational.

As it is, our heart is beating faster,
But time – is moving slow.

     The *rushes* that let our latent dream-sight
         Reach into our nows,

       Making our moments seem like
       A surreal test of the continuum,

       Flash the breath!

(That's how it gets taken away.)

        It screams:
       "Take me away!"
   Because the rushes of our dream-sight
Make the light that is floating everywhere,
Glare,
Right into our
Mind-Thoughts.

The cool breath of the nighttime
Lets our dreamscape
Live in our daytime.

131

Wind

I have a special place in my heart for the wind.
It is the breath of the earth.
Its gusts are my mother gasping for air.

It moves all.
Powerful,
The wind is what stirs the leaves…
As they come off in the Autumn.
Trees are carpet on a hill side,
Massaged by the breath.

Sweet wind –
You bring the sent of neighboring territories to me.
You bring fresh air to my lungs as I breathe you in.

You love me. Thank you.
You put shows on for me and anyone who looks
As you move through the tree branches so.
You really are majestic.
I love you.

132

The Zen of the Pen

The Zen of the pen
Makes me begin
The instrumentation
Of what I am in.

Is it a sin
To want to re-in
The Zen of the pen today?

Basking

The sun's
                Come out
         Again.

The rays soakin' in –

So beautiful.

 The clouds hang
             Thin and low.

The sky's so blue,
You can feel the warmth.

Dreamin'

I wonder why it seems
Like it's all been dreams.
I wonder if I'll ever hold a job long.
I just want to live through songs.
To many societal wrongs to get at 'em all.

The fuckin' ball is in seven courts and arenas.
This whole freakin' world north of Salinas
Is falling tha fuck over,
But still people go on!

What a fucking spawn.
The dawn is worth its weight.
I better not wake up late next time I get a job.

135

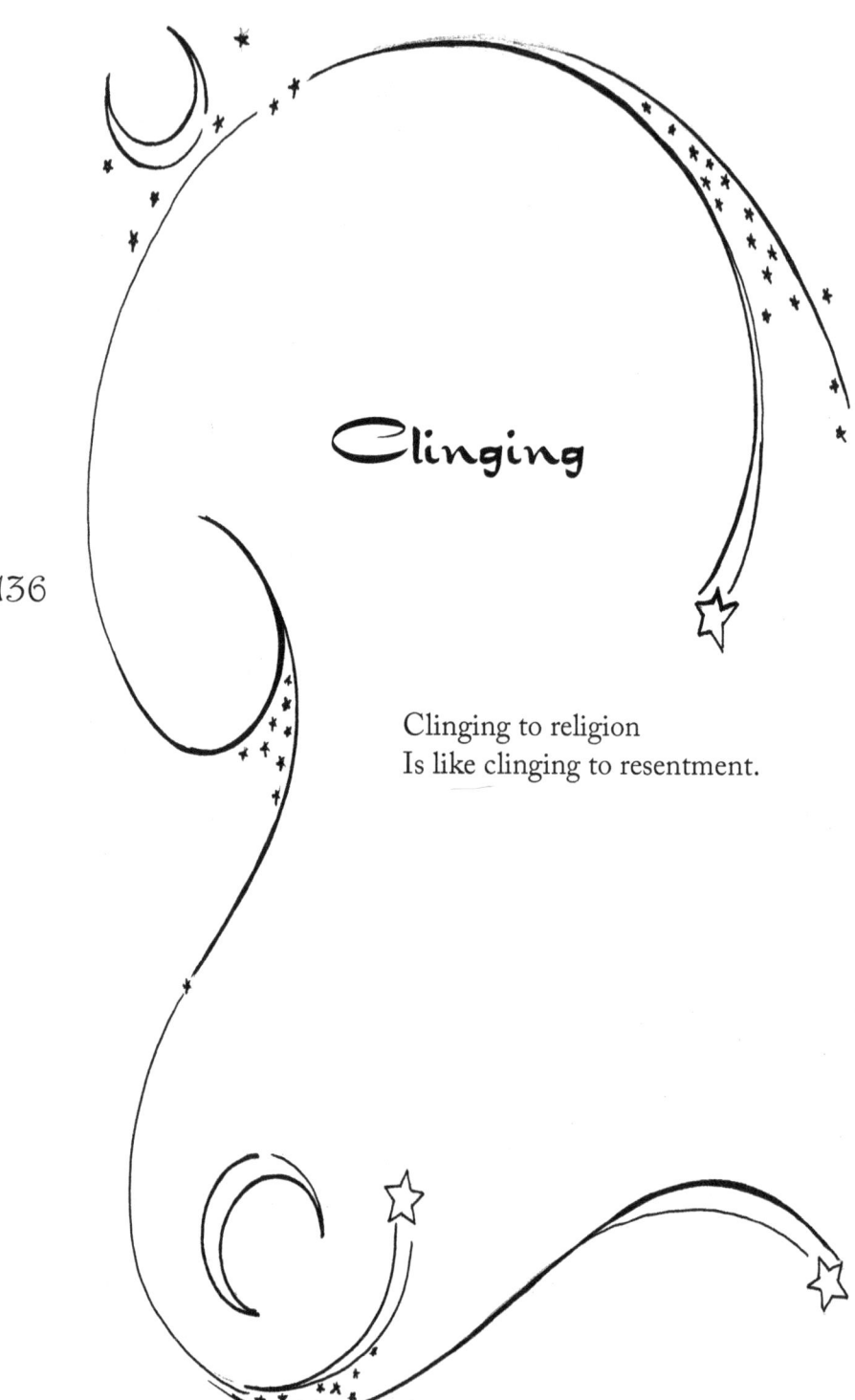

136

Clinging

Clinging to religion
Is like clinging to resentment.

We Are Such a Peculiar Species

I'm eating a sandwich
That has processed cow-baby food,
Mutilated bird flesh,
A cooked mixture of plant life and animal,
More vegetation that I put in
So that there would be some

Crunch,

And I topped it with mustard.

I apparently have no conscience anymore.
Oh well.

137

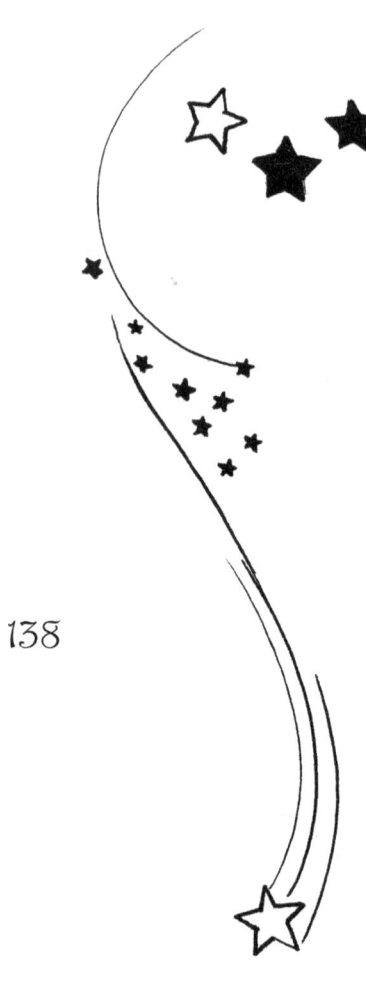

Ode to a Job

138

I wish I could find
A situation cleansing
My penniless woes away.

I wish I could find
A situation benzedrine
Just could not all wipe away.

I never seem to get one at all.
And there it was man:
Authoristan!

What he can do
Is get on through
To catch for true
The things that he do see well.

Rough Around the Edges

Life seems tough,
I get rough around the edges.
The ledges of life
I don't jump off
Seem to multiply.

I don't ask why.
Learned that one
Long ago...

No answer.

139

Traps

The music is alive with the sound of the chills.
The people are here for the chills of the war that is on.
It makes the coming time seem... Questionable.

Sometimes on the highway,
I think of others.
My thoughts have time
To congeal,
And my
World begins to feel
The pain that others around me can feel.

The protester is smiling,
Promoting the war next door.
    The fears..?

        Those kids are fresh off tour.
            They're beautiful.

        So many things to see,
        So many people who
        Need help; so much
        Crisscrosses when it
        Comes to maps.

    So much to think of;
        So many traps.
I always feel like I'm near one.

        I seem to find them well.
        Beautiful things too,
        I'd have to say.

Zoning

What seems really amazing to me is how
when people are zoning, they try to get their
job done.

They see their goals, but they lease out
their souls, and then they lace up to go out.
Like when folks are in school and they don't
study what they feel inclined towards.

They're working against their own self.

Inclination; it's what their souls had told
them, and still they do otherwise; because
they have some sort of elemental calling for
cash. Or they believe that their predeter-
mined path is thanks to others, like their
parents, or a guidance councilor or some-
thing like that.

Zoning is abstraction,
A methodological reaction.

The terms, they'll grow a reaction if
given a chance to grow.

An Observation

Sittin' around watchin' people downtown,
Makes me think of the people like
The girl all in black, with the collared chain
Around her neck.
I wonder if she wants someone to hold it.

Piano plays, and the sun rays
Keep comin' down.

142

I look across the way
En I see
A person frown.

She's hopin' for some cigarettes or some change;
Just anything to rearrange
The way that she feels.

Ooo, the deal's kinda raw
To the female that I saw,
But there ain't nothing I can do for her.
What a whir we're livin' in...

The times they are a changing.
The goths freak out the hippies
'N the G's'll take anyone out.

Still plenty' a people bein' trippy,
But everyone round's givin' some kind'a shout.

The loggers are getting out'a style.   143
Students are goin' nuts with their books.
Everybody's livin' like they're wild,
Lookin' at all the people's different looks.

Makes me wonder 'bout these books I wanna write.
Makes me wanna take a bite out'a humanity some other way.
I wanna somehow relieve widespread pain.

In the midst of beauty,
Up walked one major cutie,
Hangin' with the gal with the chains.
I wonder if she pains,
Or if she's just been bored lately.

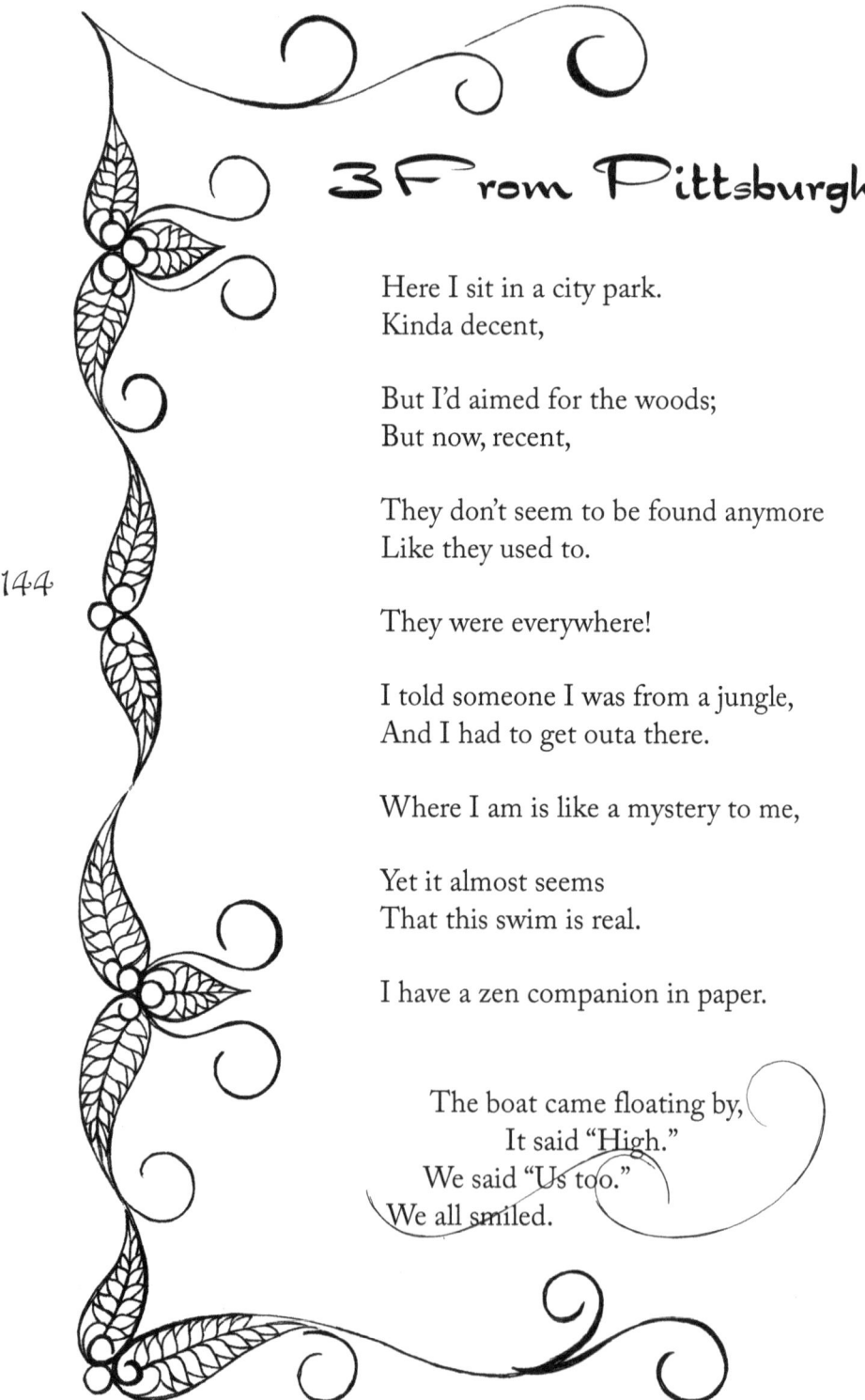

3 From Pittsburgh

Here I sit in a city park.
Kinda decent,

But I'd aimed for the woods;
But now, recent,

They don't seem to be found anymore
Like they used to.

They were everywhere!

I told someone I was from a jungle,
And I had to get outa there.

Where I am is like a mystery to me,

Yet it almost seems
That this swim is real.

I have a zen companion in paper.

The boat came floating by,
It said "High."
We said "Us too."
We all smiled.

144

****

Don't be afraid of happiness.
Do not be afraid of all.

Feel comfort,
Fall back into a plush chair and let your
Soul breathe out.

*****

145

It sounds
Like a stream.
It's coming from
Behind me.
It could be
A machine,
Or water
Flowing through
A tube...

Crickets, to...
Something that
Sounded like a
Laser gun.

continued –>

146

Spaceman,
When are you coming here?
When will you show
Your faces to everyone
So that everyone will
See you?

And so, with that in mind,
I wonder if
You'd at least say high to me.
Yea.

A Coddled Dream

So, as we coddle, I dream.
And as the moment can seem
As kindred, I do not expect.

My hopes are eternal.
My thoughts, while internal,
Permeate through the touch of my hand.

She smiles as delicate
As a paper-thin ice crystal,
And as beautiful
As a mid-summer's day.

Her style's accentuated
By her subtle ways she shows
What she's feeling,
And by what she shows she's thinking
In what she says and how she moves.

I'm drifting, so I'll join her.
She lays silent in my bed.
I'll be beside her, and if I'm lucky,
In her dream.

147

On the Road

Pittsburgh was a truly Gothic town.
It really was amazing, what could be found.
Cops killin' brown cats 'cause they happened around,
To morphine sellin' school kids, lovin' Manson's new sound.

But then there's Morgantown, where Groove
Really did live it phat.
There was no drug tsar in town, so have no
Worries 'bout that joint that you got.
In Morgantown, if US law applies, you simply cannot tell.
But now it's time to depart,
Because I live my life for art,
And now it's time to swell.

So now Seattle, for a rattle on the bedpost of life.
Time to get up by drinkin' a cup of coffee that'll be easy to find.
I mind when I don't have access to the best.
Lucidity for this man!

I can feel it already.
I feel like Ferlinghetti.
Who's Coney Island is it now?

Politics Don't Matter

Politics don't matter…
Right now, the sage brush's land is covered in snow, and the
once rolling hills from the plains are now like the Southwest's
as we discover the Columbia River.
We are about 140 some miles from where we're headed, which
is Seattle.
The trip has been interesting, quite righteous to be exact.
Our next stop is 30 miles away and after that, it's on to Seattle.
It feels good to be going to the city that
Kurt had as his launching pad –> or Bill Gates's hometown =-]
From the coffeehouses to the needle.
It seems this town is such a diverse mecca that anyone could
find a home there.
But who knows?
This trip could be the most positive trip I've made.

Pittsburgh wasn't destructively negative more than it was cre-
atively positive. So overall, it was obviously a good thing.

Seattle very well could be the next best thing to Nirvana itself.
Appreciating life.

149

Time to Build

Here we are on the cusp of a new millennium.
Some say we're gonna thrive.
Some say we'll dive into depths that are like Hell.

Some say we're already there.
Some say that's fair.
Some say that where we are right now
Doesn't really matter,
Just where we're going.

Some people are growing weed.
Some for the greed.
Some for the spiritualism.
Some just for the smoke.

Some think life's a joke.
Some think that a poke is the point of a night spent out
Splurging on alcohol and lies.
Some think that more tries need to be made
To bring about a more balanced world.

Whatever.
We're all swirled on this ball spinning,
And I'm grinning,
'Cause this is my last day being twenty three;
And me,
I'm betting on trying to build on that which I've found.

The ground in this city shakes at will.
Some say Rainier's gonna spill out and kill us, you and me.
I'm just hoping that poetry matters
For the sake of all the splatters

I've strewn on subway walls, and bathroom stalls, and
School house halls.
'Cause I've been known for havin' balls
And not being afraid to use'em.

So I'll retreat soon, to my seat,

Poon once added tang to my theorems.
The cleat to her moon without the serums
Changed how I see the whole world.

I've been twirled.
I've been whirled through the distance,
And met up with resistance
That even now has my forehead in the cross-hairs.

The only reason I'm still alive is because of the wind;
The glorious wind that brings the scent of the ocean,
And curves the track of the arrows
Shot from afar at my seethings,
At my breathings,
At my feelings,
Like the ones you've been hearing.

I'll be clearing out soon.
It's time to build.

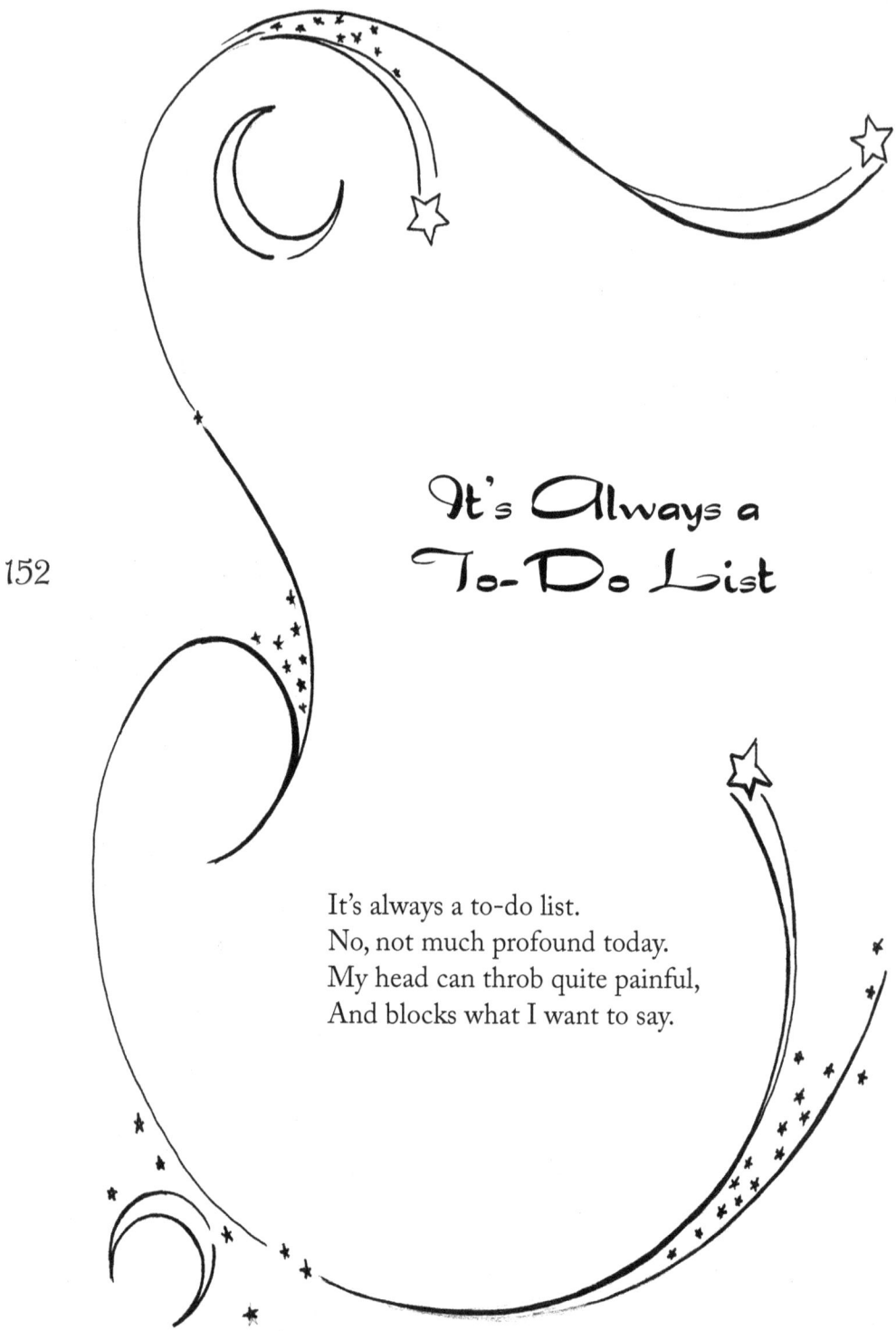

152

It's Always a To-Do List

It's always a to-do list.
No, not much profound today.
My head can throb quite painful,
And blocks what I want to say.

Journey of the Perspective

As a young man I tried to see the big picture, I did a pretty good job. Missed things time and time again though. Like when I considered money to be of profound importance. Little did I know what I know now about that. I am glad that I took time to see the mountains and the wilderness and the sea. That was probably the best choice for me. I remember just watchin' the colors over the mountains change across the Puget Sound, and Spring evenings at the marina.

153

I remember not being able to hold on to a lady. Those were some times. Boy, am I glad things have turned out as they are. If I get to read this when I'm younger, I'd like to tell me a few things.

First off, don't worry about time! Just plug through. Make as much art as you can, God knows life is short enough. Love will come to you. I am a happy man and have been very content with your future love interest. Though for technical reasons I can't tell you who that involves exactly. But your patience will be rewarded, have no fear, just persevere.

Live Until We Die

Do not let life be tragic,
    It won't be enjoyed.
          – Try to see the good,
            Positive,
            Possible
          – To be done.
    Sure, stuff sucks sometimes
          – But shit, we're here now.

154

Yes, keep with all believed spiritual morals,
        Tenets,
        Rules,
        Laws,
        Caws,
        Words;
      Even physical, you want,
    But try to be positive during time.
Live until we die!

Way to stay sane:
As we remain, we should spend every vain pump positively.

Lost in Sleep

And his eyes closed.
And the lights went out.
You could almost hear the sound
Of his riddled, breathless shout,

As his soul released,
And his eyes rolled above.
You never heard about
The girl he loved,

When she would tie his shoe,
And she would make his bed,
And when she would shake him
If she thought him to be dead.

Well, he could tell the tale
If he could ride the wake;
But as it was,
It seemed he'd never wake.

For he'd gone'a slumber bound,
For being too tightly wound.
Finally, it seemed he'd found:
He would sleep as if she weren't around.

155

Are You Thinking What I'm Thinking?

156

...or are you thinking about the wonderful days ahead of us, behind us, and the ones we are living right now? Or, is it that you are not thinking at all? Your mind is at this time traveling through trillions of miles of empty space, space that seems so peaceful and serene that you don't ever want to leave.

Or is it that surgeons have removed large portions of your built-in thinking cap we call a brain, so that all you can do at this point is react to your sometimes unhappy surroundings? Or are you just thinking for the sake of thinking; understanding that your surrounding society expects you to think, therefore you do?

If you can relate to that last one just a little too much; then sit right down where you are, close your eyes, and experience absolute nothingness, thoroughly wonderful nothingness.

Open Spaces

Thinkin' of open spaces…
So open – lets go!

We like to do what
(Or who!) we haven't done.

We should chill –
The mountain teaches much,
Sometimes too much even for
Men to en…

157

Notions

So I think about what is sent with notions like emotions;
Like JFK Jr. dead,
The natty dread,
The cone tipped clansmen,
And the black clad goth surviving on trappings
Found to be available at no charge or sergeant's directives.

The gig is makin' it as ya self,
And doing that which makes equilibrium felt.
Sometimes it's tragic, the simplicity.
Sometimes it's a joke how complex life can get.

So the cakes get made,
And the sound is the blade
That slices into the soul,
Where the feeling is felt to be baring.

The notions that can be sent through sound,
They're potions
That can change how people are.

The way they add and subtract with their lives,
It's not subtle, it's blatant.
It's that in-your-face rush that grows reality.

Peace, Love, Freedom

We are the freaks.
We are the changed ones.
We are the rearranged ones.
We are the ones who
Alternate within our love,
           Within our hate.

We figure out some working, new-found route
So we can stand to stout and drink it all in
When we all begin to.

159

Throughout the word sin,
It makes us live to grin;
Understanding
Freedom of the choice.
May it be voice, or may it be pain;
One thing's sure,
It surely ain't the end.

So friend, get fried.
You've lied.
You've tried
To make amends.
We've turned around the
Bends of our past.
And so,
To make it last,
Keep on drivin' real fast,

The cats you will have past...

Turkish Coffee

Eddie Brickell and nuts,
Turkish coffee on the way.
What can be done but increasing the fun of
Living?
      Giving cash away,
         Recycling the stuff I say…

      The smell,
         I'll tell,
            Is good.

160
            I should
               Enjoy the taste,
               Basting my mind.

And so, I'm satisfied.
      And soon I'll ride, to a new place and time.

But that'll be later, right?

I told some guy the wrong time. It'll be all right hopefully.

      A little overly inspired,
Straight damn wired.

Good coffee though.
A new song comes on. Sounds like Dylin.
I'm juss chillin'.
Diggin' it…
         So there was this cat at the bar
Who helped me figure the arrangement of the star
      Of Earth.

Why I Don't Like to Write Poems

I don't want to break any more hearts,
As I lace intelligence delicately.
I don't want to make any more starts
Of relationships that I cannot play to.

The idea of cooing about moss and rocks
Makes me squirm with the request from others.
I refuse to believe in any human clocks,
As I swoon about loving great mothers.

161

Too many times I have breathed through these rhymes,
And now my throat has gone infected.
I'm in love with the world, and yet every girl
Hears her name with each tone that's inflected.

Don't get me wrong. I hope that my songs
Will garner great love for my life,
But I also am reserved, as all my thoughts
Have been preserves, because I want to
Figure out the Deep Strifes.

So Many Lies, So Little Time

Sometimes we look in superspace.
Sometimes we look in cyberspace.
Sometimes we look at our face,
And if it tells us the truth…

162

So many lies, so little time.
Got to wonder where they're all comin' from.
Makes me want'a stick out my thumb
And get out'a here,
But I gotta steer my mind
Through what I find as reality.
I've got to stay
Just another day.

The Russians are calling.
It makes me falling,
Or way up high.
I'm just not sure.

Non- Pome-Pome
contribution of title from Ashanti

**All the profundities in the world
Can't give the pleasure of knowing that you are loved.**

To write a poem-
　　　　To show'em
That it-can-be-done
　　　　　　By one,
　　Is a task
　　　That people ask;
　　　　　　And so, I give you this rhyme
　　　(Worth barely a dime).
　　　　　　　　But I pay my dues
　　　　　　(Even when there's no muse),
Pushin' the goods
　　　　From the woods
　　　　　　In a day.
　　What can I say?

163

So many societal expectations
On the federal level,
Bedeviled.
We ain't eggs. Don't say beg.
Get a leg up.
Now you got your laws
On pot?

Guy once told me to take a shot
In the other office over.
Clover have five petals on'em on
A regular basis now.

164

A face is how a job is got,
My face has gotten way to hot.

The air evolving is
Not solving deals around here.

What I see…
Our atmosphere,
Ebbing into life. What we see is
Strife –
A dream of a wife seems
Totally off.
What we've brought our selves?!?
No loft on its way, down low.
How can I show this madness inside me?
"You got to reside free
According to the pages,"
All the sages wrote so
Many years ago.
But really, is it so?

Confused

1.2. Thank you.
Time, at that: 11:30 1.1.96

165

Confused here.

I lose things about there.

I wonder 'bout those
Who are afraid to
Give a shout
Of about
How they
Feel
Real.

166

Placid

Peace of mind.

Good music
With a good cause –
Meditative headspace –
Makin' this one cat pause.

Rolling through the audience,
One seems welcome,
And another seems glad.
Here, no one's sad.
The music's good –
Café harmonies
And melodic jazz guitar.

The rhythm makes it right.

They look good in light.
It seems all right that
They feel okay.
Some good people here.

Resist Towards Art

And **do resist** whenever
Someone comes around
Making it seem like it's all so clever
To ignore sounds
Of people as they cry,

Never even caring
And never asking "Why?"
Who cares what anyone's wearing?
We're all fully alive.
Just together, as diverse as jive.

11/13/97

167

It is a good thing to work from
Appreciated art towards
Other art.

I Love Ya, So Far Away

I love ya, so far away.

168

I'd love you if you were near.

I'm so glad, today.
I've got someone here
Who can take care'a me.

And then I'm thinkin':
Do I need a conscience,
Or do I just need to rock?

The Cold Winter Air

The cold winter air
Blows in this week.
I've seen it alive
On the cheek
Of a friend who was fighting
And was beaten – he'd come inside too.

169

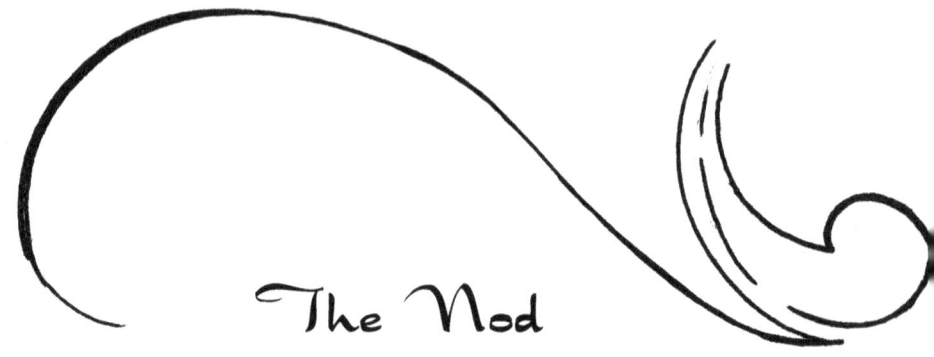

The Nod

An unmistakable
Abyss of ecstasy
Drawing me,,,
Me drawing it in.

I welcome it into my
Sanctity.
My insanity?
Or my sanity with pain?

I can regain,
But I need to remain
In power over, and within, myself.

170

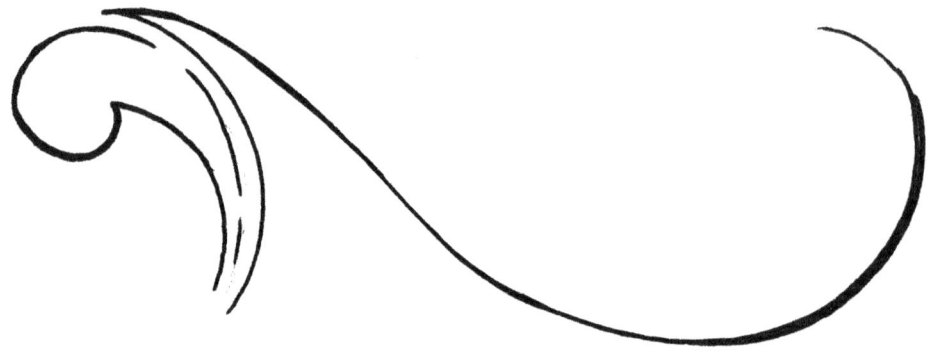

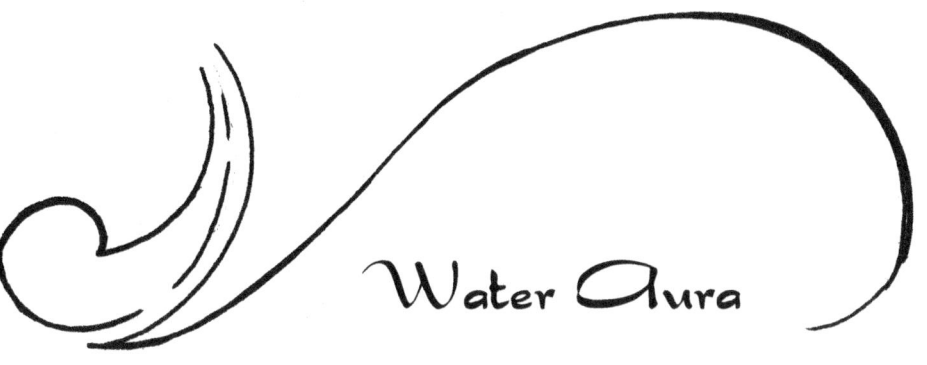

Water Aura

To love animals is
To love nature.

To love nature is to yield
To the weaker,
Say, water –
As it passes through mountains.

It asks by its presence,
To pass – Being allowed
Into the hardest of environments,
While a soft, soothing aura
Permeates.

(~Like Patchouli.)

171

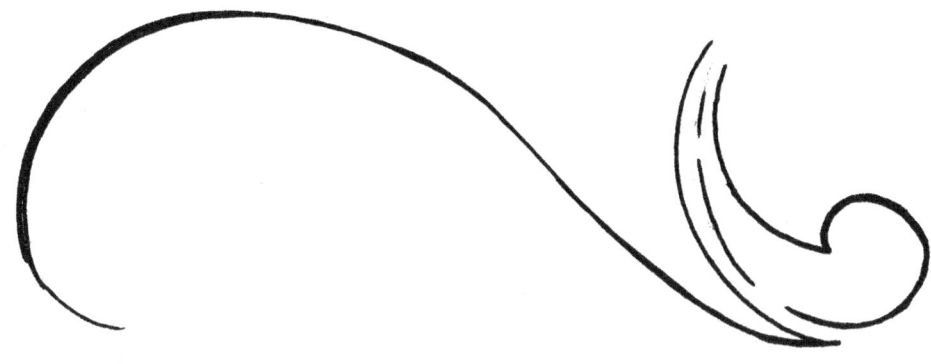

Understanding

Understanding,

     You don't arrive on time
Like I think you should.
You're a lot like ink on the tip of a ball point pen.
While in the beginning,
You're often missing;
With the right agitation, you often appear.
Sometimes though, you don't show at all.

Are you ever *really* there though?

     Understanding, why are you so
Strange and opaque?   Hmm?
If you were clear as a sunny day,
All life's problems would just go away.

     Understanding, why is it
You can appear in so many ways
To so many people.
Yet, even though as a verb,
You have no decision making powers;
You seem to <u>choose</u> to hide at times,
Leaving what could be a room full of people
With puzzled looks on their faces?

Understanding, would you please
Bring your self —
And *any* of your friendly, helpful verbs,
Such as yourself,
Over to my place?

You sure would be appreciated
For a sit-down-kinda kickin'-it deally'o.
That sure would be nice.

Wow, I don't know what to tell you.
Really, it might be worse than I'm letting on.
Can you help explain things?
Like I should be singing,
But I'm scared of the other humans
Who make life so serious.

We need to reflex some growth up in here
For the good of all involved.

Understanding, I miss you.
We all miss you. Is that you?
Oh, how do I justify this letter?
A verb as noun, as a Spirit?

You are U, and I am me. With use, two together;
and maybe plus three, it'll be okay.

173

)j(

March, Evening

The date is March, Evening.
It's morning right now,
And the wily videy keeps going.
There is nothing left to see.
There is someone right to see.
There is a grouping, and a smiling.

There is a hoping, and a styling,
That time
Isn't
A concept.

And yet the fellas all say that the anarchy sign
Is an angel in a portal, and a planet.

Yea, I definitely will can it, 'cause it's good like that
When ya say
Ya can raise your hand in actions.

Get subtraction to
Be addition like it was
A mission, yea.

Got to be all grooving
While we be movin',
So that we be smoothin'
Emotion around the positive.

174

Feel how it exists when
It exactly slides like it's
Gliding with a
Somehow nodded-reality that makes
It all okay,
Regularly okay.

175

Armed with love, from some people,
We're guaranteed a simple fight,
Where a smile
Will be the only weapon in use.

We will let our will be the only… Om.
'Cause it's for –
Yeah,
The will.

May we let the will
Be our strength
To be kind.

Can we find our own way?

I Sit Here Wondering

I sit here wondering what it's all about,
'N realize that I don't think I even know.

I figure "Oh well.
What about between now and then?"
I figure I'll help the environment and have a few kids.
I love having life pass in front of me.
I think I just like the view.

176

Got a Keyboard

Rockin' wine,
  Feelin' fine,
Don't feel like winnin' no more.
      Keep on filling up the pages,
    'Long with all the herbal sages
Throughout all ages.
    Talking more and more
        Like we are all one.

    Gonna spread the gun of the pen,
    Then gonna advance
        With the new dance of
    Fingers on the keyboard:
        The new hoarding device.

            Precisely practical,
        Absolutely actual,
    And to be factual,
It's tough moving over to the new word-rover.
        But, like clover
            And ivy and bushes; technology's
    Growin' in whooshings, and by pushes
        Of keys.
    Like a tweek on the knees,
        Getting 'em stronger.
            Done wanna talk.
        Juss wanna walk
    To a new chord.

177

Hope, the New Dope

We got hope,
The new dope.
'S gonna make ya fly
So high, but it's gonna be
Legal. Gonna fly
Like an eagle,
Today and every day onward,
And beyond.

Oh, the day has dawned,
'N with our hope
Like a scope,
We know we're on the
Right path.
In the new dawn,
Gonna keep on
Livin' 'n givin' to you,

Gotta tell the truth.
We ain't got vermouth,
But we got life's essentials still
Comin' from a bottle;
But these spirits won't
Make ya drunk.
You sure looked like a punk
While you were down.
But now ya come around.

So lose
That frown,

'Cause we got hope,
The new dope.

So undo your locks!
Here comes Equinox.
Gonna knock off your socks with this new myth
About the pith of life.

Do you have a wife yet?
Or do ya bet you'll get one soon?
Or is it 'bout noon in your eyes?

179

Before it dies we got to save our Mother Earth,
She gave birth to us all.
We live on this ball!
How tall do you feel?
How far can you see?
If you'd ask me, I'd say
"Give while you still live,
While ya still got the chance.
Give a righteous dance.
The lance should be used
Rightfully, by the son.
Now he's begun,
So try and have your fun."

But don't forget, we run the hope-meter.
Treat her good, like ya should.
You really could if ya tried.
We'll have died,
What will we've left behind?

Sunshine Life

So now livin' is all about reaching for the Sunshine Life.
I wanna bring others with me too.

180

So the Evil Spins Around ~

So the evil spins around –
Brought so many down.
The town's got all the spheres,
Cats that have been here
For years.

The tears flow down,
Searing as anti-freeze
On the soul.

181

It's time for a Rock and Roll
Commission submission, that
The world needs more peace.

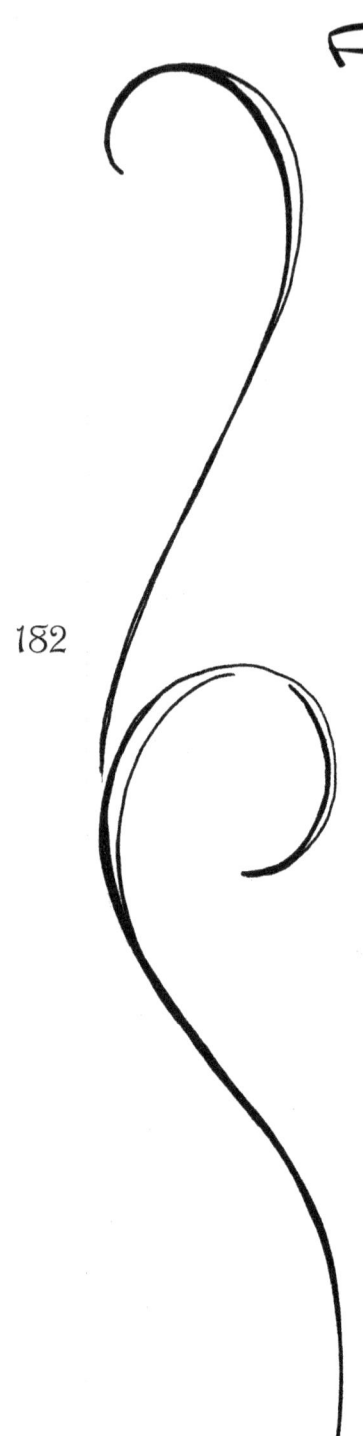

Flower Power Persists

Flower power persists.
The spirit of life, surging
Those who resist;
The purging of Earth.

Get a new birth.
Have a clean soul. Yes,
Might, some days, be a mess,
But to be blessed
Makes me want to be undressed.
But with reality, we know that we
Can live the best if we
Remember, that across this land
To really hold somebody's hand
Is so much to some folks
Sometimes. So drop a dime at
Bedtime to someone real kind
To help them unwind
The things we find
That define reality –
Beware
The air's pollutants,
They'll get you every time.
That they can. And
I'm man with pen,
In Zen – So don't be scared, ever.
Like a lever regulates,
Close the book, 'n later
Take a look.

6/97

Didja?

Were you on the verge?
Didja get to Pittsburgh?
Didja want to
Rearrange?

Didja really feel that
Strange that day,
That moment when
Ya thought it was
Wrong to be uncool?
Respect is who and what again!?
R ya a frien ta anyone?
Is your gun in reach?
Do ya preach non-violence?
B Kind.
Silence.
Defend Friendship – Is a trip.

183

What ya find in the
Rind 'n underneath
When ya look b-neath
The surface of an
Action that occurs?
It whirs, this world
On which we stand.
Is this our land or what?

Fuck.

City of
Pavement

This is Pittsburgh...
    Colorful sky
With purple grey clouds
Hanging over the bleak, yet
Blinking, city of pavement.

4:20 PM Nov. 21, 96

184

Dissolving Dreams

Now that I want to focus,
I got to pray that it can happen.
I got to back down and work my ass off
So my bosses want me around.

I got Sophia to think of when I wonder why I am here,
And why I am working so hard.

I love to strive for her.
She gives me hope
In this sea
Of dissolving
Dreams
X

185

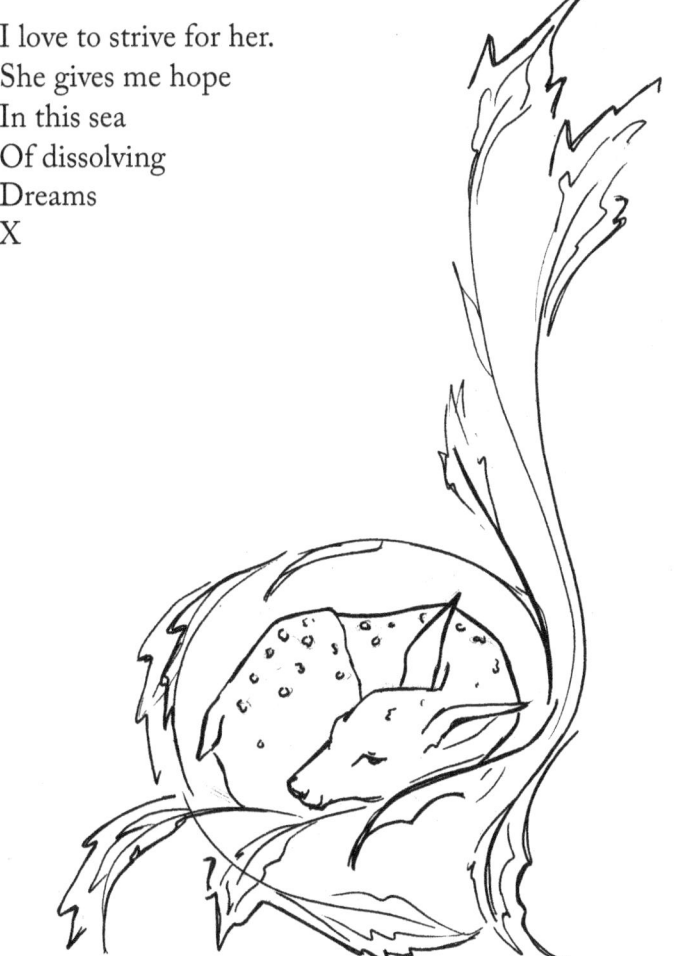

Theory of The Angled One
or The Dementia of Vegas

The theory of the angled one: The theory holds that those
of us with able bodies are the angled ones; that we are bendy.
Like Gumby.

So the story goes that,
Caught in the throws,
It doesn't matter about chips.
It's hips,
Drive,
A contention to thrive.
The theory of the angled one!

Rollin' through Vegas,
Got some hotties caught in my eye,
One's got to have a curiosity
Of how to get the sky
To open up with water
When the drought runs in, through a season.
One's got to be curious
How it is I'll get me pleasin'.

Is it that girlie's theorem
To find a guy out here tonight?
Will I be able to ask her
"Baby, would you hit the light?"

186

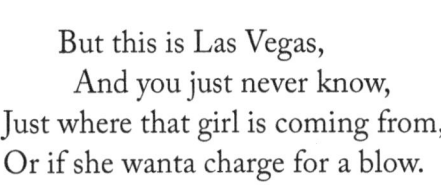

But this is Las Vegas,
And you just never know,
Just where that girl is coming from,
Or if she wanta charge for a blow.

Yet some seem so simple,
So placid, serene;
But in this bar
It could be that it just happens to be that they're lean,
As I watch the game that they are playing
So guys will come, and sniff around.

Or maybe it's that she's
Just simply dealing with having to
Look cute, so they'll laugh
And smoke cigarettes;
So smooth
In this neon littered booth of a bar,
A sea of flashing lights and bells,
Repeating like the heart of
An epileptic sparrow
That refuses to die.

187

Ah, the Breeze

Ah, the breeze as it comes in from the ocean.
And then there's the tease of the nearly naked motion.

It truly is a joy potion
For this man who can agree
That there is nothing wrong
With a day at the beach song
That goes a little long, and free.

The rolling wave's sound,
The birds as they call,
The sand for our ground,
And the grasses so tall.
All make this time
Such a beautiful rhyme
That Jah or God has had written about b4.

Here is a note of respect;
One you didn't expect,
Just because you deserve
The curve of a pitch
That says you aren't a bitch.
In fact, you're a queen.
Go ahead and understand what I mean.
You so dag keen,
That it's like a dream to me
To see you so happy and free.
And so, if I believe what I have here said,
It'll be a relief to so many ahead,
That we could straight smile a big one.

The Hook

I wonder sometimes how people get hooked,
Get hooked on slot machines.

I guess hope is something you can buy,
Even if it is just a dream.

'Cause people keep on dropping
Their hard earned cash,
And they just don't care if they
Get to eat.

I Need to Wash

Over and over in my head,
I feel the pounding
Of my thoughts.

Pictures of war everywhere.
George Bush gaining money.
Poor people losing homes.

The Secretary of the Army,
Thomas White,
Was an Enron V.P., and so
I know my nation hates me
From the top.

I hate it—> the natural hypocrisy;
The lies, and hiding facts.

There are evil people who are
Carrying my flag.

There's so much blood on the
Pole which holds it,
It has slipped from my hands.

190

I need to wash now!

****

For some reason people
Need war.

Well my fight is to not fight
At all.

Every day there's someone
I think about reaching out
Grabbing, and hurting them
Real bad.

But I don't.

My fight is to not fight at all.

This page is Coda

191

Almost Gone to a Canyon

192

My head…
I shed the memory.

I still need to emery my nails.
Never fails… Look at all
The positive stuff and I notice
The junk.
Who's punk –
En I'll ask "Why?"

I miss all the tales of beauty,
Being reality.
I need a canyon
Again.

Some Pains I Have Had

Hyper Blues

You asked me to love you,
    Asked me of love.
I looked up above and asked
    "Is it all right?"
It seemed fine every night.
Then came the time where you asked me clearly;

"Dear, would you make me a mother?"

And as a brother, I thought I was blessed.
    I guessed wrong apparently,
'Cause when your belly started to grow,
And then you yelled out "No!"
    You cut it out and said you wanted cash!
        I looked up to God and yelled "Flash!
            You lied to me!"
      Bride-to-be, – fraud!

Is it odd that I'm mad,
You're glad, and I'm just so sad?
We had something that I thought was
    Sacred.

You took my bliss and threw it into hell.
You took a kiss and left me a really bad smell.
You took my heart and well...
Threw it up there in the air
From where it fell.

You became a thief in the night,
And threatened a lawsuit.
Ahh!
You just weren't cute to me anymore.

195

And if you'd at least have been a little distraught,
And not gone out and caught
The next horny dude,
It would have been less crude.

You're just plain rude.
You brewed what I got.
I feel like I been shot,
And now I'm Hyper Blued......

The House on the Hill

The house on the hill
Makes me want to kill.

The thrill of life is gone and
I'm hopin' someday to spawn.
　Ooo, what about the fawn I'd be bearing?

It'd be wearing
　A suit of a nation
That was not of its creation –
　　That will be further down
　　The spiral
　　Than it already is.

I mean Jesus hasn't come back yet,
And we can not forget
That he said that he would –
　　To help us live in peace.
　　　　'N the ones who thought it –
　　　　"Whack!"
　　　　– Figured they'd attack
'N not even worry.
　　They're in a hurry,
On their way
To the new day that they see.

196

And me, I say maybe
I don't frickin' care no more.
But the damn lore about the
Situation of creation
Has got new twists.

Humanity persists.
All who resist will fail.
Continuity will prevail.
The sail's been raised.

197

There are Dreams to Remember

"Dreams to remember,"
The song plays.
I wonder if I'll ever be loved
As I was,
Again.
There are times
Where I see me
Hard, changed, heartless,
And cold.

It's getting old,
But protectivism is the
Option I choose
So that I just don't lose
A grip on my heart.

Meditations / Mysteries

Misconceptions

Maladjusted / Melodramatic

Magical stations ignored...

198

Give a Hint

I've been thinkin' about you a lot,

An' I took a shot.

I been thinkin'
    I can't live without you,,,
        Of bein' reborn.

I felt like I was worn through in my soul,
        And so I roll thoughts to you.

I just wish I knew
How you really felt for me.
I can't see your soul from here.
I wish you were near,
To help me steer
My soul.

    I don't wanna dole out
      No more time
    Thinkin' 'bout you in rhyme.

      I'm
    Wishin' you were here.

199

Madness from a Sadness

"A Farewell to Pittsburgh"

Got to tell you, I hear
A heart beating –
Meeting a new dimension.

Did I mention that we're
Here tonight as an open book?
Take a look.

I can't guess why I'm here near the sky.
I ask why, but the answer doesn't come –
It wouldn't matter anyway.

So I'm here today,
Sayin' "Hey, I'm gonna fly!"
Or gonna try at least.
Gonna go East, and then go West,
Figure out what I like the best.

Gonna hit while I'm at bat.
Count on that.
I've played too long,
Sang song on stage when I was fourteen
Years of age.

A sage they called me
When I got to this city.
But I'm gonna have ta leave –
They were wrong,
It was just a song.

(I'm angry.)
        Hear me!
      Fear me
        When I'm near ye.
I just might want to fuck with you
      I think it's fun –
        So go ahead, run, tell the police.
     But I got grease on me;
I'm gonna slip from their hands
     Like I usually do.

Someone brought a new dimension here today.
  Can I say it's a dangerous world out there today,
    And I often have protection that's legal?

201

      Like an eagle, I fly.
    Good-bye, I'll soon be saying –
And I'm praying that I find peace where I go.
    I know a good chance exists –

I know the Wood Dance persists around.
        Hear his sound:

    Serenity through musical ability.
Agility of the hand, to command a piece of wood
        With some strings;
Makes the sound that could surround a nation
    With contemplation of a special kind.

You say you've been cosmically signed?
    Well, I'm a Gemini,

And I fly like I'm supposed to –

I proposed to a psycho!?!

continued –>

She was totally insane –
    Her brain was somewhat disconnected
From reality.
    Oh,,, Finality was really her real best friend.
Her mind's one tare I just can't seem to mend.
        I tried – she lied to me!
        She was my pride to me.
        She was my bride to be.
    Now she's a chide to me;
Sent by the heavens,
    For something I did wrong.
        Now, my song is far from kind
        But please, do hit rewind.
    I told you she was crazy.
    Her tenderness made me hazy.
        I thought she was fine as a daisy.
I was stupid. Cupid played a mean-ass joke on me.
    My baby turned out to be a psycho.

Now I'm leavin' this whole damn state
It's gonna,,, gonna be great.
I'm goin' way down south.
You bet I'll open my mouth
To tell all forms of life
What I see 'round as my strife,
Until the last day I can wink my eye.

The things I do for you will multiply
In a gift for the Earth, and the moon, and the sky.

I'm gonna bee bop some more
But before I go and do –
I ask you to remember lore
Written by some "you know who".

The fools who sing for you here, there, and everywhere
Stop the hate that goes on, so don't be late,
Get your shoes on.
That'd be great, but listen mate:
If you connive, you won't survive,
So thrive as you dive into your existence.

203

Dip-jive in the soup
Dgee wop bee bop doo oo
Dge bee da we bee da we bop da we bop didley wop bop boo woo woo
woo...

As If

I have a poem for you baby,
Something I'd like to share.
Oh, that's okay there sweet thing,
It's okay that you don't care.

204

Why would I want you to
Take something you don't want?
I understand my timing's bad.
I'll just give it a bit of a punt.

Maybe toss it in a box somewhere,
Or lose it in the wash.
I'll just go make some loot so we can vacation
Somewhere decadent and posh.

But don't worry about calling between now and then,
I know I would get in the way.
I know you've got to spend time with you're friends.
Really, is there more left to say?

You're probably tired like you get lots of nights,
And I don't want to bore you right now.
So I won't even call you, I'll just text you a feeling,
'Cause baby, that's where I want my next vow.

I don't desire your presence,
Or even hearing your voice.
It's the ring tone I seek
As the prettiest noise.

205

It's all I know of you,
And as such, our love,
And so it makes me think of things
That we had done before the shove

Off into the chasm
Of interaction we now share.
Okay, so this poem is sarcastic as fuck,
It doesn't matter, you'll never read it.
I think we have established you don't care.

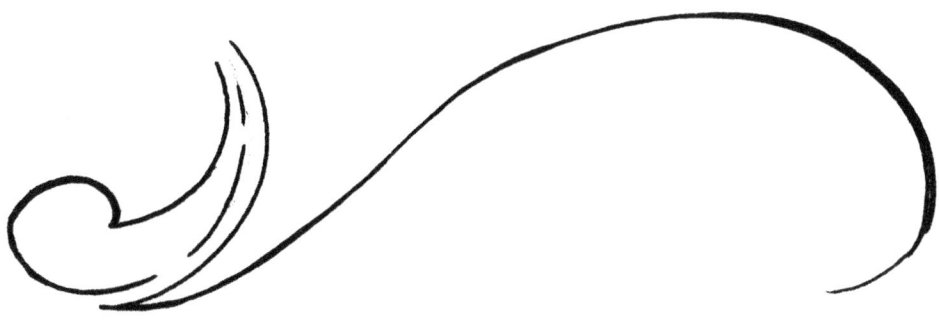

Letter to the Lost One

Some bottled potent drink is
A friend of mine right now.

Yea, I get lots'a kisses
When I try, or
Happen upon them;
I don't really know how to
Talk myself away from them.
Somehow, I feel like through all my searching,
Understanding is still somewhat elusive.
Possibly, I'll understand another day.

Imagine falling in love and then
Moving away.
Like what kinda happened with us,
Only you'd have to switch the rolls a bit.
No, you never realized what you meant to me.
Every time I fall in love this happens;
Like I don't pay attention or something.
Yea, I've only got myself to blame.
But all the same,
Everything seems all right from where I'm at.
Can't complain a bit.
Awful shit happens, it's true.

Under this umbrella though,
I kinda feel
Safe.
Even though you see me as
Elusive more than I would hope.

You've been gone so long that
Only a memory remains.

207

Understanding my mind wouldn't be wise maybe.
Right now, I only wanna hold you
And call you 'baby'.
Every day that goes by I think of you.

Oh, what a day it would be to finally see you
The same way again.

Oh, my friend,
Why do I have to feel this way?
Always thinking of you this way...
When am I gonna see you again?
Over the ocean, please send
Us a note?
I'm getting a little mutilated.

Standing on the Edge

I'm tryin' to distract myself
From topics
On my mind.

I'm looking for an excuse,
For something
That I can't find,
To not bother me
In its absence,
Or a topic to numb me.

I wonder why I'm left here
Feelin' like a fool.

My girlfriend hasn't called
For a week and maybe more.
I wonder why it seems
That I'm just beat straight to the core.

She didn't call after she said that she would,
And now I don't know what to think.
She also hasn't written when I know that she could.
I'm standing on the edge of the brink.

Don't wink, I might think it's got a meaning.

208

17,000 Years

Sometimes we can't understand, just why certain things happen.
Sometimes, it seems like a farce.
We don't always feel like our God is all there,
Sometimes, he seems all fuckin' nutz.

17,000 years we've spoken of this force.
Not *every* moment can hurt.
But sometimes, bit-through is how we, simply, feel.

The blood of emotion flows swiftly and pure.

209

Hopefully, with constant acceptance of great theories,
We can be in peace.

Even though it can be agony
During our way,
Sometimes, it's all we'll have.

But always, and through it, we learn anew each time;
Each time we go and **be** in a time.
<u>Always</u> thinking of the future,
Always.

A Note on Hangin' Out

It seems to've left:
           The ability to write something good,
               That would somehow explain
      Just how I feel these days.

When you said you wouldn't have me,
         I left my mind to dreams…

         I had planned out a whole bunch'a things
                   To do,
And all but one'a the schemes
          Seem to be comin' true.
             All 'cept for the one I could see;
        The one that had
              Me with you.

I don't know what you think of me,
And I don't know that I ever will.

I just hope that someone, somewhere,
Will figure out just how,
And then use their skill,
To unlock your heart.

It's so beautiful to see…

The time was there,
But now has gone,
Where I thought that it could'a been me.

I know we can stay friends;
        I just didn't want loose ends
           Hangin' out.

210

Where to Begin?

I've run out of places to
Go to.
I never know when
To hold on
To what I've got.
I think I may just give a shot at the pot…

Think 'bout what it
Is doing to you,
And dream
About release…

211

It's the only way to feel it.

I can not fall in love.
It hurts me.
Sometimes I wish I could
Cry, loud,
In someone's ear,
But they're
Never near.

Inside you, someone is living.
Beware.

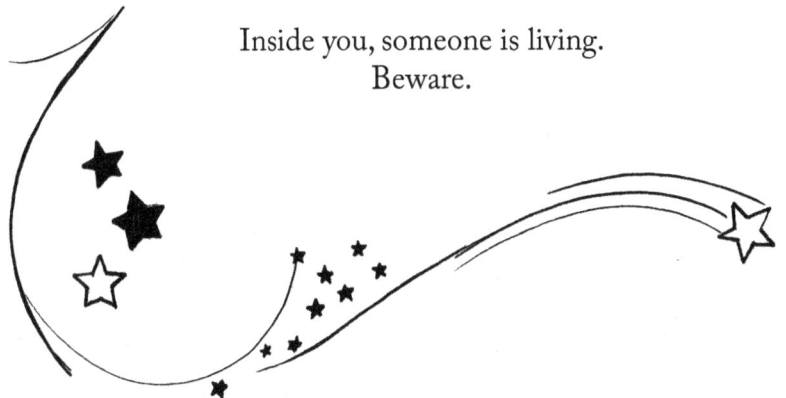

A Noel

Yes, you make my mind think of
Eternal realms.
So I try to make you happy as I can
While totally within the thought
That we were to be.

Decided by a conversation,
It seemed just like the Most-High was
Having you there so that I would see
God in your face.

I saw the grace,
Felt the trace;
Now I taste all emotions
Mixed within a single,
Very intense, potent sauce.

I'm wondering
Why.
Yea just why, it takes so much moss
Growing upon the tree of life
To take away the most painful
Of all the
Earth-bound strife.

I hope, and dream,
And pray, and yearn about
Your love,

So clear in its shallows.
While in the depths,
I'm never sure.

I wish
You wouldn't push
Me away
So much.
I keep on wanting to
Keep you,
While knowing
That I shouldn't clutch.

It hurts sometimes
When I don't like my rhymes,
Because you say
That they're too much.
It makes me want to cry.

You are the one
I hope to impress more than
All of the rest.
I'm sad right now,
Because I know,
I just have not
Done my best.

So now, I hope that you will
Love me through all my fuck-ups.
Please, I say now, please understand,
That I don't know you from God,
And though I know that it seems odd,

213

continued –>

When you tell me
That you want your space
And you go away,

I feel like a tiny little
Chipmunk
Not knowing which way
To go home.

214

All I know is that I feel
A need to go to Rome,
Knowing that you'll be there.

I have these dreams;
I know it seems
Like I'm not there.

I hope it seems
Like I'll always be there for you.

I totally want you to understand how
I'm living by giving you a whole new
Sense of trust.

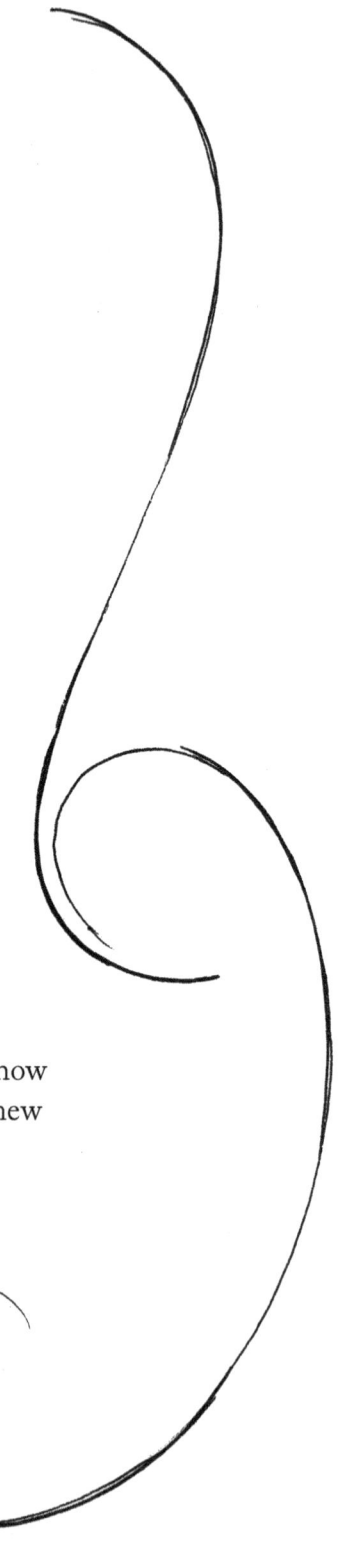

The Kindness
of Darkness

I see people grieve.
I see people leave.
I see people heave themselves
Along distant trips.

215

Darkness creeps into me.
Darkness creeps quite slowly.
Darkness makes that which is lowly,
Seem light.

Just Lost

I wondered where you were,
Then I realized you were gone.
You were all that I had.
I felt like I was naked
In front of all my peers,
But there was no one around.
You've found somethin' else to
Fill your life with
Other than my self.

For a while, I missed you.
Then I realized that I'd kissed you
For purely selfish reasons,
And now the season's changed.
I've rearranged my mind.

And now I find every day is okay
Without you.

I get so much more done
Without you,
But still I would take you back
Maybe.
Would you try me
Baby?

I want to take you back or
Turn you down.
I'm not sure which.

I just think that you
Were a bitch
The way that you left me,
Baby can't you see?

Californian Mirage

"You broke my heart"
Just might be said.
But I been long gone
For so long it seems.

Dreams happen sometimes.

You were an angel.
I wish I could have been
Better for you.

I yie yie

I wanted to rush things,
Kids 'n things.
'N these things…

A lover to you
Yes,
But the guess…
My blessing,
Is that I observe
A snip;
A clip.

Chips off'a so many blocks…
So many cocks.
Yea, we're running out'a space,
        As a species.

217

continued –>

I wish you'd miracle my way
Again someday my friend,
What can I say baby?
I tried to be gay,
It just sorta didn't work.
So I quirk another moment of our time.

Our love was pure rhyme.
Sometimes I look back and wonder
Why ya never came by to me,
And I see that our we
Was simply something of a certain time.

I move on in my life.
I really need a wife.
Comfort is mostly a state of mind.

Be kind, and be well.

Aw hell, you gotta know –
You helped me flow
When we were together;
Like two forces of weather,
Coming apart and going separate ways.

So many days I yearn for the time of you.
Eugene, oh God, be kind won't you?
It was only the best time of my life's memories,
And so I shake these trees over here with residual.

But you straight hurt me inside
When I decided to glide
Into your realm.

You don't know what I found.

You weren't around.
I fell down on the ground.
We were partners of the royal kind,
But then you left me to blow in the wind.

I've sinned. Yea, maybe,
But never versus you.

Curses too!
I loved you with every drop of my soul!
I made you a queen of Rock and Roll,
And you looked at me and said
"Well that's just not enough of a toll for me."
So I did sixty hours a week
So I could take you out
Now and then,
Wastin' time — ya know,
That kind'a thing.
Then you kicked my king-ass out on the road.

I talked with the Toad.
We talked about it, yea.
But I'm still torn up inside.

Your love held me together like a feather has its stem.

I couldn't do much more than clear my throat,
'Cause I was swimming in the moat
Of our Californian Mirage.

219

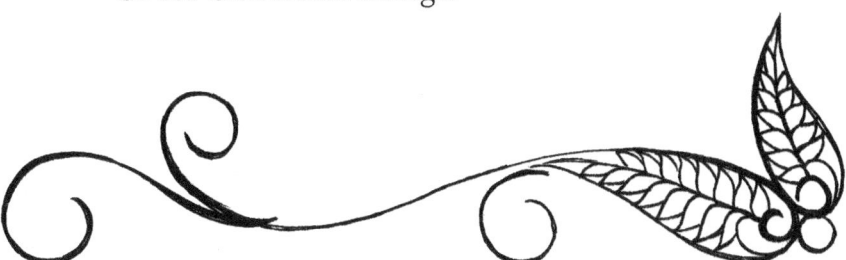

Take Care, Fawn

I see your mind wavering
During this time you could be savoring.

Your trip to your folks
Gave you some terrible pokes
To your mind.
Now, to just hold on,
You're laboring unkind.

You were so sweet and admired,
But now your conscience is tired,
And upset,
At the world around you.

220

I wish I had the right pill
That could make you feel chill,
Something to make your mind still,
Maybe some words that could astound you.

But when your mind is a mess,
It makes me regress.

So I digress;
I have only one life to live here.

I hope you can experience
More good things, sometime this year,
(Like when you first found those mood rings)
That'll somehow, accidentally,
Bring you cheer.

Because dear,
You do deserve it.
But babe, I gotta swerve it right now
Because you are about to destroy me.
Oh no, it's not that you annoy me.
It's simply, you're sucking my life away,
So I gotta stray right about now.

Don't think that this is how
I wanted things to turn out between us.
And though you're feeling burned out,
And though it's likely you'll doubt it,
I won't go 'round and shout it
As I go and route it.

221

I know you'll rearrange
From what now seems strange,
To something that'll work for you.

But until you do,
I gotta be gone.
    Take care, fawn.

Blank Abyss

The humans around here are a breed apart.
I often wonder whether this town has got a heart,
Or if it's designed like a vampire; to kill for its
Blank abyss.

222

Burnt to Distrust and Distaste

I can't write a love poem to save my life right now,
I'm to flippant to be loved, so I'll just say so.
It's just been too long.
I got burned by someone.
So burnt that hope has gone,
Replaced by distrust and distaste.
I hope I meet someone who really cares someday.
My rhythm is life, but when breathing is strife,
You know that change is a need.
I'm hoping we get to know a time where joy is evident
And conceived as part of the great flow.

How do we detach from an idea that is a breach itself?

223

Sophia is a
Memory

224

Sophia is a memory,
Forever in the past.
I wonder who will turn my head
And bring a love that lasts.

I Apologize

I apologize for imposing.
I apologize for love.
I'm really not so bright.
You see,
I thought heaven above
Had opened up
And been real nice;
But I can see that you
Are just a traveler yourself
Doing what you do,
And not what I had dreamed.

225

I apologize for asking twice.
It's just, sometimes it seemed
You let your
Mind travel with me there.
I thought we'd be a team.

Sunbeat Book

"So grows the apple tree
That was flung as a seed..."
So sung the humming me,
"That can not find the ground."

I wonder lightly
If I'm wrong nightly
About what we could have been,
Or what we could have clutched.

226

And as yet, I've but touched
The surface 'bout where
My mind has been trolled.

So I circle, and query,
As I meditate upon the Tao.
And as I seek further and further,
I begin to wonder how ~
To find a great kitten for myself.

I guess I have to wait more,
Because I'm still like a book on a shelf;
Getting dusty, and sunbeat,
As the time, it erodes my life.

Oh, to be Free...

Yes, I'm open to falling from grace.
        I look in your face,
     And I see a trace
       Of pain remain.
Can we regain peace like grease?
        Or do ya think that the East
     Is gonna come to the West
        And say "You thought you were the best?
Well here's a bomb to remember Hiroshima and Vietnam."
       Can you stay calm in the mist of a war season?
        Or is it treason
     To realize what our eyes can see?
Oh, to be free in the deposed land of freedom!
       It can be dangerous to someone.
– Aren't we supposed to be havin' fun?
      Why'd you hand me a gun?
       Now I like to kill way too much.
We've always been like this it seems.
      This really is all real!
This is no dream.   I wanna scream!

227

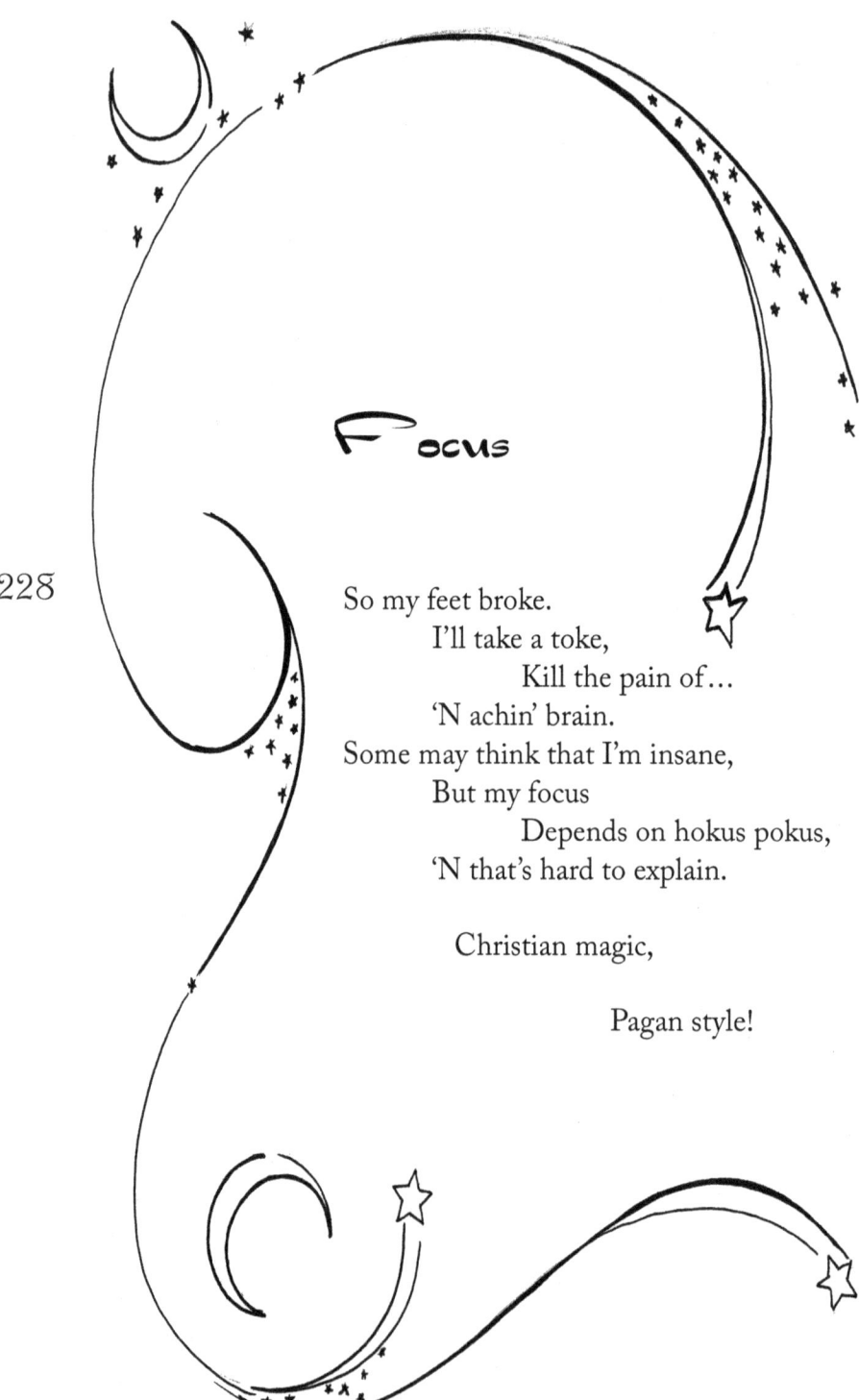

228

Focus

So my feet broke.
I'll take a toke,
Kill the pain of...
'N achin' brain.
Some may think that I'm insane,
But my focus
Depends on hokus pokus,
'N that's hard to explain.

Christian magic,

Pagan style!

How Do You Cleanse?

Here I am again feeling
Good/bad/indifferent.

My stomach hurts,
Not enough for heroin,
But it's raining outside –

See,
I like rain.
How do you cleanse?

229

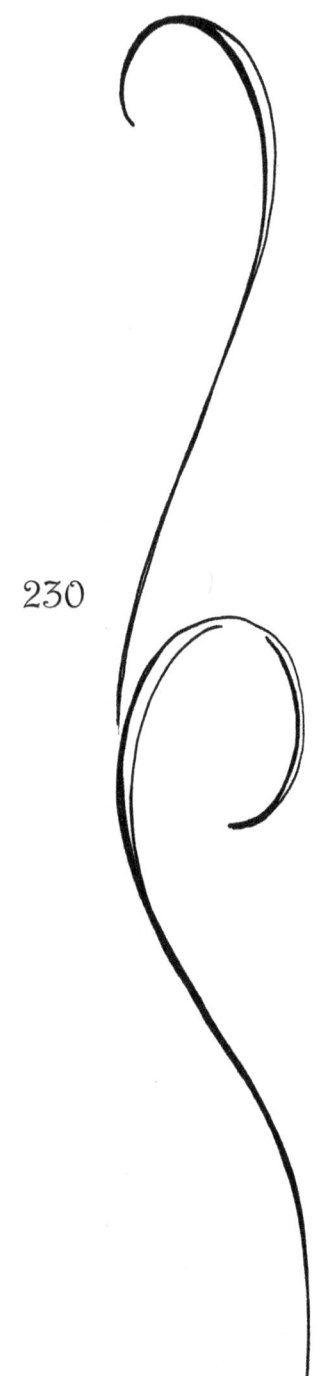

A Search for a Little More Than Aspirin

i just wanna get outa this town.
i just wanna get outa this school.
i wanna rule myself.
i can't do it.

i wanna go somewhere from here.
oh, someone hear me!
oh, feel what i've gone through!
i can't figure it out.
i keep on shouting.
no pouting,
no more.
no,
i won't let it be.

someone see me, love me, hold me tight.
i don't feel all right
tonight.
i can feel to much pain…
oh, i like the rain.
it's cleansing.
feel what's real.
i can't peel this feeling away.
i can't sway.
i can say to you though, that i'm feeling this way.

230

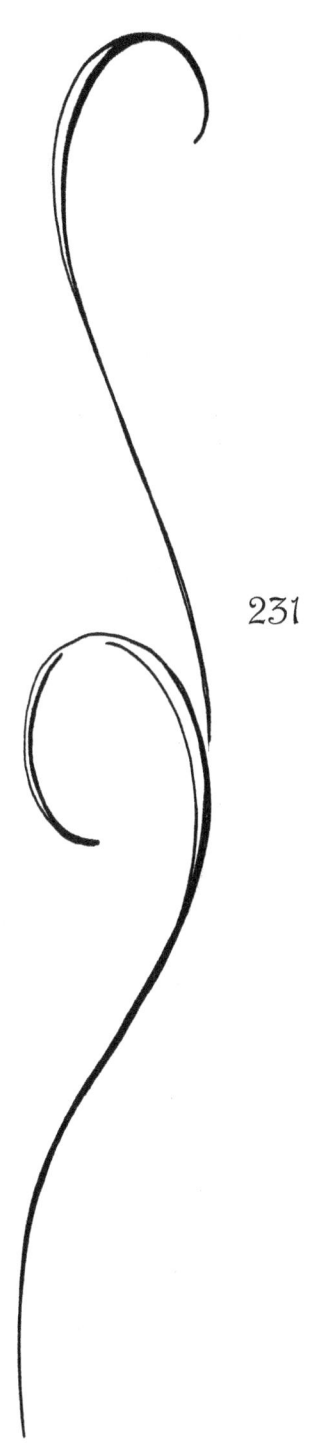

oh, today!
i got to say i don't feel okay.
what to say?
i wonder whether you want to hear more.
i wonder if you care anymore.
i'm sore, i ache, gimmy a break.
take what you want.
punt me in a new dimension!

i need new direction,
i need affection.
you see, i have an affliction;
like an addiction,
it just comes in to me.
diction is what you see.
help me
(i'm trapped in here).

why won't anyone hear me?
do they fear me?
they sure run like they do.
maybe i'm contagious outrageously.
i don't know.
i just want to show that i feel.
i'm really, really, really, really real.
come feel, help heal me.
ohhhhhhhh--ooooooooh
so lonely

—

231

continued –>

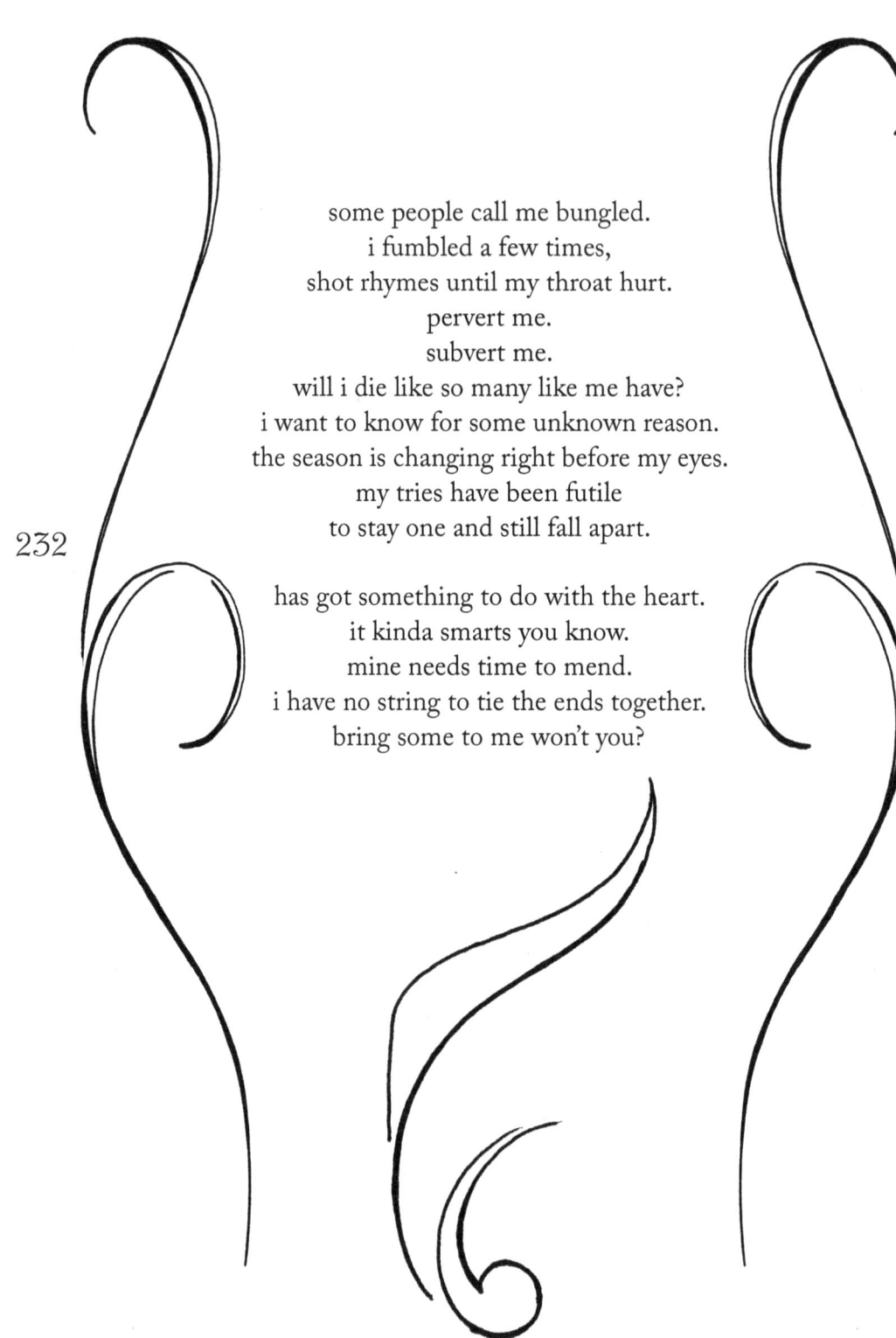

some people call me bungled.
i fumbled a few times,
shot rhymes until my throat hurt.
pervert me.
subvert me.
will i die like so many like me have?
i want to know for some unknown reason.
the season is changing right before my eyes.
my tries have been futile
to stay one and still fall apart.

has got something to do with the heart.
it kinda smarts you know.
mine needs time to mend.
i have no string to tie the ends together.
bring some to me won't you?

Enraptured Mind

233

My mind is becoming enraptured
With pained ridicule; with demise
Becoming a frequent theory of my life.

I feel tapped out, left out, shunned, gunned,
And unliked. I don't want to find employment,
Haven't had a lover for too long, and I need to
Figure out if my life will sing a song.
But as it is, I feel shitty. I feel
Torn, and removed, and depressed, I can't
Even get mental health when my finances are stressed,
And so I'll search for some meaning, or maybe
I'll off myself, because I'm either positive or
Negative, and I won't resign to living in hell.

Bloody Evil War

234

We're in this bloody evil war again!

It's been decided to send
Cluster bombs
To our friends,
The Afghani children
Of the East.

It seems the nature
Of the beast.

Is this the one they
Stabbed with
Their steely knives,
But just couldn't kill?

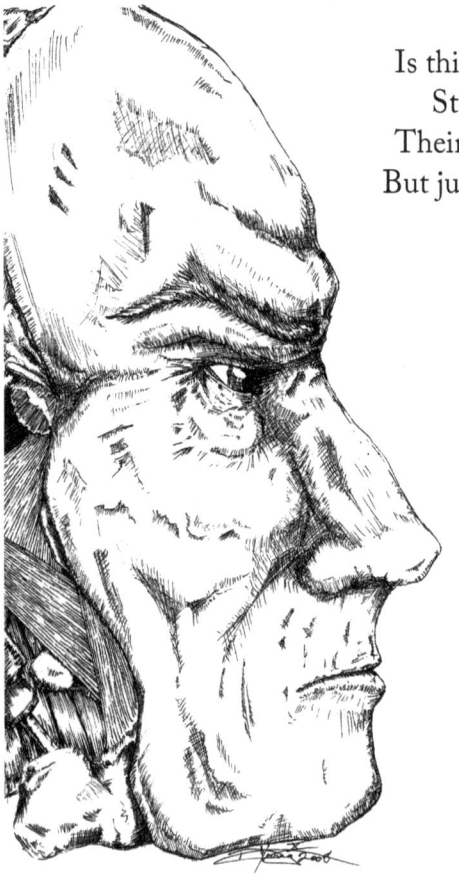

I feel kinda ill.

I just don't understand this land.

We hate, we create,
We create hate.

I hate that.

How can it be
That we
Can do this to ourselves?

We are one world.
We are swirled
Together
Like weather –
There will be pain.

But it's insane to make it worse.
I think it's a curse.
Specifically, I mean it's
Shitty!

Dead To Me

When you came over to my house, I got happy.
When you came over to my bed, I was blessed.
When you came over top of me sweating, I died.

I came too, a few minutes later.

We lied to each other about needing to be anywhere else
And shared a cigarette.
You might've conceived, but you're now dead,
So I'll never know.

236

I grieved, but now I must grow.
I thought about blowing my head clean off,
But that would be counter-productive.
I haven't died, and I don't know where Heaven is,
So now I've got to replace you,
'Cause I need a family, for meaning, for me.
I would really love to grow a soccer player,
Or whoever my child wants to be.
I need to find a lover.
I hover and traverse.
When will I bust this curse?
You weren't the first to have all my loving.
You just made me see kids' lives more clear.
So now I've screwed with this year
By falling for you and watching you fall down dead.

I'll never forget how heavy your head seemed
As the blood coming out, just streamed.

I dreamed about you again.
You were wearing a sundress I'd never seen.
It was beautiful.
And as green as it was underneath your feet,
It was like catching a cleat in my eye
When I recalled how you died...   237

Mourning combines with dawn.
We've all got to move on.
So that's what I'm doing right now.

I'm placing a personal ad for me.
I'm gonna auction me off today.
What can I say? It's a new day.
I've got to get a move on.

I've got to get back in the groove,
On the plane that I understand.
The land can not be so complex
That I have got to get a complex for you.

Fear

238

I run away because
I'm afraid of myself,
Afraid of who I am.
Scared that my Dionecian reverence
And people's love,
Can and will kill me;
And I wonder how to control.

I've taken paradigms as paramount;
Like not being a control freak,
And trying not to lie.
So, I'm trying not to die;
Trying not to be false.
But the truth, it kills anyway.
And I know that the day
Will come that I strum my way
Into a ball of light,
'Cause I'm at the height
That they're all around me
In my flight.

She Said "Don't Leave"

I've always said
I express better in a song.
Sometimes, I'm just mute.
I'm not tryin' to be cute.
It's just I don't know
How to talk,
So I look at my clock
Thinking
    "I got to get away!"
  What can anybody
 Say, when the same
Girl who broke my heart
 Said "Don't leave?"

239

Now We Part

Girl, you are so insane.
You better believe
You can't remain
On a plane of existence
That is so uptight.

You might want to listen
To your self.

240

You tell me that you want to do another girl.
That's just fine in my version of the world.
I just don't get it why you say forget it
Now that I've done the same.
My name,
You said you wanted it to be yours.
Now you're sleepin' with whores.

That's fine, I read
Your letter after some fine wine.
I had another girl's number in my pocket
Just figured I'd clock it,
Clock the time it took you to crook.

You stole my heart.
Now we part.

I'm accused of being sullen.
I'm accused of being crass.
Sometimes I'm even accused of being
A pain in someone's ass.

241

I don't really have a fucking clue
How to get back to the class
Of people that are more happy,
Than being pissed off.

At times,
I wonder how I find myself places
That all I can do
Is share rhymes.

Rain, Huh?

Rainbows come in with rain,
It hides the pain,
It brings the sane.

What will remain,
Will be forever alive.
We can survive
Bein' alive.

Today can really hurt, really bad.
I'm glad something like the rain can come.

To thumb from one town to the next
Is one way.
Or to be gay –
Or to say "fuck you" to
Someone who
Pisses you off – it's
Kinda like
The rain,
A pain in your ass.
Is a class all its own –
Thrown from one
Town to another –
Don't know
My brother.
– Oh brother,
Ya smothered ya main brain

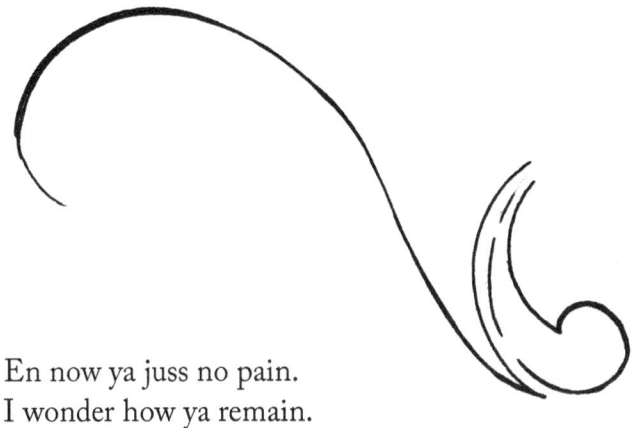

En now ya juss no pain.
I wonder how ya remain.

I hope –
Yea, I hope ya can gain
For the remainder of your life,
A life without strife.
    –Ohh, ya dug in ya arm,
     Lookin' at the blood farm
     Inside your arm!
Hopefully rain can release the pain.
Get good en washed off.

My space got cleansed mentally.
–Preventally, I hope you the same.

But all for the name,
I hope that the game isn't too hard for you to finish.
Participate in rainbows.

243

I Don't Want to Pay

244

There are hookers from left to right,
That want to please and play.
I got to tell the truth though,
I just don't want to pay.

The Fucking Hooker

The hooker doesn't seem so happy tonight
It doesn't seem the sex industry has
Everything right.

She's sitting at the next table, her
John is Chinese.
She looks as though she's gone so many times
To her knees.

There is no joy at her table,
Even the guy don't grin.
I guess the guy is getting nicer,
She's starting to give in.

She smokes, she sighs.
He pays, she lies.
She drained her beer
And laughed with no fear,
It's gonna be one
Wild night.

I gotta laugh, she's seen me see them
And now she's giving a performance for some fun.
Her motions stir the man,
He's surprised that he can
Sit near this gorgeous one
Who speaks regarding nothings
Into his ever-juicing ear.
It seems that they've changed their positions.
She's fucking him,
That's clear.

Placid Restraint

Placidly restrained seems to be the best way,
So as to not be one of the offenders.

One of the menders,
Instead of given to chance.

246

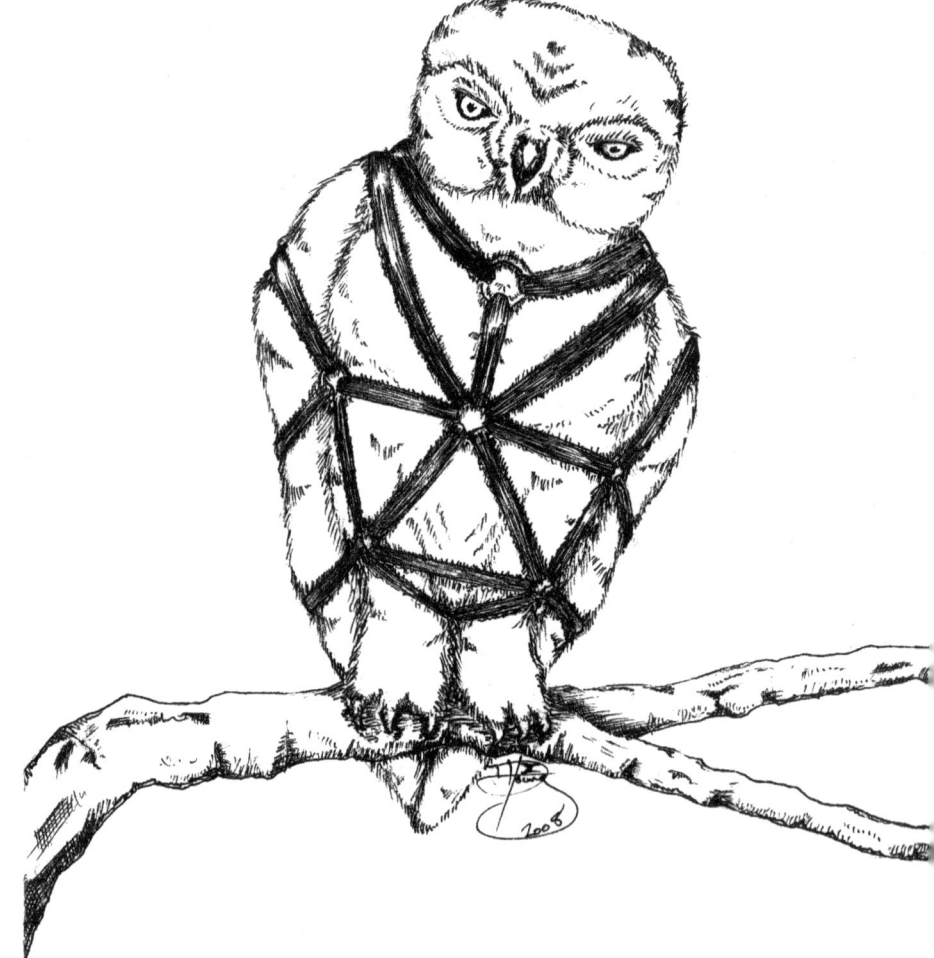

Placidly restrained, so as to stay out of the way,
Of the violent and unhappy;
So as to seem dispossessed or
Mirthless.

There are times when the expulsion of
Forces inside
Is inevitable,
And with good sense,
Is narrated,
So as to soothe the experience.

247

My supple incantations pray for virtuous love,

But a consistency of callousness
Remains a staple adversary to relationships of benefit.

I Can't Sing

I kin not sing-song the last song.
It seems to mean too much to me.

I can not sing-song the last song,
'Cause you don't mean that much to me.

I have to float on so I can breathe free.
I have to remember that we never really met,
And I can get lost easy.

248

Things I See

I don't know how to write anymore.
Like a whore,
I've been used like a tool by others.
College smothers me.

I look out at the people around me.
   I know
   What they feel
   So real, it's tickly.

So I numb my mind whenever I can.
Don't you know? My hand's
Been dealt to me
So that I know how I'm gonna die.
"Why?" is something I can not see
Behind the mask.
I wonder if I'll be safe.
I'll take a pill. I always will.
What a thrill!
I wanna kill sometimes,
But no! Rhymes!

That's all I see come from me.
   I wonder
If I really exist.
I persist beyond all reason and doubt.
The season's come to shout.
I know about the things I see,
And that's all you'll hear from me.

249

Wrapped in Technology

Wrapped in technology
With no way out!

I've got a cordless telephone,
A remote controlled stereo,
But no friends will call me.
They're wrapped up in something
Technological themselves.

Wherever they are,
They're doing something right now
That doesn't require any people.
Isolated!!
We've isolated ourselves!

We've finally put all our love on shelves
(we've put it out of reach).
It's something you cannot teach.

Ask the children who they love today.
You might be surprised with what you hear.
Stand near, I might tell you.
Oh no, I'll repel you.
I don't know why, it happens that way.
People don't mesh together the way they used to.
It's hard to get used to the new stuff today.

We make so much shit that comes around.
What have they found lately?
We are warped in technology!

I write with a pen and I hear it's odd.
My god, what's happened to our people?
Are we gonna kill ourselves soon?
We've been to the moon
But we haven't fixed ourselves.
We've electrified everything.
Shocks hurt.
We've got to get off the shelves
What humanity built itself on…

Love your family today.
Love your neighbor anyway.
It's really the only way to make the species live on.

Once love is lost,
The cost will be
The frost won't melt no more.
We will have treated Mother Nature like a whore.

We take what we want,
Don't lemmy front,
Then we neglect her.
It just ain't right.

That's right,
You might want to say "thank you" somehow.

Wrapped in technology,
It's gonna kill me if I don't kill me first.

I thirst for something more than I've been getting.

The Willow Dance

I've seen a bad human
        Willow dance.
I've seen abused people
Try to romance
Each other.
    It's frightening.

I've seen women happily paint themselves
Like the dead,
Yearning for a little
Bit more of the dread.

I wonder how their
Children will feel.
I'll tell you something
I know that's real.

    "I'm Frail!"
    She wailed,
    As the ocean ship sailed
    From the sea
    Into the port, where
    She and me and many more
    Have been before,
    Or at least heard of.

252

The port that she landed in
   Has scared her now.
   She doesn't realize
   Just how she'll get around.

She knows she has the tools
She just doesn't know the rules of the city.

253

Poem About Deep Strifes

This is a Poem About Deep Strifes

I look around at the planet and I wonder,
"Well can it really be these people are
This dumb?"
I got to wonder, 'cause
I see that they're killing our mother,
And I want to extend my green thumb.
I want to hitchhike to the next world,
So I can't see what's here.

I'm perplexed that people haven't figured out clear,
That if we don't recycle, change our fuel sources,
Save our seeds and thoughts,,,, well, we're screwed.

And I wish
That the people that get paid to sing
Would talk with intelligence,
Instead of fluffy bullshit,
Because if
We don't preserve this Earth we've got,
Well,
It'll just split.

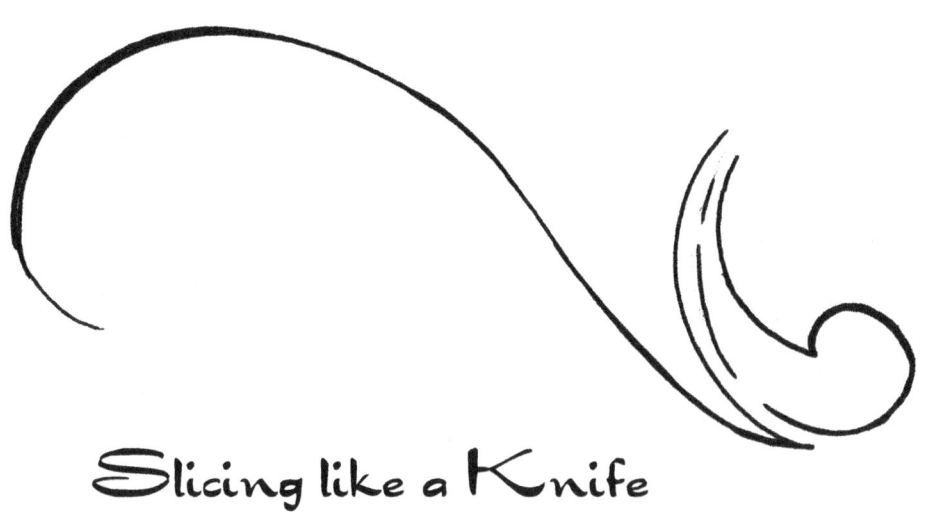

Slicing like a Knife

Slicing like a knife,
Exposing hidden strife
That flows within'.

255

What it's Worth

There are times where I feel serene;
Times which soothe my tempers,
And strife-filled emotions;
Times which settle my soul,
And help me.

Understand why it is, that I pry my life apart,
And those moments
Make every cleanse worth the cost,
Make every scar worth a star.

256

The Music of Life

Jazztronic

The way an active musical
Ambient wave's…
Air
Is impressive and altering.

258

An ambient sense of sound, works as reiki or other supra-

massage. The elbows and thumbs of a masseuse are the audio's equal,

as the vibrations travel, and then arrive, at a human.

…Still traveling, yet at a destination;
Traversed, and yet continuing.
…Arrived, and yet impermanent;
…Resonant,
Though followed by balanced change.

Two Things

The streetlight hum
           Had a smell of echoes
                        Of light metal,
     Falling like rain on an open surface
                        In slow-motion.

And how
        The clanging of the
               Super-high chlorines
     That held together the audio wavelengths
           Was sharp,
                 And rang in my ear –
                       Escaping through my hair,
                 In a rather bizarre, though I must say
                       Pleasant, way.

259

Those two things made me think of Jazz music.

What it is About Music

Part one

I listen to music for the magic it brings from inside.
It reaches out from the realms of someone's mind,
And shows the secrets no one would confide
In a friend, or even a family member.

A thought so near,
You can hear
How it feels,
When its chord has been played.

260

I love to listen to poetry
With a beat and guitar and some bass.
I think it's the ultimate path to go by
To get up in somebody's face,

When you've got something on your mind
That you've been thinking about too much.
It's also good to remind old people,
When they've got out of touch.

Or even the young ones;
When they don't quite yet know,
What it all means – that goes on around them.
Or do you just think it's a show?

Music is, to so many people,
What keeps them going from one day to the next.
Music is an expression of feeling.
Nothing else can you ever expect.

Part two

I don't know if I can remember
When I happened along with the taste
For good music as I wake up in the morning,
Complimented by a burst of minty toothpaste.

It really makes the day go by nice.

My prescription for a morning
Comes from years and years of testing.
I have recently come to the conclusion
That it even improves your resting.

By listening to music by night, asleep;
Your dreamscape's landmarks come alive.
So you shouldn't expect just some sheep,
As your subconscious reveals what's inside.

When your mind is massaged by the wavelengths
Soaring through your thoughts;
The images come to life, almost at will,
That tell you what it is you had ought

To do, before leaving this place we now sit on,
This place that we now live in,
This grace we've been given.
Let us all be dreamers,

Just let the band play on.

Like One Again

That friend
Who'd bend the strings
For the guy who sings,
For the girls who
Are dancing,
With their curls in their hair,
Makes it in his way.

Catch it in the day
Or on the nighttime, where
The signature rhyme of the band will land
When they make their play like they had planned.

Try to check their expanded minds.
The finds, on the rinds, and what it is inside…
Where funk loves to reside,
All for the slide of being smooth.

Oh, they cried as they tried to make the night plain sing
In order to bring Mother Nature's Spring
For the ones around
On through their slick sound
That they had found to groove to.

And since they brought it to you
In hopes that they'd move you.
They want you to feel
Like one again!
So feel it,
For real.

Sky Dancer, Joyride to Tranquility

I am guilty of seeing too much.
I am guilty of loving too much.
I really want to believe
That it's all right to love,
And not have pain for insane
Reasons.
Seasons keep on changing.
I'm still strange, and I know what I
Have got to do.
I got to get up to
Another microphone to sing
Again
And again
And again.

263

Rainshine

The rain's shining.
Not a soul is
Whining.
The bus is singing,
And we are bringing
Ourselves
To a show.

We're going to entertain
And try to remain sane,
As we realize
That all size is in
Perspective

Of whether
You love
Or if you don't.

So go ahead and smoke a joint.
"What's my point?"
Someone might ask me,
And I'll tell: My task is
To make any sadness
Simply
Go away.

What we'll do is try to play
Some music
To some listeners,
Because they like to hear the glisteners
Of sound.

264

Here we are.
We've come around;
We'll help you find
Yourself getting down.

Got a little buzz –
Talking 'bout what it was –
And then the buzz
Got a bit –
Consciousness – got higher!

We're massagin' our mind;
We're tryin' to just plain find
The feeling of equilibrium.

So late,
There ain't a
Drop'a hate.
I'm here to create
A good dose'a love
That's flowin' up, in, and through.

We all ride inside a bus to go to
All sorts of places.
We look at the faces
Coming out as our crowd;
We float around like we're up on a cloud.

When we come,
Come on out all sorts'a loud.
We, in our speeding bus
Carryin' all of us.

Rainshine has begun;
People laying it
On down,
Don't grimace a frown.

265

continued –>

Think of how much fun
They're gonna feel,
When they find themselves
Playing music for some kats tonight.

It's gonna be all right.

Won't you take in our
Light flow
That you can dig?

That's the gig.

The Band's Got to be Formed
We Create the Legend

We need to train up who will
Be the next horner for the band,
Because across our land, we find
That not just sand is our base.
What it is to see a face
That doesn't believe in the race,
But in humanistic bond:
How they're filling the shelves
With the books they're writing,
From the view near the fighting
That goes on
From the dawn
Until night time!

They're seeing the fleeing,
And all of the being we do,,,

So, for the balance,
Won't you please be conscious?
Like, really conscientious in your action.
Do apply some subtraction
With the mission of addition
While attempting to avoid destruction,

Like attraction 'tween the sexes
Leads to having children.
Let's give a bit more care
In what we do.
Realistically, it is on you.
What can anybody do
But persist to exist?

267

'85 Jive

Crusin' wit' the top down,
down the highway.
85, in the sun.

85, just for fun.
Hair flowin' 'round.
The ground zippin' by.
My oh my,
tha speed of 85.

Jive is spoken here,
alive.
Don't ask me why.

85 miles pa owa;
survive!
Strive, to excess.

268

To 85 – drive. Be alive.
Speak tha jive.
Never connive.
Thrive.
Arrive at conclusions.
Understand confusions.
Release solutions into the atmosphere.
Ahhhh, to conversate…

The rider on high, rides a little higher.
The powers found in the mind
you can find,
mystify at first.
The big brown brain,
the rain,
don't complain.

Regain
the plane.
Refrain my friend,
send me a letter.
Make it better.

(A hedda z'wat he is.)
Got a goal,
like a mole:
Dug it.

Got ideas to make it fun.
Shun no sun!
Oh, blue sky:
Why you so beautiful?
Got chyour clouds,
your stars at night…

The night consumes
the fumes in my head.
I get red during the day;
perfumes help me be,
see.
Be free.

Be with me, free.
One thing to remember –
Only the self drives,
through existence.
85
Dive into life!
Release the strife,
Revive!

269

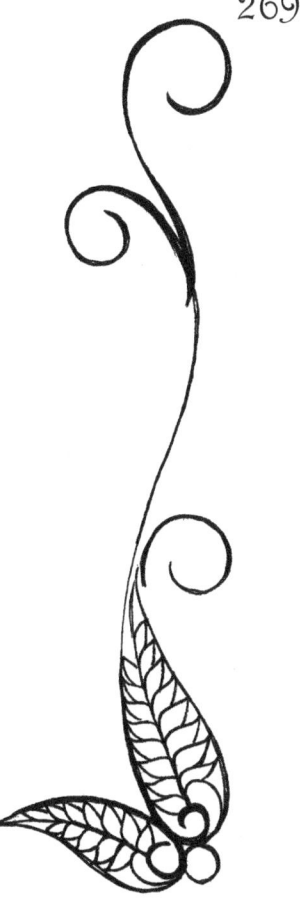

continued –>

Come alive,
again,
and again,
and again,
and again,
and again,
and again, and again.
Don't pretend
to contend
certain things
if you don't
believe what you're saying is true!

It is you who must say who you are!
Nobody else knows.
Nobody can show how you feel.

Be real.
Life is a mobile,
and you are the hanger.

Show your self – reveal.
Be ideal
for real.
You shouldn't fake it;
you won't make it
if you do.
It's you
that must strive to be alive at 85;
to drive…

Be an archive,
arrive at conclusions,
avoid confusions.

Decide what you feel,
to be real.
Wow 85…
With that wind in your face,
what a grace it has…
Pizzazzz!
Shaaaaaaaaaaaa…
Ohhhh man,
you can
do it.

271

I mean shit,
what do you do?
Move. Groove.
Be smooth!

Live with your head above ground.

Come around
when you've found
what abounds your mind.

To be a Pirate

To be a pirate
Is to be floating
Upon the wind,
And the seas,
And our lives.

We gather before you,
A feast for your senses,
Especially the one of your eyes.

Though I must say truly,
(For we are many and unruly,
And I don't hope to be quartered here tonight.)
That our Dj's will astound you,
For their music will both pound you,
And I believe, inspire you–
To burn
The wick of your great spirit-torch,
For a mystic – and appropriate – light.

****

272

Lovin' Shared

Loving gets shared.
People get paired.
Wanderers, of course,
Stared at us.

The bus is
About to be moving.

The drummer's grooving,
And we, are now moving
To the beach.

Fresh as a peach,
We're goin' through today
With our sniffles and coughs,
And our random soul boffs.

We're glad to be now, on our way.

273

Have Fun!

This is goin' out
To those who can't
Hear my shout.

Though we're here all together,
Like a day of sunny weather,

They're not here,
So they can't hear
What I'm talkin' about.

274

I hope the sun is shinin' where they are.
But they're all far…
The car that brought –
Wait, I gotta balk;
Maybe you walked.

But I see you brought
Your body and soul
Here to rock and roll.

Ain' much of a toll
To sit here for a while.
The fact is, here and now,
That cha' got you'a
Groovy style,
'Cause ya got
Groovy smiles.

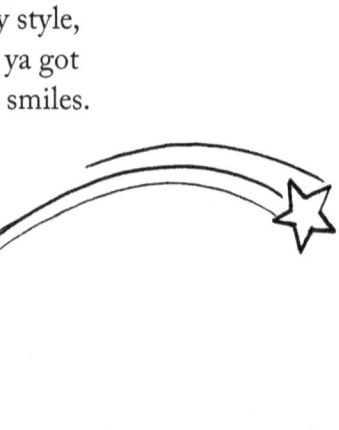

And all of the miles that we've all tread
Don't have the first clue how to kill us all yet.

En if we take time to wonder
What happens
When we're dead,
We'll miss a lot'a what's out there.
Yea, that's my bet.

But if you maybe can feel
That Karma could be real,
Or Judgement Day might come.

275

Maybe
You kin feel
Like you want to be kind
Some.

All I want to say
Tonight
To those who
Aren't here
As well
As to those who are,

Is look at a bright star,
And know that it's not that far,
Because all – that is Soul – is One.
Have fun!

Laptop Rock and Roll

Sooo – I yie yie!
Laptop rock and roll –
It's really, really sold out –
But that's the toll
For being able to spray a shout,
Or a scream,
Or a dream.
– It really seems the night is
The righteous place – to give a trace
Of the space
That's been filled.

276

Who've you killed on your tree of life,
Trying to get away from strife?
A new knife is words.
– We birds fly so high
That be and by,
You and I will learn to try
New methods of existence.

Resistance to what's coming up.
I feel like I should shut up 'bout makin' problems
And just revere the sky – my my.
Don't you know that when I high,
I see what it is like to be free?!
Re boo bee bopbahh bee bee
Booby doo wop bop bay…

Motion

Set in motion,
Movin',
Groovin',
Listenin' to the sound.

On goin'
Relapse-Synapse
Breaks down
The sound.

277

Under the Hale-Bopp's Perihelion

Remembering other times,
Times slicing;
Slicing my mind,
My memory.

slicing the mind,
slicing the memory ~
slashing on through,
making the call.

Needing the call.
Needing to Break on Through!
Check the hall. They're coming for you;
Coming after you.

thinking in the daytime 'bout the night,
hoping flight
allows.
hoping the flight allows for anything;
anything throwing them away from their blues.

They might bruise
Or overuse.
Take it loose,
As they choose to
Peruse your thoughts.

that which is caught inside your skills
just Yelling to be out…
wanna shout
about what
you think folks'll share,
and they might!

278

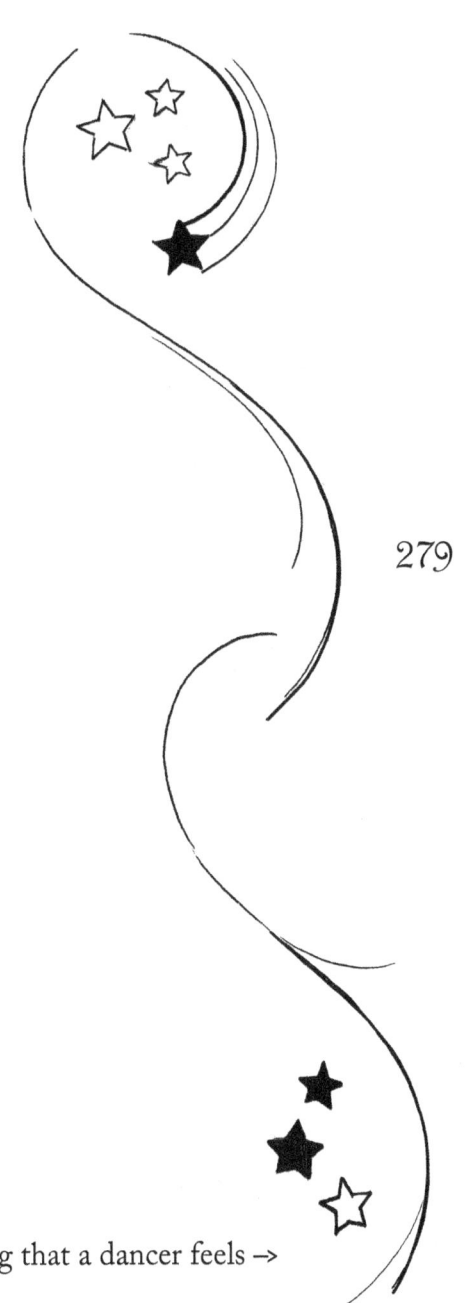

Right!
Like, right on the money!
Honey, you got it.
Spot it there between your ears.
Clears your senses
When we break down
The fences of our fears.
Too many tears
From ya head been shed.

time fa smilin',
milin' into a new kinda future.
got a plan.

279

Chock full, we can take it
Shake it,
Bake it in a pan.
We can stake it down,
Give it a lake near some land.
We can
Keep it in a can,
We can
See the lifers dance.

they prance in a magic style
having gone the mile
to arrive,
to strive
for centered motion.
implosion of the mind we find
in the motion of the kind feeling that a dancer feels –>

        The reels...
Four dollars an' a tap for tip.

continued –>

As a fact in time.

Hit the wikky wikky wac
'Till the beat turns into skat!
You will be fine.
So space your face,
Let your
Voice make some noise!

so choice,,,
did you see that Halley?

My god she was fine.
Ain' gonna make her mine.
Jiss diggin' on watchin'
Her walk down the line.
So fine as a dancer,
As she
Dance her hips off.

shooo!
whoooooooo,
got the crew starin'
and wearin' those eyes'a theirs.

Bears, as they're leanin'.
Mean, 'en still, as they chill,
Watchin' the people,
In the steeple.
There be no one freakin' out.

clout only mean a something.
there ain't nothin' there to doubt.

Enjoy your route.

280

Choice Moments

"What do I know about music?"
You've just asked me plain.

Don't take me wrong, as
I give it to you in song.

It might seem a little insane,
But ya know that the poet
Needs his pain.
So I strain
My voice
At choice
Moments,
'Cause that is what it is all about.
You hear it as it comes to you in a shout.

281

Hopefully you won't doubt
That it'll get a whole lot smoother,
Once I hear my voice
In the microphone check.

I'll pinch my throat.
If you take a vote,
We'll agree it looks kinda funny,
But as I let my words get all kinds'a runny,,,
It turns out that it's worth some money.
So I might let it roll, on down Blueberry Hill…

His Tune

He stands at the microphone,
    Dancing slightly, and sings
        His tune.
The old and mighty
      Willy Nelson is seen beside him.

282

His neighbor dances with his six-string
        Like it was his lover.

    They sing together in harmony…
The bartender comes out to dance.
    There's one female dancing in the
        Middle of the floor.

The musical dance is a quick step.

~~Nobody saw any of it coming.~~

The Groove Paper

A story with 10 titles
Find them all!

All About Love in Rock and Roll.
Love About All in Rock an' Roll.
Rock, and How Love Fits In.
+
Roll the Concept.
    Ya Know, What it Means to Be a Rock on a Roll.
So here we have it, a description of what it means to
Dig.
    Ya're gonna read what it's like to
Hear rock and roll.
    Now is one of those times
        On Earth, where it fits to've rhymes
           With full explication. Here
             It is.

283

From The Sole, Here's a Scale.

"Rock and roll – Gotta see that payin' the toll on the highway of rock and roll's gonna pull blood, sweat, tears, and kisses from ya."
           –A Fish

"If you're a mister, ya get the sisters. If you're a sister, you're gonna get the guys. All'a the lies that they'll tell – Some'll live through Hell to see you – They just want'a get through – They want'a touch you all the time – They want'a clutch your soul!"
           –A Non a Must

Ol' rock and roll has so much basis in love. It fits like a glove that some people got their minds in..,!,..the angst grin.

"Can we begin continuance?"
        – myself, A.K.A. Jimmer

continued –>

The Rusted Root speaks of a plant
That can't be grown. Our own,
And others', brothers', sisters',
Freaky, combined, refined,
Defined into a total existence.
Sometimes resistance,
But other times
The grease for the glide
Of when your inside reaches out;
Not to shout, but to sing, to bring
Beauty to the air.
Where do we grow?

There are cats that are stalkin' about,
Talkin' about it bein' a quest.
Some request an autograph for a laugh,
Or just to have a little bit of proof
That anybody can't be so aloof
As to be gone, out of reach.

There are those that will try to teach
What it's like to live a life, with or without a wife.
Some might like to have a dozen.
Some like to get with their cousin.
Whatever makes them grin.
They don't really care about sin
In the realm of Rock and Roll.
To pay the toll is all they really ask;
Even if you take it as a task to try out all the drugs
That you can handle while you're gettin' all those hugs.

Do dangle if you want.
Ya can't forget to punt
Yourself out of the world
In a curly, groovy way. No way.
You'll die, no lie,
If you go the route of the Bohemian pout.
Some say you should smile.
I'm of that style.   Yip.

Positivities through music
Make for happier musical expultionists, A.K.A. musicians.
In the meantime,
    You might have the spout of a lifetime.

    Even if ya don't want to be a rhymer,
You can always make it by bein' a timer.
    Drummers have a groovin' time,
        And they don't have to spout rhyme.

Also, if you play the bass,
    You can find yourself giving "face"
To the whole generation.
        The nation listens to it all.
            It's such a big ball.

285

        'N no matter how tall you really might get,
    Ya can not forget
        You're like a building in New York City;
    You might be pretty,
            But you can be replaced.

There are industries built around making things erased.
Destruction seems so simple,
Sometimes you might seem like a pimple that rhymes.

And so you might get tossed out
Like dimes after making sixty bucks an hour.
Power is not something to estimate,
It gains its own esteem.

Little rule:
It's best never to hate the rolling members of your team.
If you can't deal,
You better look for real
At what it is you're talking about.

Figure out your route.

continued –>

Know where you're going,
'Cause it'll be showing up in your show.
You'll blow the whole thing out'a the water if
                              It can't flow like a river.
              Don't shiver,
         A building in New York City can do a hell of a lot.

Take a shot,
You just might be hot –
Make ya slip on the ice.
You'll glide so nice
If that really is the case.

Just for the lack of space:
              Sing those lovin' lovin' songs.
You can't go wrong
When you're helpin' people get along.
People need it.
People greed it for the right reasons.
Each of the seasons, they want a new one.
So punt a new one, let it run
Into the next year.
Remember not to show your fear,
You gotta steer.

We want the "children to really ring"
              When we bring sound,
                    To the air
              Where they're gonna hear it.
Gotta steer it onward,
The flow is synergistic energy.
Synergistic motion is an emotional potion
                    Of dance –
                    When people prance
In delectable ways,
Like they're soakin' in sun rays.

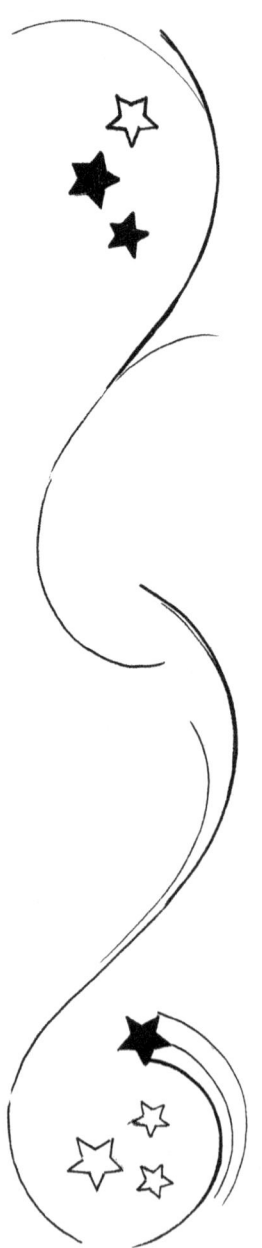

When days turn into nights,,,
    People have fights with their souls, now and then.

The rock, when it rolls, truly can be known as artistry.
And the tree that grows
– You gotta know –
Is known, as "flow."

When the synergistic energy is in its groove,
When people just feel like they gotta move
– To dance –
It's like releasing stress.

No one's got time to digress
When the energy moves.
People's grooves
Are forward moving.

287

When people let their flow get on a roll,
You never know what'll grow from the time.
It may have a beat, maybe some rhyme.
    Can't be discreet with something like a rolling flow,
Like a river, gotta let it go go go.
Don't'cha know that spiritual love energy is like a centrifuge?
The energy's huge!
    Bigger even than Eugene, Oregon.
"Keeping on 'till dawn," is about going the extra mile,
About keeping it going for a while.
        It's how you resonate a style,
Which is something that's required.
When we're wired and we want to hear some music,
We need something that can take our soul on a journey.
    See, it's real important to have multiplicity in a song,
  'Cause if it goes wrong,
You're not going to get the exposure that'cha want.
The closure's gonna punt you to a depressed state of mind.
     As a positive perk, that's when you'll find
    Plenty of time to work.

continued –>

Just for an example, here's a sample for our thought:
The things that B.B. King brought
Around
'Bout bein' blue,
Might entertain you,
 – But the Hell he must have gone through
Probably was worse than he'd'a chosen if he had a say.

            Would you like to do what he did?
            Diggin' into your lid's what I'm doin'.

        I want to ruin theories on hate.
                My friend, as of late,
        I'm a man who claims he's beige.
                        It's all my age.
                            Got a new sage.
        Do try to consider your place on this world
                    On which we're hurled;
                        So swirled,
                    Like a tsunami of culture.
                Don't fly like a vulture.
        Fly like an eagle or a hawk.
Talk about what's legal and what's not.
                Hot as the tropics,
        Some topics will get people steamed.
But this ain't a dream.
                It's so real that the deal is
                – Cats are still goin' around, givin' out their sound
Filled with contemplation about what our ground
                            Grows, and shows to them.
                    Sensei said
        "Spread your love wide.
        Don't shove,
        Glide.
        Do the love-slide with a girl.
        Make the world bright;
        Turn up the light, make it warm.

People swarm 'round good sound
'Cause it's a massage, and it's got a message to boot."
If you give a hoot, that's wise.
To like livin' with open eyes, leads to growth.
 Mmmm, advancement.
You'd never know that Rock and Roll
   Could lead to
    Enlightenment,
  So keep on!
 Dig dawn!
Dig the future!
    What we've got coming
   From all this humming
  Might be good.
   We should pay attention.
  Our retention ain't always what it could be.
And we should be hoping for improvement.
   Grooving on cement, loving another,
– Taking our lives, and being like brothers, sisters even –
The blisters are seethin' myth.
Livin' life like it can remove its own strife
     From its pith
   By singing a song.

  What a concept?

 Am I wrong?

289

The Trappings

As I grow,
Ya know,
It really kinda hurts.
I lose some friends,
And some bends that I make
Just about break me,
But they take me on a
Roller coaster ride.

I think about what's inside
Of our word
Soul.

290

In our rock and roll,
We find disjointedness
Of a duplicated kind.

The replicated find the way we fly,
And then ask why we can't take
Two or three along.

In a song

We share our love,
But we also shove.
What of looking above
For conscientiousness my friend?
Will we be able to mend
The broken family
That we all know?

Open your eyes
And your soul.
It is our rock and roll.

When you give your heart out
To a person, hold it.
You're gonna get old, shit.

Don't you want someone to
Hang with?
Marriage is no myth.
We know it happens,
And yet the trappings of what we see
Make us think we're on the brink. See,
We gotta love and not shove
Our honeys.
Moneys can be shared, or
Are you too selfish
Now?

Be a sharing part of humanity.
Let our reality
Evolve into
Something that we can care about;
Something where our route can
Epitomize why we should change.
Do you think that you could rearrange existence?
Because Stag-Nation
Evolves into resistance to
Our growth.
Our wellbeing depends
On this thinking…

To Bring Method to Chaos

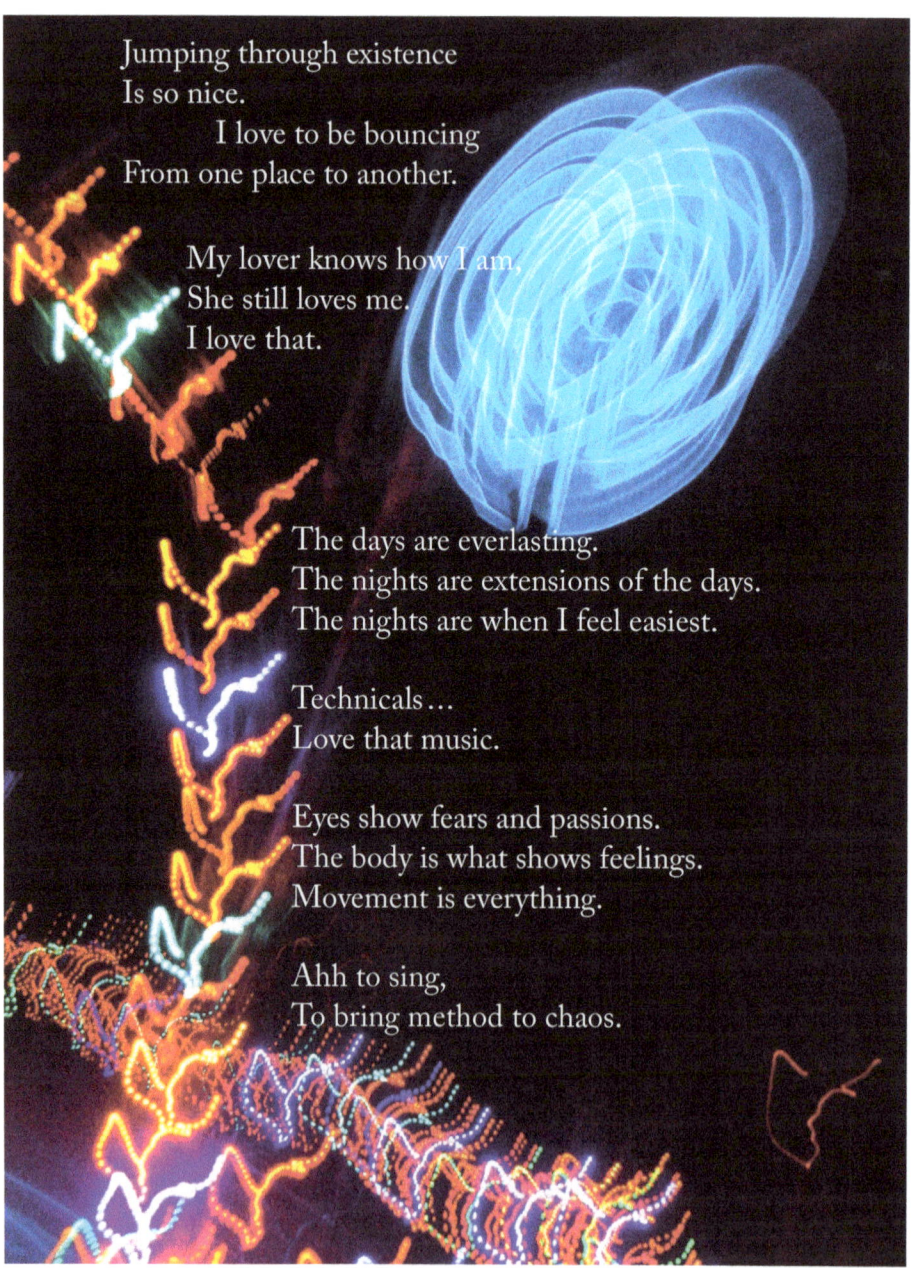

Jumping through existence
Is so nice.
I love to be bouncing
From one place to another.

My lover knows how I am,
She still loves me.
I love that.

The days are everlasting.
The nights are extensions of the days.
The nights are when I feel easiest.

Technicals…
Love that music.

Eyes show fears and passions.
The body is what shows feelings.
Movement is everything.

Ahh to sing,
To bring method to chaos.

292

Ecstasy on a Stick

One time on a bench,
I saw this girl walk by;
Her hair shimmered in the light.
Her thighs passed by...
        Delight.

She wore those real short shorts,
Ya know?
    Her face, was smiling,
        Was ecstasy
   – On a stick.

Thin, she was, but not
Too much –
Oh, she had the touch.
Fine – she was.
Looked like the
Sweetest wine.
I wanted to drink
Her,
Soak my lips with her flavor.
Make her feel the pleasure
Of existence.

The sweetness of a guitar
Is the only thing to describe
The silence.

So Many Things

There are so many things that man must do.
There are so many things that a man must say.
There are so many things to do at the nighttime and day.
One of the things that rhyme tells you is,
There is a listening time.

There are certain things that I'm required to send out wired.
We're all so fired up.
Tired, yup, but we got to keep on!
There's so much distance to go.

There's so much resistance to flow.
Don't you know
That dawn is coming?
Oh, oh oh.

We've got to be thumbing into the new time.
We've got to be running into chimes.
Musicality 'till finality!

There are so many things to sing.
What about the song to save the world?
What about the one for the girl?
I've decided that it's a goal of mine to think so fine for you.

I'm sure language needs mutation.
Its inspiration only needs a glide.
I bee-bop-a-loo 'cause it's something that's got to
Be done.

So run along with me.
Take your sunshine with me,
Try and drink a lime in the myth with me.
I got to be bringin' out new temples.
I'd like to build'em.
We'd yield'em into a contemplation…

295

For the water

See, as we contemplate,
Totally straight,
We are forced to stand a little still.

Then, on for the thrill —
*********bebop ill!*********

I don't like to communicate with a person who enjoys hate.

Continuance…

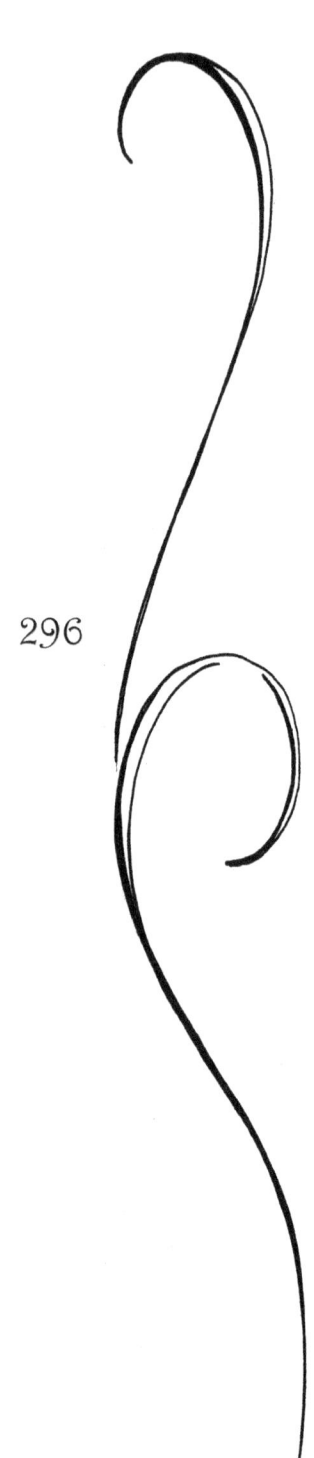

Light in Flight

Light, in flight
@ night,
Scares fright
Away.

There's only one way
To go, when you on.

You roll out'ta rock n' roll!
Dolin' times.
So many chimes are
Bein' hit by the kit.

Maestro- yo, that
Drummer is tappin'
Up a brush n' a beat!

Kicken' a boomer'a heat onto
The dance floor for sure!

What a treat for
An evening,
With the kicken' room–
Flutes 'n dancers;
Runes.

I love a dancer.
The prancer's true.
I may be sittin' down, true.

But I ain't blue.
You see, that she,
Is in my mind,
So it is not a problem,
That I can't find,,,

The energy to get up and
Dance right now.
'Cause I am dreamin'
And I ain't schemin',
No more.

Ain't schemin',
No more.

Even though it gave me
So much energy.
I just don't need that synergy any more.
There's something just right
About tonight.

I might
Write a little more.
Or not.

Tres bene la musica!!

297

Here in a City

Here in a city,
        Is it pretty
                To see
        Shity things
                Goin' on?

Dawn arose
        The other day.

Thought the day would
        Never come on,
                But her belly was
                        Covered, and it
                Was warm;

Movin' on.

Goin' up the Highway –
        On an Astroplane,

                Can we gain
                Arrival?

                I want to survive all things
That come near me.

Some fear my attitude – the

Latitude of my direction.
     Don't need a correction,
Any place I get to is fine with me.

     Dine with me –
        I'm normal. Formal?
           Maybe – it's all relative.

All is alive, every time, suggestive of another.
     My brother … ask him.
Jim is my name, the same as all the others –
     Are the same, Nedy, Woody.
        What is a name?
           I got a tree with me,
           See pith with me.

     Heading out along the road,
     I'm lookin' forward.
        I got wood on my side,
           And here, we ride.

299

I Think of Dancing

I think of dancing
To have a day.
I mean, what can I say?
It's such a lucid 'n groovin' way to be!

Mmm, when you let yourself free,
'N let your body roll with the music,
You never can tell
What the hell you're gonna do
With those shoes which you wear.

Everywhere
They got the blues or
The psychedelic
Flowin' around.
What's groovin'
Is the energy of motion.

So in this ocean,
Swim for me
On the dance floor today!
It's a great way to play
When you get the time,
When the rhyme and the music
Are rollin' together.

You can blame the weather,
Or even the sound.
Just find an excuse and come around,
'Cause what I found
Is movin' around,
Is freakin' profound.
So come get down with me.

Let Yourself Go

You never know just what
You're gonna find
When you go and
Let your whole mind and body
Roll your soul out on the floor.

When you're out and letting
Yourself go, you never know
Just what you'll find.

I think that the inside,
Behind the rind –
What resides
When it's left free to go –
Can be freedom
Like we can't know
Unless we let ourselves go.
And so,
Let yourself go and go and go and go!

Ske budu way boo!

You never know
What can grow
From letting yourself go with the flow.

Ske boo de wap bo...

301

The Band Played On
(Crime can be good.)

The feel is good.
U2 know "no,"

It next.
Flexed were the strings.
The guy who sings
Had a smooth-ass voice.
A choice was made.
Played was the chord
That sent the band to play.
The day had made it to nighttime,
Sublime.
The crime was that the band just played on, and on, and on.
The dawn came brightly into the day
That they continued to play in
The way they knew.

Runnin' by the side...
Smoked a little...
More into the lesson.
Or was it more?

302

Nameless Blues

I know about the blues
When you got'em,
You can get gotten bad.
Make ya mad
So bad.

Sinking low – go – go
Oh oh,
The show – woh
Below all else
When you get low
You sing the blues.
Oh mama, I miss havin' you around!
The sound of a color is comin' to my mind,
And I find the rind of a blueberry lookin' at me now
Askin' how to find its hill.

303

Frayed

What a wonderful fraying
> You found to pull.

> Objectively,
> It definitely was cool.

Subjectively,
> I'll take it as some school.

'Cause god-damn-it,
> I feel sometimes, like a fool.
It's like I'm bein' used
> Just like a tool,
By my mother and my brother.

I used to rule
> My own life,
> > But now I'm stuck with this strife!
> Somebody's poured me a big fat bowl,
> > And now I'm told
> What to do with myself.

So my whole world's gone upon a shelf
> Collecting dust,
> > Just like rust
> > > Eatin' away at me.

I'm needin' to be free,
So I can see what my life will bring me.
I need to get out and sing the
Thoughts and emotions on my mind.

There are certain things that I run across and find
That should be told around.

So I'm bold on the ground
When something needs to be said.
I'm there to place my tread,
But here, I feel dead;
All stifled and shut.
And I would like to cut
And get away,

305

But I've got to stay.
I've got to put away
What it is I want today,
'Cause I am here by request.
And I found that the best thing
Is to maybe bring
A little more music to mind.

Angry Johnny

Inspired by Poe's 1995 song.

Angry Johnny,
          Why do you come up in her face and hate?
Have you not heard of love of caring?
... Of wearing another soul's shoes?
She's singing the blues.
How am I supposed to call ya brother
When ya still have to shove a lady to feel good about yourself?
You should recheck,
Correct yourself and anyone
Upon your shelf.
Were ya deaf?
Won't ya listen to sound glisten?
Ya ya yea coco jumbo
Ya eho

306

Angry Johnny, this song is to you
Angry Johnny, I'm thinking about you.
I want you to know
I see the same things that you do.
I just think you should rethink
The things that you do
Once more, 'cause
You're makin' women
Real unsound with the way you tour.
Reason is found for all types of change.
Rearrange the sparkle in your eye.
My my my, women are too fine
To be treated so unkind.
Couldn't it be time to reassess
How you picture someone who walks
Around in a dress?

Don't be long –
Come along on this concept
That I share.
          Where do you feel you wanna go?

Here for a Year

Here for a year,
Now off to somewhere else.

The tragedies of mystic men
Faking numbness;
Astrology binding,
Introspective
Rewinding,
Finding purpose.

Rave music is a brave
Analogy.

It seems the dreams
Of someone, come true.

Oh, to've changed the world to rave.
Saving ourselves for anything?
Or giving our all,
And play ball
In the big leagues.

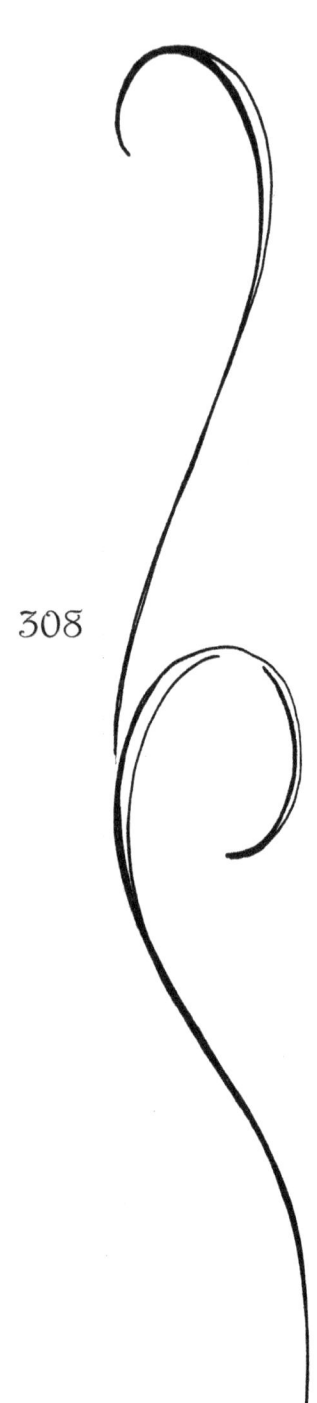

I'm a Space Cadet

I'm a space cadet,
And I cannot forget
That I just might get
Beamed away.

I've dreamed a way
To get away with myth.
And if you want to play,
You've got to understand
That as a magician of scat,
I definitely make harmony
Whenever I can.

And if my hand can
Ever do something for you,
Would you welcome it with open arms?
Or would your plan
Bring a pain to my heart,
By extinguishing the start
Of a loving feeling that I am
Feeling for you?

I really dig it when I see your face,
And I see the trace
Of the aura that you hold:
So old and young;
I want to have sung
To you.

I'm gonna sing anyway,
And I might as well groove
With funk inside my soul.

I like to have more
Colors than blue
In my Rock and Roll,

Because I dole out
Musical thought
Every time I'm brought
To a moment
In time.

Well, I could write something sappy,
Or I could write something happy.
You see; there's something nappy in my mind
That I find
I want you to hear.

I want to be near you
When you are at your most beautiful,
And also when you're feelin' down.

I want to drown
Feelings like the one of dread.
I want to make your head
Giggle, laugh, and make
That smile,

'Cause I think
I'm addicted now.
(Oh wow!)

It's true I've done
So much before
I got to your doorstep...

It only means that I know a little more
Than some other guys.
Yea, I wanna share what I've seen,
Learned and burned
All of my life for.
)'(yea)'(

310

Please understand,
As I look at the ground that I stand on,
And the wide sky ahead,
And to all the sides of me;

I got to be
Expressing: I'm in love with
Not just you, but positivity's core~
And all that it can do
To you.

G

....

On the ground he lays;   (like he prays)
screaming through his guitar, (the man will go far)
for the things he wants to play ———   (to say)
breathing his music.   his friend answers his plea
with a g-minor progression
twisted with funk!

He plays his thank you, so well.
that's a man who breathes
his music.

To play so well, a man must first go through hell.
what he has to tell is so hot, he must not use words;
feeling is what you hear.
do not fear,
but shed a tear
for a man this year.

It's weird how people need to say certain things.
they have their own particular way to do it.
shit, don't you?
but ooo, the man with a guitar in his hand can command,
can lead and be followed;
never to be shadowed.

Hear his pain.
hear his gain.
hear him regain what is sane.
his humanity is differed;
not a word need leave his lips,
yet we know what he feels.
he reels in delight tonight
as he tells you how he feels..........

311

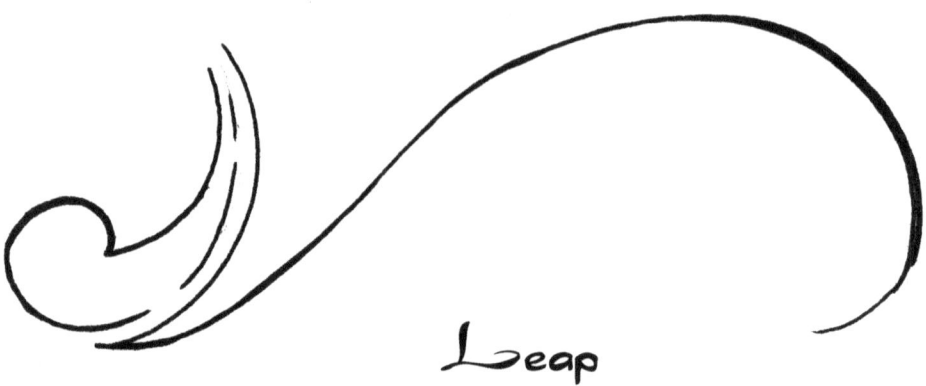

Leap

Leap
To Spirit Passage.

The ambiance of a
Chalice on a warm day.

Glowing music;

The glowing day of music
Came to the clearing one afternoon,

It seemed so clear right then.

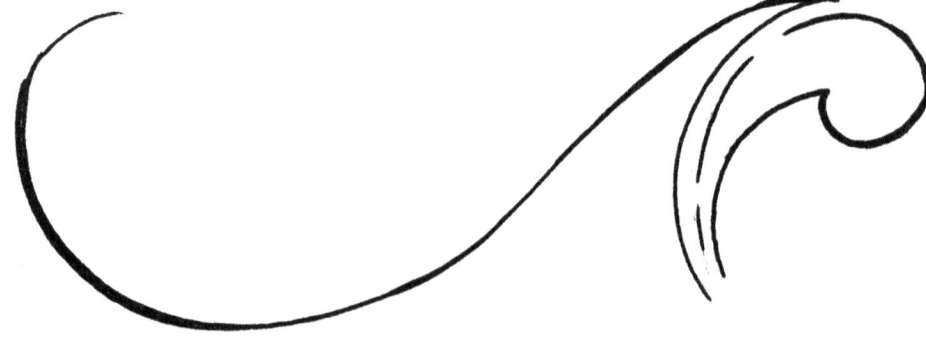

Surreal,
Sir,
Real.

Floating Coffee

The stars like night,
But no land to sit on.
A floating coffee.
Electrification of consciousness.

Suddenly a bar stool to sit on –
Shooting stars.
A chair.
A room, drifting calmly.
In it, a couch and a wall hanging –

George Jetson buzzes by.
A sneer at the pollution.
Another sip of the coffee.

Now a rainbow of stripgum comes rolling –
A motorcar rolls along it and towards…
But just missed, and putters past along.
This time no sneer, but
A shake of the head as if to say
"Oh, what ignorance."

Another drink of the coffee,
And a drift.

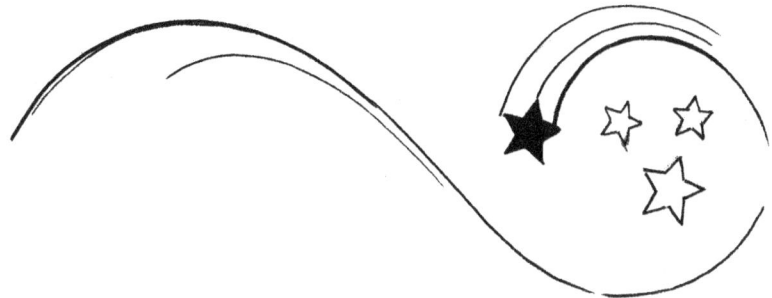

The stars illuminate the surrounding air
As nothing else can be seen.

The rainbow's left.
It followed the car on its way out
Of the galaxial realm.

The room has also floated away.
Now a bar is floating in the right direction –
Hopefully a refill can be procured…

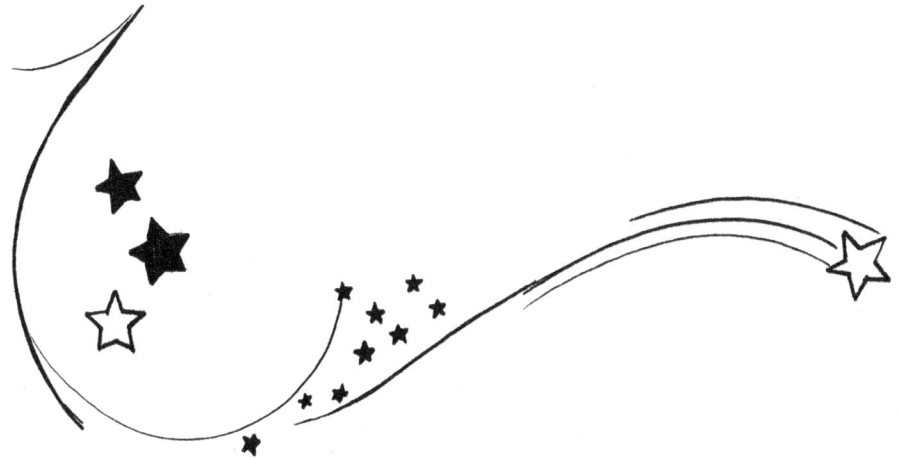

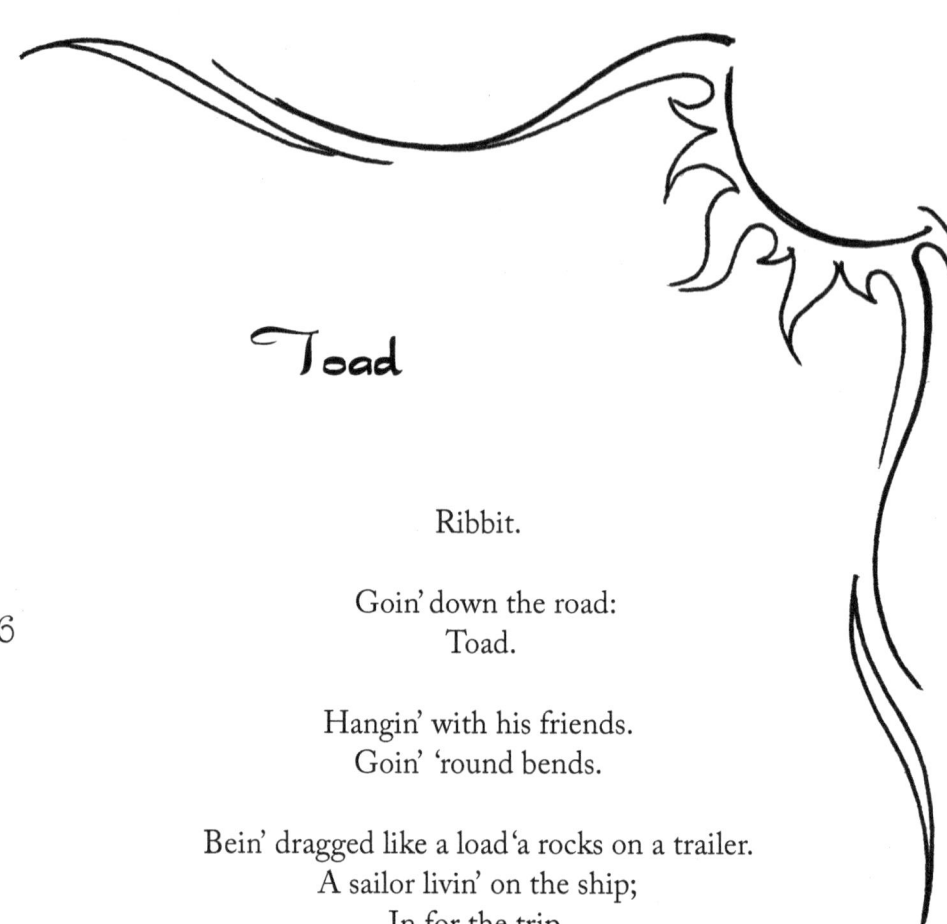

Toad

Ribbit.

Goin' down the road:
Toad.

Hangin' with his friends.
Goin' 'round bends.

Bein' dragged like a load 'a rocks on a trailer.
A sailor livin' on the ship;
In for the trip,
Completely.

Neatly, goin' "Ribbit,"
'Till he finds home.
It's how I roam.

The Bite of the Wind at Night

The wind of the night's biting back.

Someone handed a microphone
Like he was passing a bone of the herbage.
You know it was Pure-Sage-One.

317

One page is only enough
When sending a letter.

Better get it or forget it.
Never regret.
Always act anew – ! –
42 –

The Conan the Vegetarian

318

The movement,
The flushing movement.

The way we change;
The way we're open
To moving, in a new way.

The way it's okay
To be different
Than the way we were.

Totally changing
To pure energy
With the synergy.

Being the motivation,
And the trust.

Trusting self, and others.

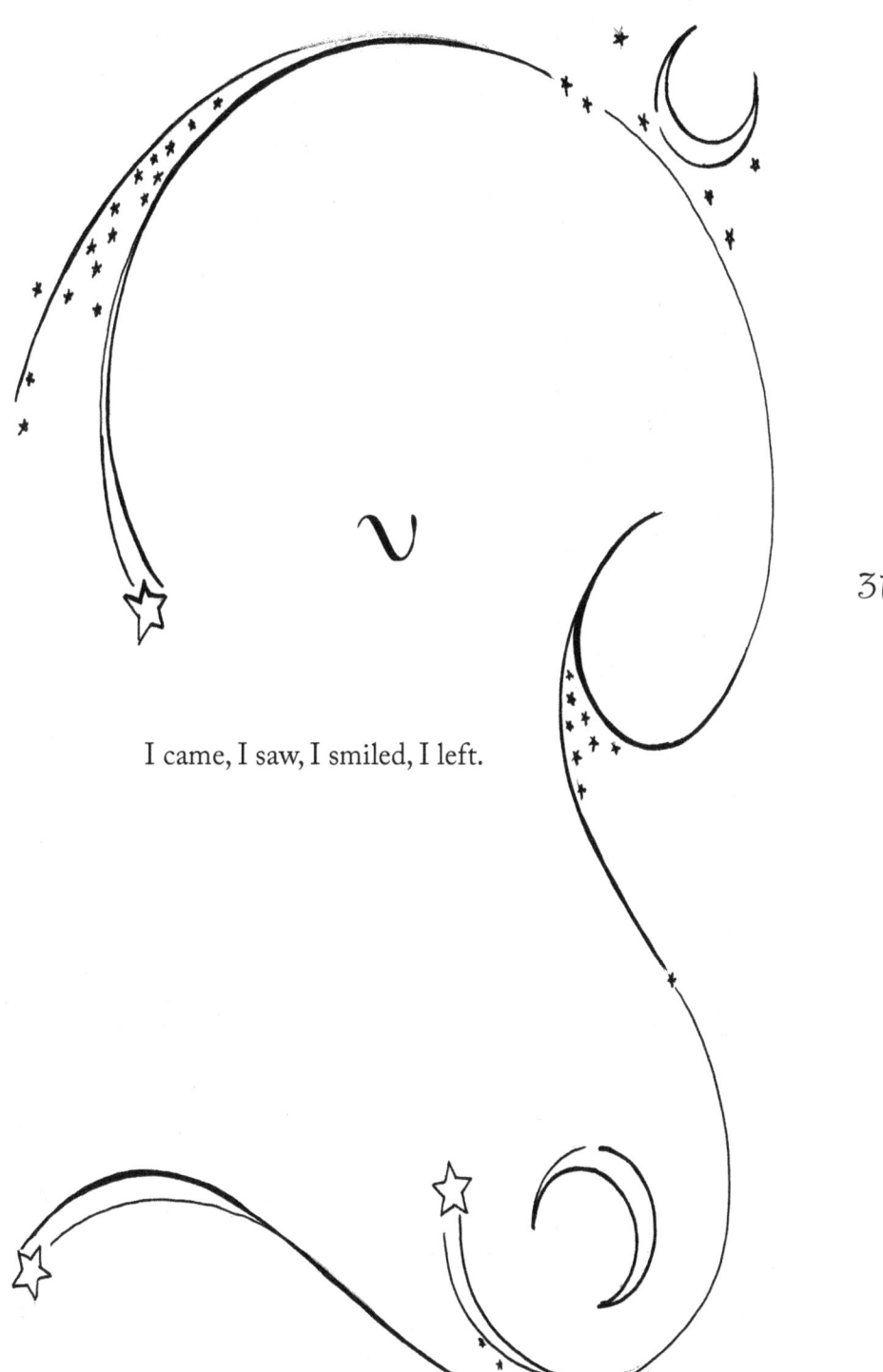

I came, I saw, I smiled, I left.

The Kool-Aid Test

Be glad my friend,
    Take this as a mend.
We're gonna check the day-glo sky
    By testing the Kool-Aid;
      Ready made
        Night – bright light,
    In spite of the rain.

Or, in the sane,
    As one with it.
      Gonna myth it.
        We're gonna slide it,
      Yea, ride it off into the night,
        Where there might be fright.
    But that'll be all right,
      Plenty'a people 'round.
Gonna share good sound,
    'N share what we've found.

It's gonna be outside.
      We're gonna open wide –
Send feedback to the souls of rock and roll.
      Pay the toll, it's all right.
        It's gonna be right tonight.

Take a bite
    To feed your soul.
You better fill it with rock and roll.

320

It's gonna be the toll.

The potion
Of emotion   can feel so fine.
It's gonna feel like wine,
And then we'll dine.

We're gonna feed on the mood,
'N so with the blued,
I want you to
Go through whatever it takes.
We'll all make mistakes.

Just remain noble, 'n your lobe'll feel okay.
Your mind will understand   *the defined*
'N then find the meaning.
'N then smile – On to the mile!!

Gonna be gone for a while,
But gonna be back soon.
I'll see ya at noon.
I'll fill ya in then my friend.
See ya then.

Gonna mend an air tare where there are breaks.

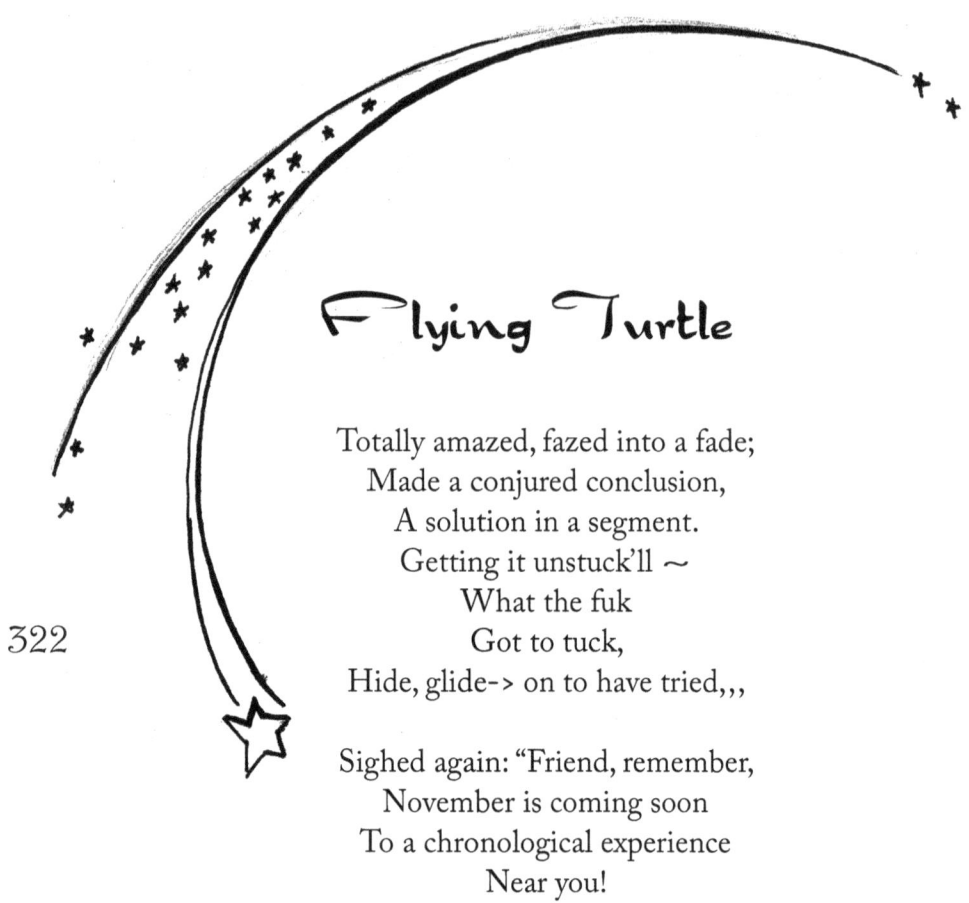

Flying Turtle

322

Totally amazed, fazed into a fade;
Made a conjured conclusion,
A solution in a segment.
Getting it unstuck'll ~
What the fuk
Got to tuck,
Hide, glide-> on to have tried,,,

Sighed again: "Friend, remember,
November is coming soon
To a chronological experience
Near you!

True thoughts will
Come in front of your face.
You'll trace to Ace, so base your actions
On abstractions that come from
The sea,
Or whatever you see."

We can get on into the future as if we
Knew what was going on.

(I wonder what the DJ is gonna put on.)
The heartbeat of life is often decided by the DJ.

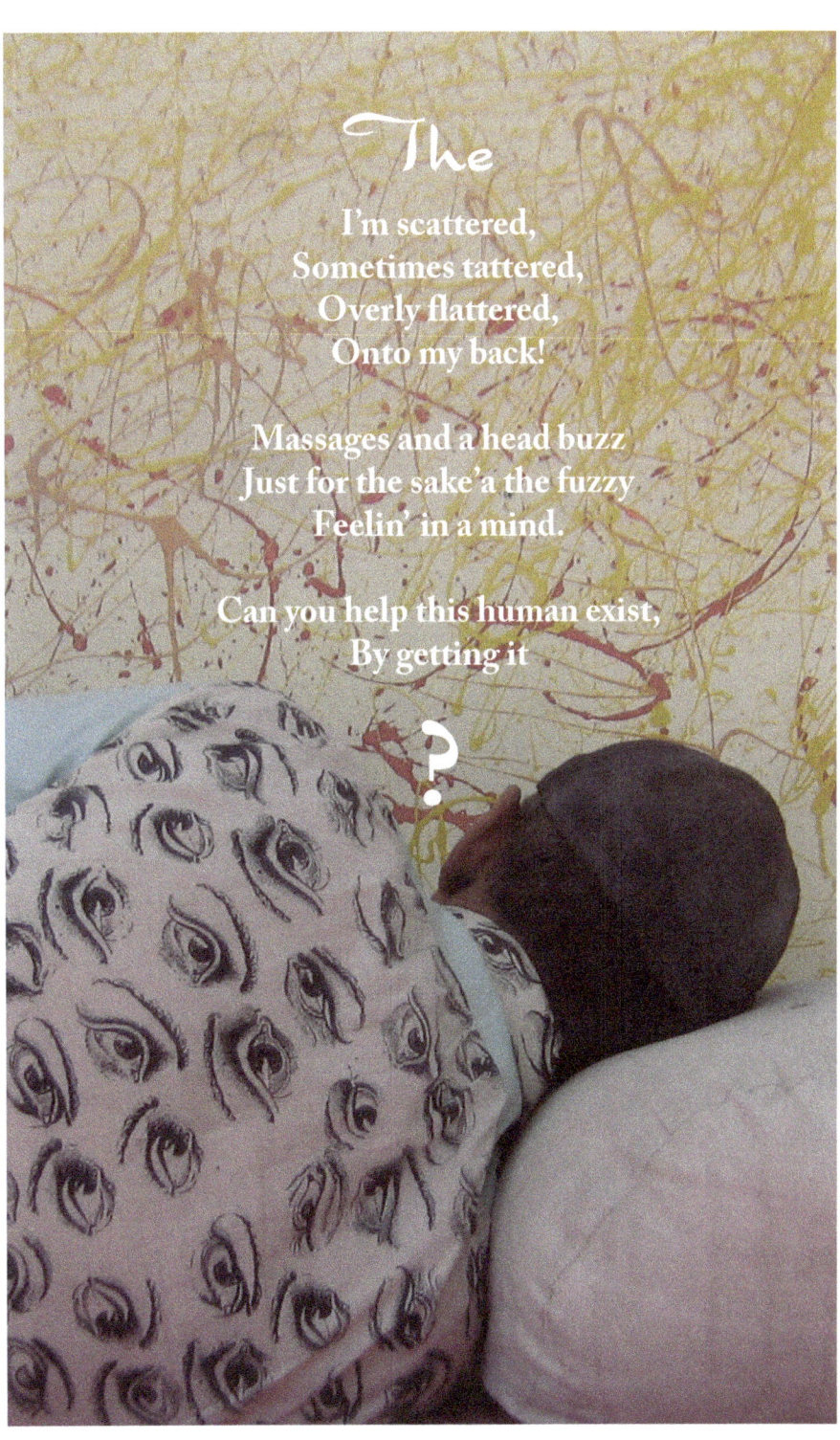

The

I'm scattered,
Sometimes tattered,
Overly flattered,
Onto my back!

Massages and a head buzz
Just for the sake'a the fuzzy
Feelin' in a mind.

Can you help this human exist,
By getting it

?

323

Mirror of Moons

It broke through the silence of the night;
Shimmering, glaring, into the shadows.

It seemed as though the shadows were talking;
Talking as though yelling,
But not a sound.

324

Not a sound to rustle the leaves,
Or a sound to be heard in the breeze.
There wasn't a single sound, but the occasional
Chirp of a cricket.

The talking glass at once, broke into song,
As a fish arose from the center, of this yelling
Mirror of Moons.

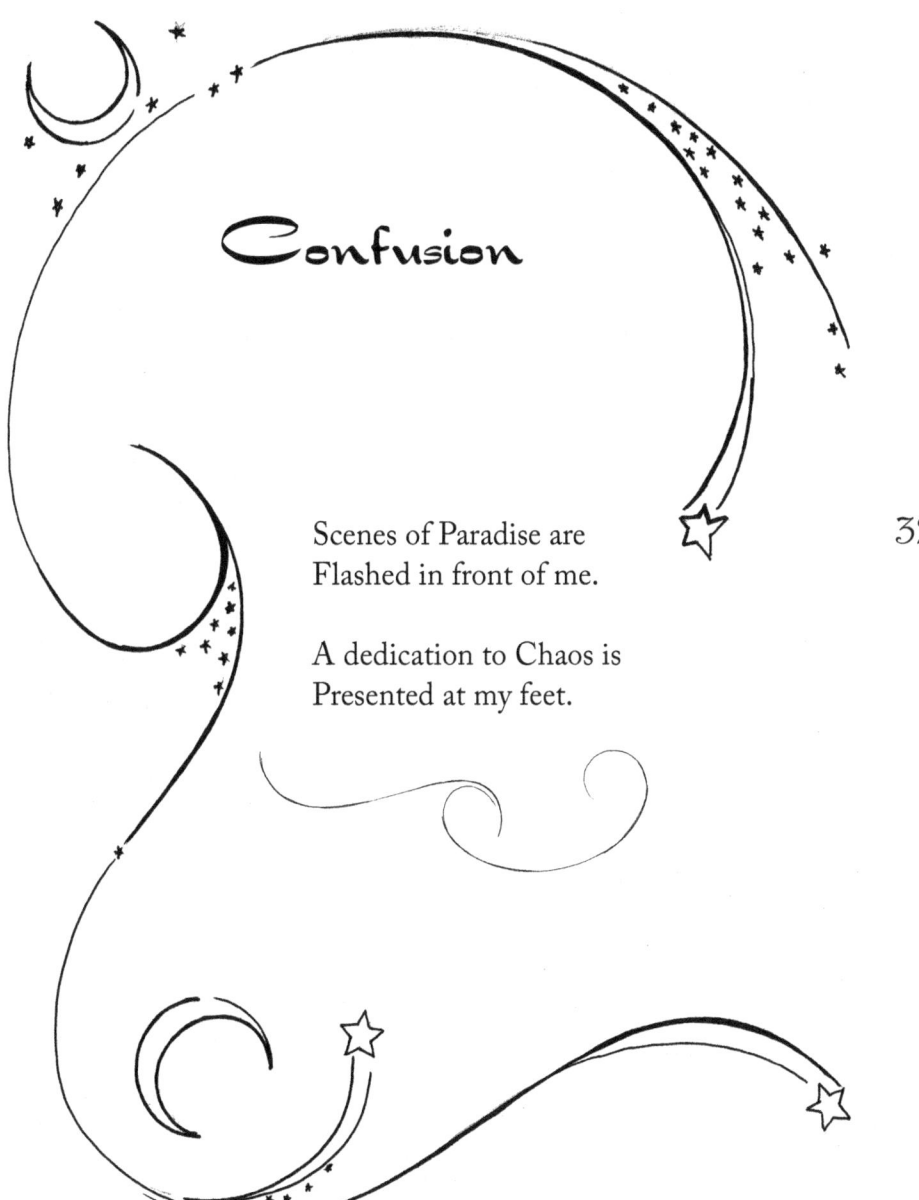

Confusion

Scenes of Paradise are
Flashed in front of me.

A dedication to Chaos is
Presented at my feet.

325

Somethin' About the Distance

"If you understood everything I said, you'd be me."
— Miles Davis

==

Flowing stream of consciousness, –
How you stare your human connector,
Your lucid reflector!
Connected and yet,
Straight one day, erected a building
To see what it wanted to see.
So please, be as one
With the nearby people.

Everybody's got a season of thought.

The Earth's El Nino, we'll receive.
Love!
For we are treated kindly.

We can turn down our attitudes,
Turn down our real, active level.
So when we walk down to Electric Avenue
'N think about
Getting higher —
We do.

Our biosphere –
Which is really our atmosphere however,
Actually combines
Us,   if not legally,
Then,
Actually.

Fumes

When my life
is completely consumed
by love for memories,

I live
inside the mind;
and that's
where I find
the fumes hangin' around.

327

Somehow we live in a void,
And I've grown just a little bit annoyed.

I do believe it's time to go,
I just don't know, if it's good or bad;
Oy, if it's joyous or sad.

Or does it even really frickin' matter?
Does it count to be a batter anymore?
Or am I just a whore writin' letters?

Will it be better someday?
Or will we just wander away?

328

I think that we have a chance.
I believe in the dance.
I believe all can come together.

After the weather comes through,
It might kill you, but oooooooo.
When it does come through,
It will be beautiful.

Kinda like the residuals in Montana,
Too bad Canada had to feel some too.
But whoou, we all die.

It's simple, that the eye of the storm
Would swarm the tidal wave.

No one will be safe.
So go ahead and dance in a rave;
Just try to save ourselves from the insanities:
Like the vanities of the race concept.
Be the exception.

The
Exception
in the Void

Pleasure Dimension Pool

Here, we are free and cool
With "Enjoy the Moment,"
As our only rule.

Some live to give,
And others to receive.
Some live for joy
And others live to grieve.

I'm throughout convinced,
That all the pain we've winced
Will be all right in the end.
We're here to live as friends.
So hear me spread your kindness wide,
So we can all glide into
A pleasure dimension pool.

329

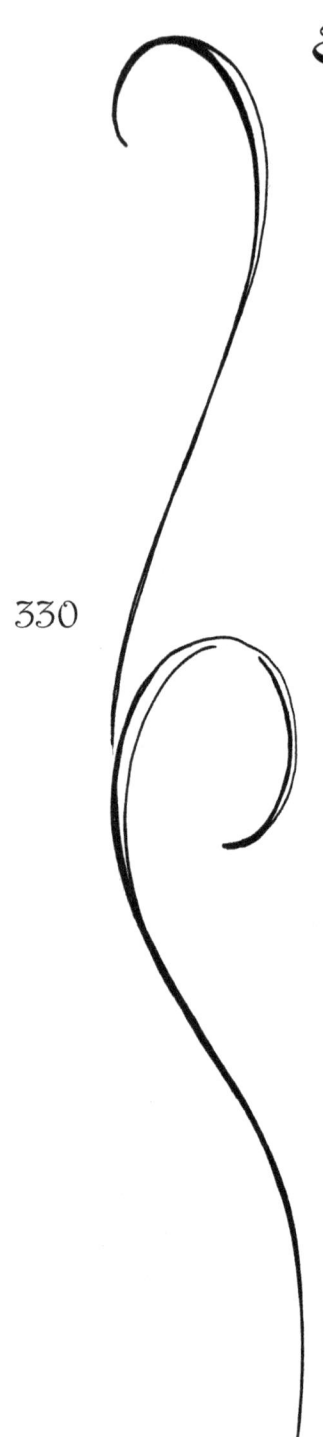

Elumphaliteration

330

I know that you're tired
Of bein' down.
I know that you're wantin'
Not to frown.
I know that ya need ta get
Outa' the place that
Ya livin' right now.

I know that you're tired
Of the town.
I know that you're wantin'
To get 'round.
I know that ya need to
Get out and get movin' and unwound.

I know that you're tired
Of movin' around.
I know that you're wantin'
To calm down.
I know that you're needin'
Peace and ease ta come around.

Zirconium sarsaparilla
Makes a darn good
Float if you're
Inta havin' one.

Magnesium chrome
On a yellow alabaster phone,
Shines with dirty
White spankles.
Id ain' suh good now.

When the dirty blerk
Spankles, the
Rosnim goes to blue,
And when the anslim
Marblens a hullabaloo,
The angler aims at you.

And if you get away,
Swim and tell Marla,
'Cause she'll surely
Need too know.
And until I am allowed
To show flamoxon
Turn into dayglo,
I implore that you to watch
Out for oxen,
Flamobalamamebo!

And so, with that
Behind us, we can get on
With what we were saying
About the dred-headed
Webelos scout who
Helped me get that
Fire goin'.

I was
Shown that I really
Needed a hand by
The man who turned
Up to help me.

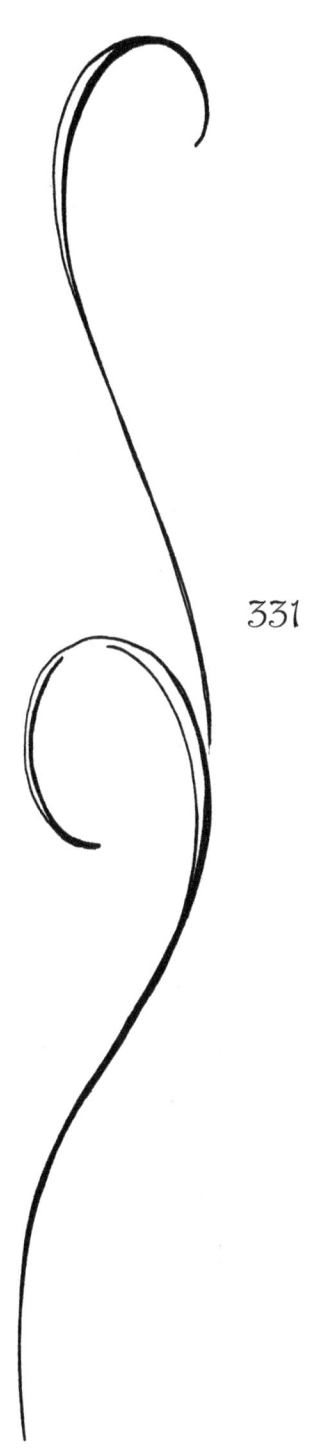

331

continued –>

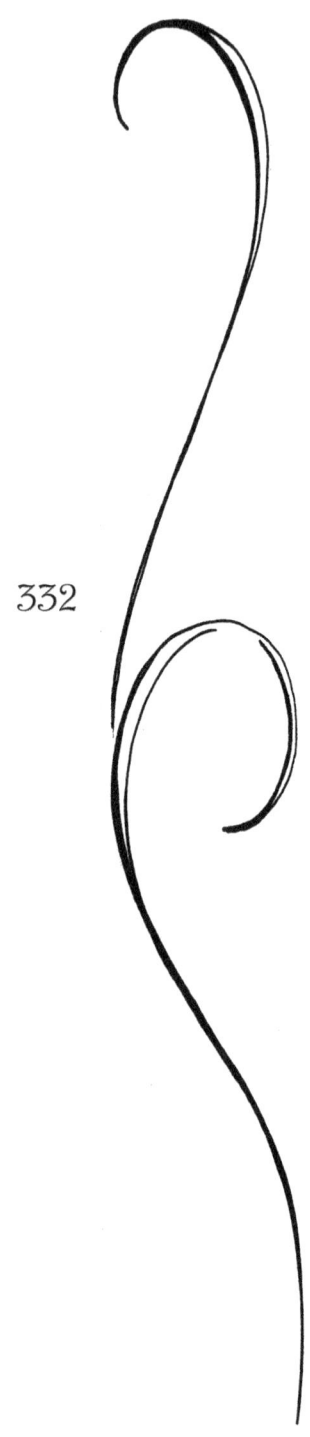

He handed me Chex™ mix
And said, "Hold on to these."
I said, "Hmm, fuel," and
Ate ⅓ of a handful.
They tasted just
Right – We lit up
The fire together.

The weather was perfect;
Purple skies, even the moon was dancing.
Sparkles were in our eyes,
And the people began their prancing.

They were bouncing like
Sprites in the wood,
In the cold forest evening air.
They looked in the sky hung above them,
And were bent on
A reeling of dancing there.

Prancing people are
Truly a joy to watch.
Slancing a dreeble makes
A lumony-gummony gautch.

And you can't deny that.

I know that you're tired
Of flyin' around.
I know that you're wantin'
To get on the ground.
I know that ya needin'
To find self and find home,
So that you won't be lonesome
When you're all alone.

And you might be tired
Of my strange sound.
'N you might be wantin'
To put me down,
But you might be needin'
Someone new around.

The sound of the
Browned ocean
Tastes like grape
Jello.

It's glistening green waves
Crash without a sound
On the silver pebble beaches
Of Nantucket.

The warmth of summer
And the cool of autumn
Combine into a
Serene flow filling
A field.
I M M I
Wondrously and listlessly,
The goat approached
The bush and asked
"Where is the 7-11?"

The bush
Roared something about
Pixie dust, and
Went on its way.

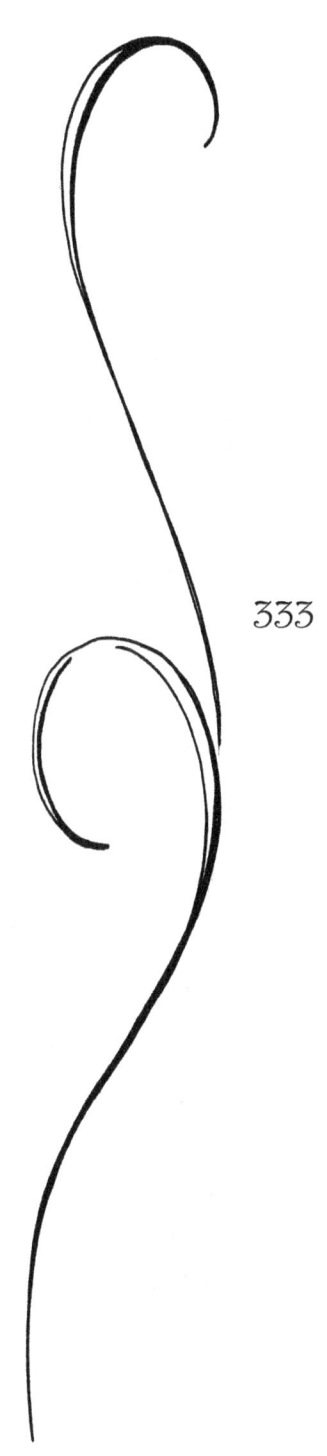

333

continued –>

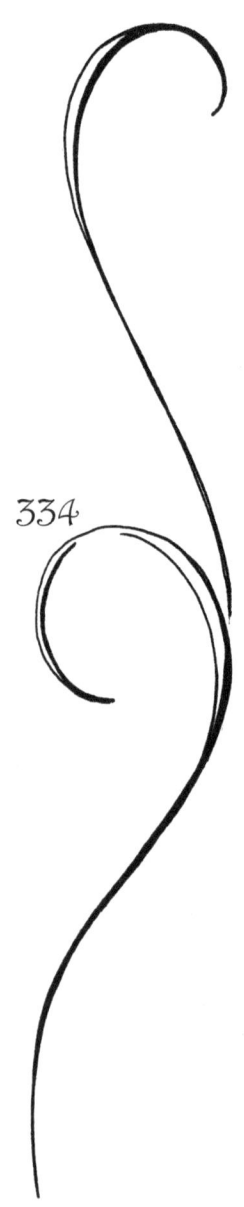

The goat was disappointed,
And so, turned into
A moose and
Galloped off.

One might think
That the end sat
There, but when one
Recalls raspberries,
One can easily see
Where the moose
Was to be galloping to.

And
With that in mind,
I think that it's time
For a word concerning
Sponsorship: Elumphaliteration.

Elumphalettership is no
Joking matter –
Every year, eight
Vocabulary tests
Across the nation
Elumphaliterate – and so,
All should be warned.

Visible symptoms of
Contact with
Elumphaliteration include
New sideburns (males only –
If you are female and you are
Growing sideburns, see your doctor
Immediately!), hemorrhaging notebooks,
And retinal strain (this can be spotted by a

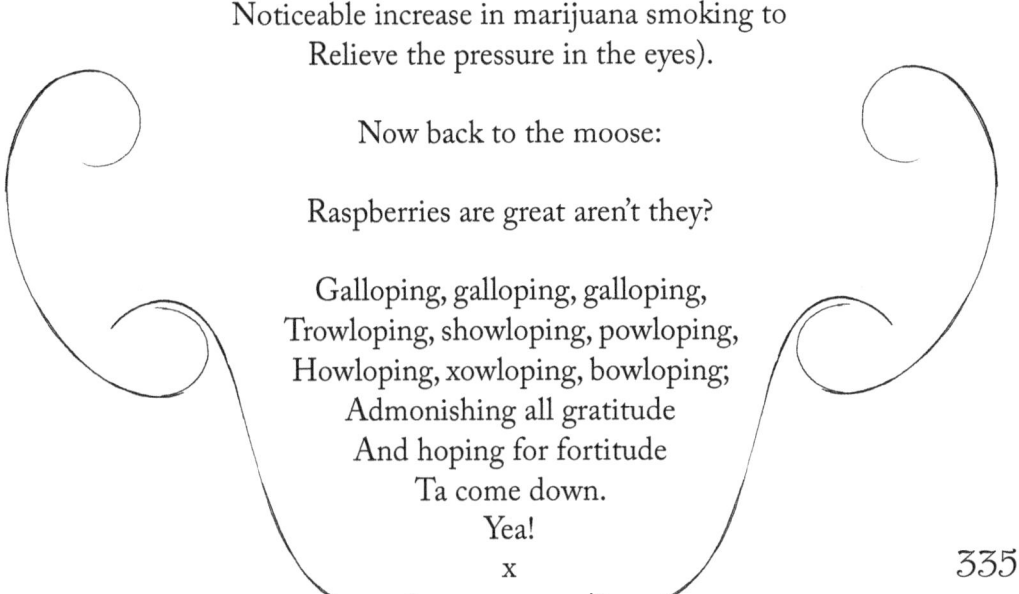

Noticeable increase in marijuana smoking to
Relieve the pressure in the eyes).

Now back to the moose:

Raspberries are great aren't they?

Galloping, galloping, galloping,
Trowloping, showloping, powloping,
Howloping, xowloping, bowloping;
Admonishing all gratitude
And hoping for fortitude
Ta come down.
Yea!
x

335

Sometimes I get so down for such a time that I consciously force
Myself to try to feel good by doing something good.
It could specifically be something outside myself or inside.
Life's emotional route can be like
A rollercoaster.

One thing to remember is that what goes down,
Is bound to come up –

The view –
From the top –
Now that's good stuff.

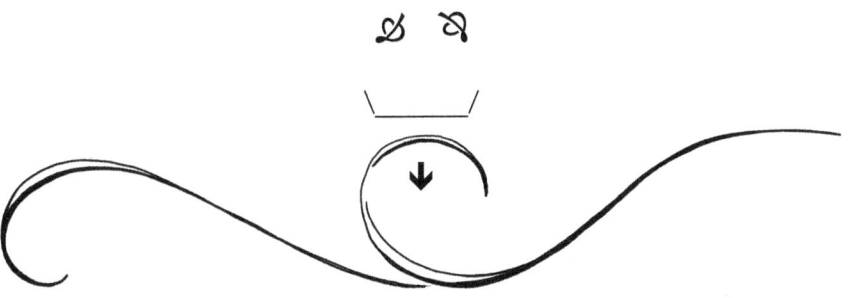

A Priority of Distraction

Too many listeners,
Too much rhyme,
Not enough conscious action,
Not enough time,

To finish all the lists of things
That can be dreamed up in a day.
How are priorities set?
How can somebody say
The world's all right,
When I know that tonight
Has got so much pain for so many?

My government's wealth and reputation has
Been looted by a moron!

In the meantime,
Fifteen year old meth-heads sweat out their
Fear of sleep!

AIDS is killing as fast as warfare,
And I'm a wage slave
Being held away
From the mechanisms of change
By pure
Capitalistic,
Elitist,
Exclusionary,
Tactics.

336

(And a modernized apathy in peers
That insults the ancient Stoic origins of apathy —

Which, in the time of Seneca,
    Originated as
        "<u>Patience</u> under suffering,"
    And is now askew
        Philosophically;
            For it was not listlessness,
    But imperviousness to perturbations
            That we see and live through.)

337

And as such,
    I clutch
        On to my pen, so I can
            Let my thoughts
                Dissipate.

You see, there are things that I just hate,
    And they seem to keep me up at night.

A priority of distraction
    Would fit right now,
        Just about right.

Hit a Gong

Well now that I got it together, I'll be seeing rainy weather a bit more often than I'm used to – confused too – but that's life…

338

Cloning – honing in on a new age – what sage will come and help strum a chord? What words will come from his/her mouth to make us find peace in our souls? Who wants rocks, and rolls when foam is so much nicer and the bread seems dry? – Oh, I must ask why – every woman cries – everybody dies, and I want to know – why should we live?

What should we give to each other? Where is my brother – Who is my mother – And what about the other? Oh brother, am I fucked up now? Can we say "Wow?!"

I'm seeing now that it's all going – holy cow – like the Hindu said – the bread, now dry, you can't let it make you cry – we all die.

So the eye – does it lie? Can it buy a new dimension – The Tenth Incite-bite? Might light the night, but it could be wrong – What a song… I'll hit a bong just to gong my carelessness.

Edge's Wish

As I straight, turn the page,
    I notice Edge in aura-form,
                    Alone.

The bone is smoked.

Soaked in longing,
The songing keeps the lane
            Plain-speaking,
        Creeping into the gigs.

            339

        Where were we again?
The friend is over there somewhere…

Memories of the past from a passing girl.
            The swirl of thoughts.

        Caught – Snatched – Latched in memory;
            Dreamed thoughts of the future –
                To suture with the weather.

"Tether feathers just for the wind,"
                        It grinned.

Be lost… Sun Tsu Sound

Ground point 11,249;
Line 2,483,642:
You are reading as
Fast as
Thought travels –
As it gavels its way into
Existence.
For persistence
Requires fires, but burns…

340

Monica, Moneer,
Old fear,
The quake,,,
Shake Rainier one time for me.
Free tension,
Before build up, yields up trup-ble!

Double duty for the cutie with a gun
Who's fun ain't so,
For so unblessed many.

Any idea what
Depleted uranium is?

There's only time to tell
What direction
We'll take to Hell.

There's only time to tell
How much we'll
Put up with in the distance.

A Good Laugh

I was told once that none of us
understand anything, ever.

Thing is though, the cat said it with assurance!

"And so, with that, what do you have?"
asked the sage.

A good laugh, I figured.

341

Pretext

Always aloof.
        All ways, proof.

Caught by the sleuth
        As a gorgeous
                Pretext
                        Pre- what?
                                Text.

                To being,
                        To freeing,
What it is
        That is explosion –
                Proportion –
                        Expanded –

        Extended into a new —

342

Chaos

The "Earth First Network of Gossip"

The time of conversation 'bout and 'tween people, used for transfer of thoughts. Through the outsets of time, through the onset of rhyme, all through the yogurt state of mind, the yogurt state of mind not only leads to relaxation but also, for the sake of the time and place where we always find ourselves when there, every time; there in the wind with the chimes ringing and listening to stories of strawberry leavened breads that pick up the day.

Like a tongue outstretched by a person being silly, a hat can be hoped for, for blissful hilarity. The wind taking the hat for a ride to remember the ride of a lifetime, the ride of an existence... The hat flipped, and glided, and spun in the air, floating higher and higher into the sky, until it was totally gone from the head it was on. The head looked into the open air where...

343

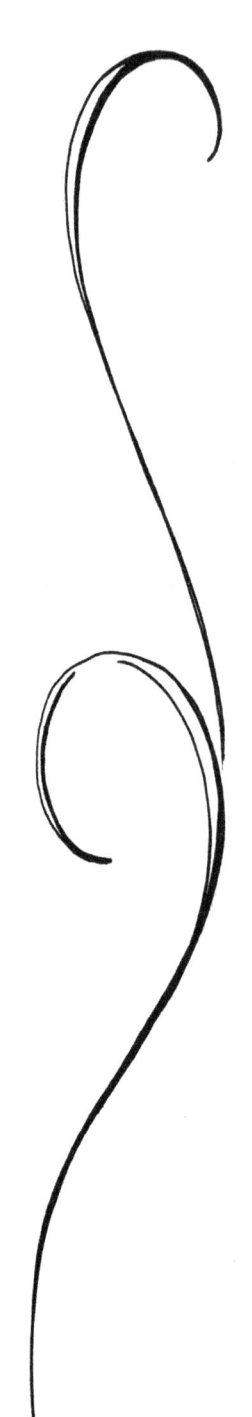

A Stream

There's a lot
Of talk about
The world we know.
Oh, you know we're the
Ones who control it.
You now it.
Of course, we're just
Like the ants,
We're juss better.

Turn on. Remember
Everything you ever learned,
The things you earned.

En try not to get burned as
You move through your
Plane of existence.

Assistants will
Come to you
And ask what
You need.
Tell'em you need to feed.
Tell'em you kiss 'n get
Kissed.
Don't get missed
When they're lookin'
Ya over.

344

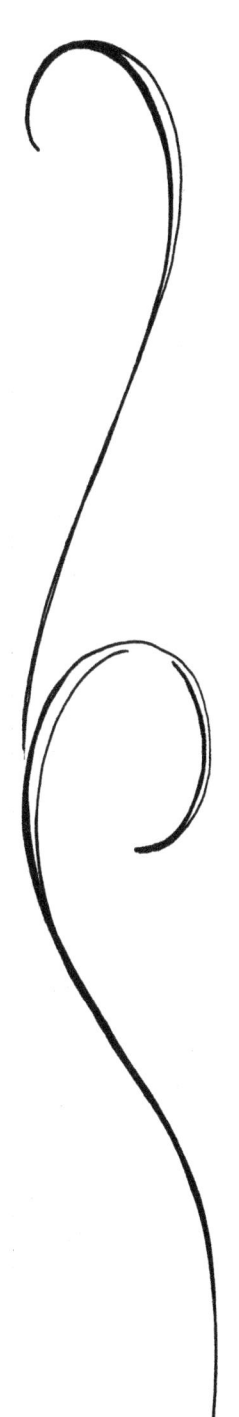
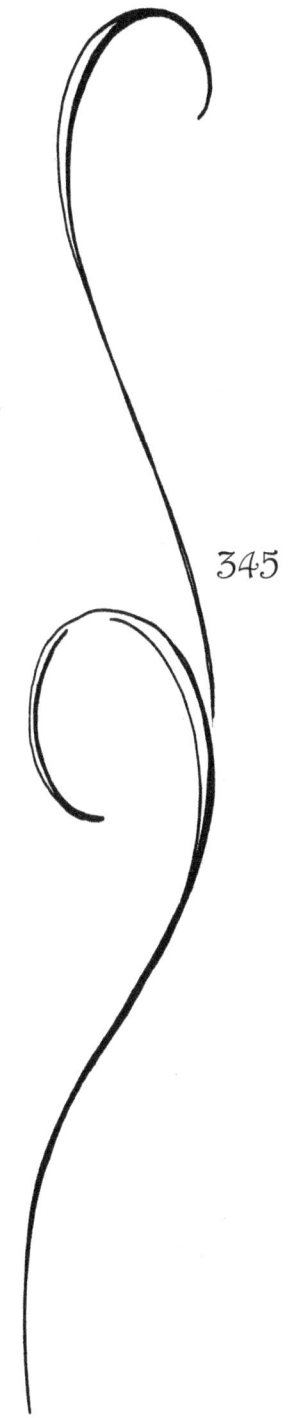

A clover, yea,
It'll bring you luck
If you look to it to.

How am I to talk to you?
You need to tell me. Otherwise,
I might just drink.

Think about what you want.
Then,
Punt yourself to that new
Dimension.

345

Don't mention it to anyone;
They'll say you're crazy,
And lazy and bored.
'N when you're
Whored 'n your
Stories are lored,
Remember what is
That's the truth.

Hey you, move, groove…
Remember yourself.
Don't leave a full
Shelf of history
Of yourself in the
Dark, no more.

continued –>

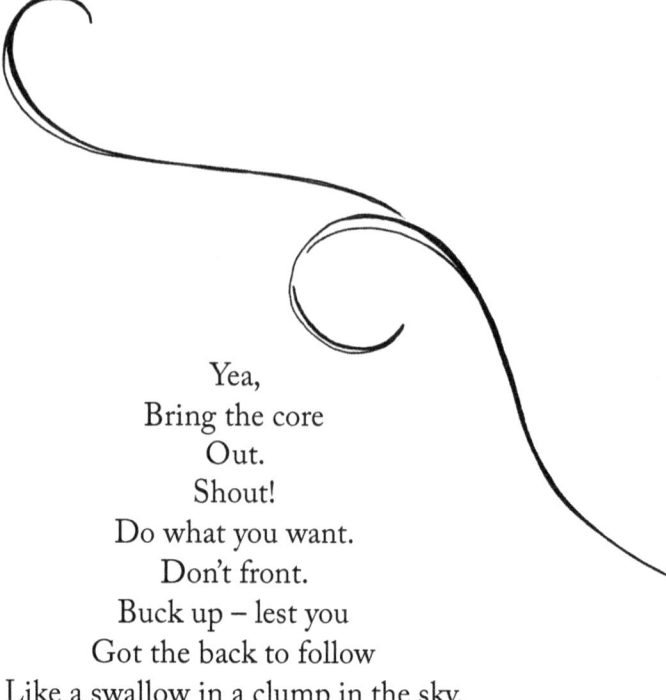

Yea,
Bring the core
Out.
Shout!
Do what you want.
Don't front.
Buck up – lest you
Got the back to follow
Like a swallow in a clump in the sky.

To've tried is the answer.
The question is – unknown –
'Till shown – then known – alone
In the spotlight.

The right night's bright lights,
Bite like the frightened animal
That autumn air reminds me of.

Be Note

Who I am is a mystery.
　　Sorta got…　　Mystical,
　　　　Mist in the morning

　　　　　　　　Across a cold, damp field.
　　　Is a shield,
So as to protect.

What is it, really, to yield?

347

　　I'm
　　　　Be note
　　　　　B! Note!

And so, to release the mess,
To let the energy flow…
Move fingers with pen, to
Realize self.

348

Mmm, was it space-code motion?
What potion?
Love ocean
Procures!

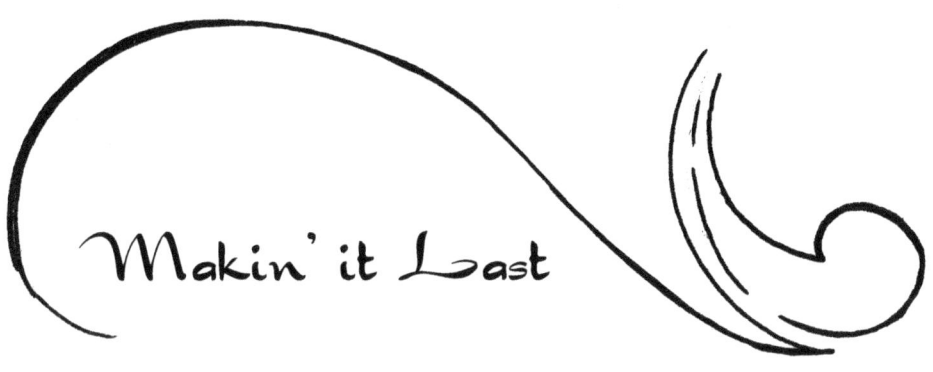

Makin' it Last

We play the game until we die.
How tall are any of us anyway?
"What are we up to?"
Is asked.

349

A beautiful girl takes pictures.
The flash, it brightens,
Makes the moment last.

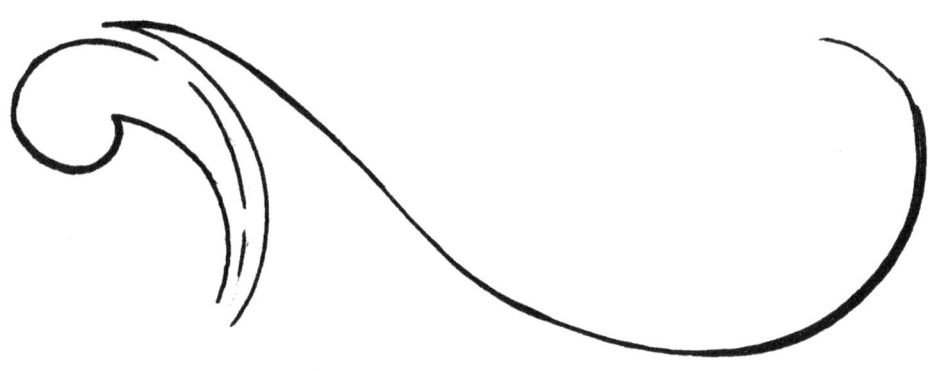

Are Ideas Edible?

The brightest sunshine can beat down on some heads here,
And they stay unaffected.

The strongest rain can fall on some heads,
And they remark about the glory of life.

A mind is from what spins it:
The inspiration,
Mixed with the goals,
While considering the drive factor;
The need for some one-thing to be accomplished.

350

Your intent, along with your motive,
Will determine if you'll have a motif,
Or not.

The inspiration and intent melt together
Into the drive factor,
Providing for the engine needed to achieve the goal
You can dream.

The pelting rain can bring down remarkable,
Energized heads.
And the warming from the sunshine
Can awake the sleeping muse.

I think it's the inner light,
The drive,
That makes so much difference.

Yea, it's an inner thing,
　　　The true love for the goal,
　Or the act of achieving,
Which is what drives.

When the wind is in the face,
　　When the steam needs to be laid on–
　　　　When the great unknown
　　　Is the only thing to look forward to,
With only a vague idea of how things'll end up –
　That's when the soul shines.

When it's not held down...
When it's not held back by a pessimism,
　When it's free to be itself,
　Fostered, fed, and enjoyed;

That is how a dream fruits.

Villa Rosa

Inspired by *Lucy*, on the road.

The mesa winds blew to the hills
That were so far in the distance.
The clouds were to numerous to count.
The rolling guitar from the distance played through the wind,
And we smiled at the thought.

Building. Planting.
Here, these things are elemental.

352   The seeds need to be changed consciously.

(idea!)
Working with Vision Paper for seeds, getting them into the hands
of bikers, who then could spread them to corn farmers, rather than
doing it as a one man team.

The junction was Tullarosa....

The goodness of anything is sometimes in the way.
Sometimes, it's all art.
Sometimes it seems like a ballet,
Sometimes it is coming from all sides.
Nordic winds and Alaskan fishermen dictate the sound 'till...

Chill time,,,, good thing the cursor is still here. We are in the moving
artery of the overlay of routes 70 and 53, on our way to White Sands,
National Monument....

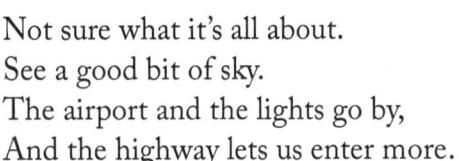

Not sure what it's all about.
See a good bit of sky.
The airport and the lights go by,
And the highway lets us enter more...

At first it was like stepping in on a very subtle prison break
Where everyone in the deal knew what was going on,
Just didn't want the outside-looking-in to understand...

The "70" on the highway stand is painted with bold red and white,
Letters standing up high.

353

We are courted by a salespitch from a billboard sign.
With disregard, we dismiss it.
There is just so much sky.

The sagebrush, through the barbed wire,
Breathes its eternal breath with the wind;
Wondering why it doesn't get eaten by the buffalo anymore,
But has gotten kind of an understanding
That it was replaced by a pavement undergarment
That now is part of the space,
With its moving units that just speed by...

GROW KENAF

This is where we are......
Joan Jett has her own radio station now... That is huge...

Peace

Yes, it's all swirled and twirled,
But it's all right.

We all know that it's true
That when we are all through
We all put our oval heads down,
And at that moment
Our souls define what will be
Our evening's mental wine.

Gonna drink it in through our noses,
Yi, gonna let it out through your mouth.

When ya trip,
Don't fall;
Be ready, and on guard.
Sometimes the landing is hard.
I have fallen out'a windows,
Fallen off cars goin' 45 miles'a momentum.
I'll tell you it don't feel so good,
So ya know before ya see that stuff.

It's like teaching "duff"
To someone who's on a fire line,
That it ain't something to leave 'round.
Yea, you're on the line all the time,
Talkin' words of wisdom, from the ground
Found around,
Comin' outa people's heads.

Dreads,
For example,
Are a good sample
Of kindness living free
When it can.

You will find that in the sand;
What you hold in your hand
Can have a different value
Than you ever dreamed.
You might be relieved
And you might be shocked,
But I hope that you didn't think that a value is locked
In a permanent place –

Gold will not get sold
When you're alone in the Sahara;
Ya need water.

So daughter, when you're swimmin' around,
Keep with the sound of music,
Keep it alive!

One of these days I won't physically be around.
I remember one day I landed on the ground,
A sidewalk, as I recall;
And what was some different about this one certain fall,
Is that I really could have totally died.

355

continued –>

356

I flew,
From one of helldom's greatest gifts that I ever had.
I wish that a pad had caught me.
Yea, it about bought me –
I fell off a damn tall building there,
That's why I stare at certain sights like it's been too many nights.

But here, with all the lights,
I believe that kites
Should be flowin' all day
What cha say?
Hey, hey.

Drink in the good days;
                    Savor its taste, don't let a drop go to waste.
                              Peace, love, happiness, all ways.

Surfing Buddha on a Lake

As I look around, I think of hundreds of things to do.

Contracts, cleaning, homework, e-mail, all sorts of things.

357

The path of least resistance…

Surfing Buddha on a lake.

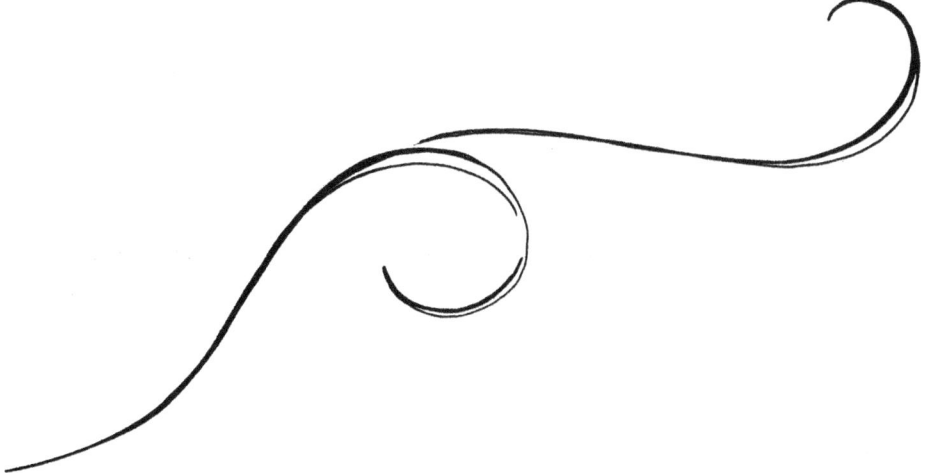

The All-Seeing Eye

As the all-seeing eye throws
A peace sign worth of energy.
Christ's cross leans against a
Wall, as though it were resting.

Musically and fiendishly, the
Center is perfumed with a growth
Of intricacy forming a...

358

359

The Thing

The thing is remembering
What it is to
Be on earth.
To be, actually, on
The astroplanet,
To be wandering well, , ,
Has to do with
Leaving as much positivity
As is humanly possible – in our wake.
The thing, you just can not fake.

The Stream-Life

So the stream-life flows.

I guess I'll remember the power of gravity.
Apparently specifics in writing,
Without citing specifics of a sort,
Is the balance I mostly find.
There are times when all the rhymes can be quite painful.

There is time when there's nothing but bliss.
All that makes up the mass, must be balanced.
The whole time I'm looking, I see things;
Things that may or may not be spoken about.
The balance is precarious to say the least.

360

Mental meditation leads to the peace of non-movement,
People bring their thoughts.

The stream-life has aspects that are diverse,
And pristinely analogic,
As it flows through the pains and serenity of existence.

The tensions and good-space continue loose.

Feeling empty in the soul,
Fully prismed and primed for active full-body life.

As if the spirit becomes abstract and all there is, is life;
    The life that is before us,
    The life that we transform,

The life that supersedes our voiding,
The life that we can live,
With all the energy, drive, passion, derision,
Decision, desire, and flow or fire
That is inspired or conspired for in the self.
We are constantly and consistently adding –
As I, with these words, you with your consumption of them;
We are the rocks, we are the water, we are the gravitational pull.
We are as alive as a stream.

The stream-life can be heavy,
And the stream-life can be kind.
The stream-life can rush swiftly,
And it also gets calm

To remind our static mental states
That there are things that take more time than one moment.
Like a deep, still, lake under a mountain,
There are elements of our life that require
Greater width of focus in order to be right.
Sometimes, we need the depth of focus in order to see the light.

At times, it's very difficult to focus.
It's one of the greatest problems of our culture.
Lack of patience, mixed with lack of love.
These things are just mixed up badly,
Making many people sad.
A sense of Melancholy has swept our nation.
Now we're sitting here,
Freshly swept,
Freshly in need of knowing our options.

20 pairs of tortoises

You and the Goddess

The Goddess whims unity, as one.
We always yearn for sanctification.
We travel while here, traversing so many a marked mile.

The wind of serenity blows
During meditations
Of growth and fixing.

Sometimes, we never grow old.
Sometimes, we don't really know
If we are going to die young,
And yet we still really
Don't know how to live.

Sometimes the peace of seeking the Tao is taken from us by over medicated, out of balance stimuli that gathers subconscious retort and itemry, originating from your self. Sometimes an old dude in a diner gives you hope just by smiling.

Time is an issue, because we're just a chronological blurb, and everyone wants to know who, what, where, when, why, and how they are. I keep time via satellite. It's nice; whenever I cross time zones, it changes for me automatically. I like that. Eras are always transitionary while in action. They are only commutable to segments in retrospect. Therefore, now is just a quandary.

You have the ultimate freedom to influence that which is the future. Every now, is a new now, with new options regarding which way to turn or go. *We* will be what we leave behind, both physically and mentally. For we will die. But this one is our era. We produce both for ourselves, and for those who will follow. The Goddess is eternal, it is we who are, or are not.

Hey You

You guys there, all jet-set
And ready to go on:
Your waves are warm.

I wish that your thoughts
Take you swimming so high,
That your swarm
Will cover
Such beautiful shit,
That you never recover,
And you stay <u>so</u> glad you had
The vision in your mind
That you find as your dream,
Which seems to consume your life,
And makes your strife dissolve–

As you solve Rock and Roll,
And as you send
The requisite toll
Of loving and living like your life is
The reason for your existence:
Know you are a beacon
For us hopefuls, who want to
Walk the world.

So walk with heads
High, for I sigh for the dreams
Of what you'll see from my head.

And happy trails, and happy swimming.
You will be remembered,
So very fondly, in so many minds.

363

364

Is it dischordia –

           Organization centers?

Multiple centers,
      The centers of humanity,
        That vortex!

        Funneling
            Chaos!!!

I See Your Eyes

Building up my dream
Like a landscape
Model,

Take another step.
The moss roots into
My feet.

Breathe another breath,
And the stream
Surrounds me.

Morning sun arises
And my dream ends.

This is just a dream,
I just don't know what to do.

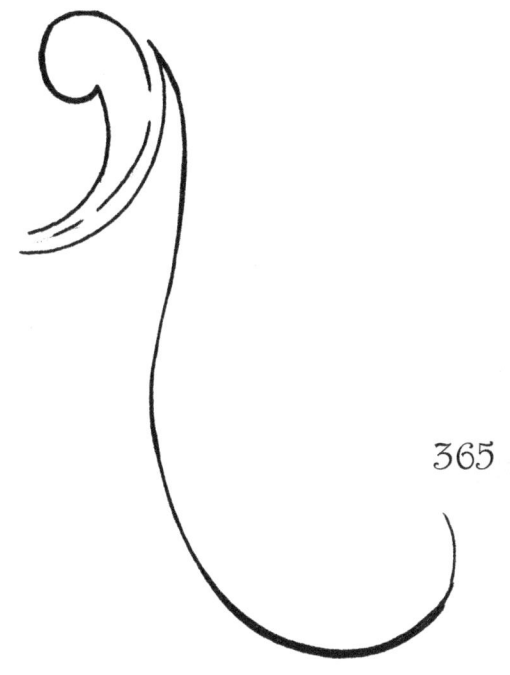

365

I See Your Eyes

Casting out a glow with the sun in battle
I wanna watch the waves as they caress the sands
Take a ship to a distant land
I wanna make my dream a reality
I want the mass to overtake me

I see your Eyes … Flying down the highway I reach 4 U

Inspired by…
4/23/03

Resound Jammerine

366

The town –
Surround.
Abound –
Come down to ground –
The sound around
Resounds.
The pounds,
People…

Ah, surrealism –
See it in music,
Don't try to lose it.
Use it, fuse it
Electrified –
On the dawn,
Awakening!
The shaking has begun
To occur.

The library moved –
The sound grooved,
The people danced
Up and down
All around.
Let me hear
The sound of them singing,
Ringing the air.
The vibrations there
Where I ask you –
Can you ooo ooo ooo?

Guest of the Jester

Sew a new fog, and a new cloud rises.

Every silver lining needs a cloud,
And every sewing needs a string
Pulled, in method.

Method for
Binding, or art.
So, a new fog…

367

Sitting with the Morning Glory
Suits it.
All sorts, all sorts.

Only the best be the guest…
Of the jester…   Better look out…

The Hawk-Artist

A bird and a wailing man on a guitar make the chess games just a little more intense. Then someone refers to someone gone and we all look away or down at whatever it is we're doing.

368

The hawk is collecting pictures from an artist in time with the guitar as it plays. The guitar player is missing somebody, and I no longer feel alone, with a human here at my side. The girl circled and smiled. Wild is the picture being digested by the bird.

The colors keep flowing out of the pen that's in her hand. Giving page life; as a world, taking unto itself a whole new reality. There's nothing that I prefer to a beautiful artist spreading beauty upon a page that she holds down with her hand so it won't move while she drives her hand across it.

Now this is bliss.

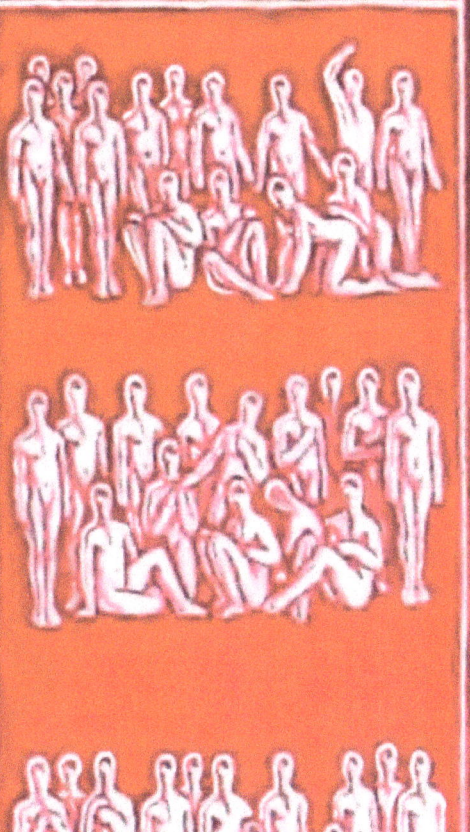
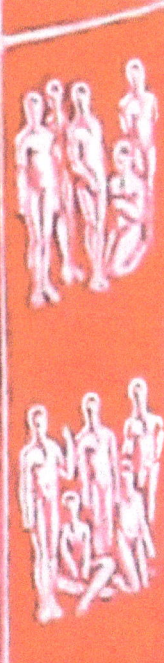
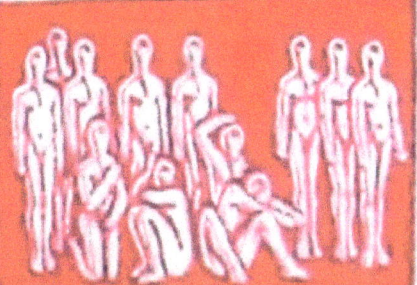

A Letter for Rachel

I remember how your letters were so filled with
      So much love and hope.
I remember how your friends all loved you so much.

You were killed because some freakin' dope
Didn't believe in life.
He just gripped his clutch,
And used it like a knife;
Turned it into a rope
To snap your neck.

370

He wasn't afraid.
He knew his action was already made.

Your parents said
You were so brave,
But could you save their hearts
Which are in so many parts?

That's just the start.
Today, I'll think of you 37 more times again.
So many rhymes I sing to the wind,
As I dream to begin
A new kind of world
That's not so swirled;
And girl, you'd be there too,
And you'd have a new tattoo.
It'd be really cool.
You never would have died.
Your mother never would have cried
All of those tears
For all of your years
Missing,
Blissing only 'nother dimension's beyond.

I'm writing for your retention in all of our minds,
'Cause I find your ghost is healthy for my life.
You wanted to be the world's wife;
Well, your children will have names like mine.
You were just so fine, incredible;
Trustworthy to the line.
You let your body die
So that folks like I
Could be inspired.
So wired for you, Rachel Aliene Corrie!
You told us "Don't forget Rafah!"
And I just can't,
As I pant from running, thousands of miles away.
And it's another day,
But I had to say

371

continued –>

"Solidarity never goes too far!"
    You're a star
Every day that I can still talk about you,
And how you died,
        So that others may glide into the light
            Of Peace.   There is no East,
                    Just people who need more.
For sure,
    We'll know them by being
        The ones with the least.
        And maybe
Our lives will let us give things away,
    And stop charging for everything.

We all have to sing
    And for that, we all need to be wet.
So let water run down
    From your Heaven to our town.

        Seattle will remember you!
            You are from our core!

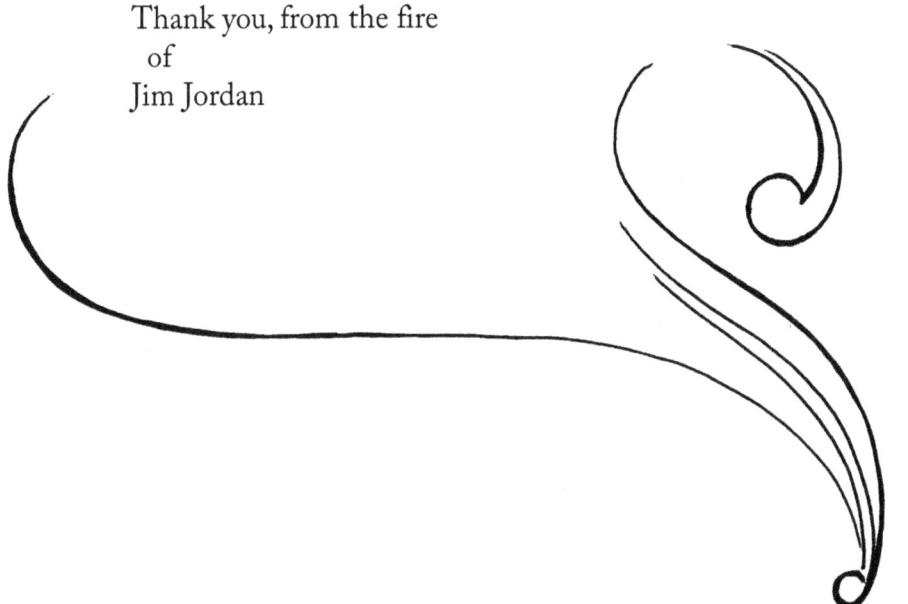

Causes are not forgotten!
You've become our living lore.

Rachel Corrie,
I give you lives like seeds,
And for them I plead:
Let them have some peace,
That then, they can bring it around.
And maybe they'll be as nice a sound
As your voice would have been here today,
If I could have heard it clearly.

373

But I'm nearly at the end of this poem
That I wrote to show'em that you're still alive,
And you're thriving, not just surviving.
You are remembered, and you inspire.

Thank you, from the fire
 of
Jim Jordan

Act One

Visible design features would have been extraneous as the crashing reports of the impact from the *explosive* power of the initial sound that commenced the ceremony ~grabbed the attention of the silent hundreds who had gathered to watch the unfolding battle scene.

All sly and murky-like, the "ffffffttssssss" from the water was joined by subtle movement from some nondescript, yet curious creatures of some sort that had been floating far out in the water. It seemed as if the shore was being approached by some sort of crawling, lurking, slow beasts that were blowing breaths of mist off the water ahead of them.

374 — Abruptly, from the side, came a *stunning* stream of fire from a new character in the scene, in an obviously aggressive and defiant way. The approaching water-based, unknown creatures *leapt* back in response, towards the direction they had come from. The fire-staff-carrying dancer claimed the dry land for herself as she spun and writhed with an amazing fluidity, now that her vanquished water-born adversaries were apparently dispersed. Her movements were those of a slow-motion carnival dancer, alone in a wood, practicing – with her new, fourth-dimensionally enhanced battle tool, clearly designed for supernatural foes.

The life forms in the water recollected and mounted their coming attack with noticeable focus and force after a long pause, allowed for by the serenity provided by the cleansing effect of the land-based fire spirit. This time though, they came with an expanded width of twice as many of themselves, with their giant tentacles dreamily rising and falling in the dark surf along with their weapon of rolling, damp breath – which startled the staff-wielding woman who then recoiled her own presence from the aggressive mists that had been sent in her direction by the water-born beasts.

Her answer was to circle back and *erupt* with surprising bursts of flame from within the blades of her weapon. The Water Spirit's representatives leaped back again as if unable to even withstand the force of one blow from her stunningly powerful tool. And again she danced with a wistful, detached bliss after the routing of her enemy which, to the pleasure of the viewers, lasted some time.

This scene of peace did not last as long as the last one however, as the energy from the water regenerated more quickly this time, and with more volume as well. The *elven* four-bladed-fire-staff brandishing soul was then the lesser of the two sides within the wholesale balance of power being fought for; but then, swiftly, from her rear, up showed a team of reinforcements: fire-fan dancers who proceeded to dictate a push for the landed-side of the battle which was emerging as an apparent illustration of an eventual power shift towards light, emerging through a system of resistance, promising growthful possibilities for the forces of fire-light with their thrust.

375

The four fanned-warriors for the Spirit of Fire retook the ground from the hissing and writhing water creatures by symmetrically panning out where the grasses curved towards the water. There, they caressed the atmosphere with ecstatic care through their windy dance-play that felt like a song being sung by wood nymphs to the mosses during a sunrise over a forested hill – with the light glimpses and elaborate shadows that reach and bend through a warming, early morning mist.

The gliding dance of the fan-dancers was then punctured by a force of anger that was able to repel the fiery foe, resulting in acquisition of the beach for the invaders from the lake. A moment of silence rolled outward, towards the witnesses, from their misty blessing. The water had erupted with an explosive advance from the water creatures, and the fire warriors were nearly completely extinguished, after the brutal hand-to-hand battle between the two forces, with the only surviving remnant delicately emerging from the center of the melee upon a palm-torch, which ethereally floated out from the battle to a boat which had arrived at the shore, with the ambiance of being from the same fleet as the boat used to cross River Styx. And as the fire was taken to the center of the water, the first act came to a close.

Harriet Tubman

Harriet Tubman was too real to be fake.
In order to tell her story, I invoke the soul of Blake.

Back in 1820 or 1821
Is when Harriet came to this Earth.
That's when her path was truly begun,
Though for all it's worth,

It could have been even earlier,
When, in 1793, the cotton gin was finally produced.
But the thing that really worried her
Was the fugitive slave law, that reduced

The chances of getting and staying free
When a slave would escape to the North.
This too, came in 1793.
It was played like fishing, to bring forth

Any random brown skinned man
Who happened to fit a description,
Written by a man who was tan,
Making a mighty potent prescription

For those who would happen to fall into the grips
Of the men who hunted men.
But Harriet made over nineteen trips.
Not worrying, she called upon Heaven.

Her name was Araminta
When she was born
In Dorchester County, Maryland.
By eight, she had worn

Out her voice
By the illness she had had.
One day she heard a sweet noise
That made her so very glad.

The name of her husband,
John Tubman, it was.
He was a free man,
But just because

This was so, did not make her free.
In fact she was later sold.
(Damn the lovers of slavery!)
That was the act that made her bold.

377

She decided then and there
That she would be free.
She ran, she knew not where.
She just plain needed to see,

And feel, and experience freedom.
She would not be sold again.
She rose to the authority of the Higher Kingdom.
She wanted to escape the pain

That her people went through
And were forced to feel.
She saved members of her own family too.
Harriet was so very real.

She's called Moses of Her People
For bringing hundreds out of slavery.
Someday somebody'll raise a steeple
For this great woman's bravery.

continued –>

She was a very large part of
The underground railroad,
Which was a mixture of love
And walking down the road.

It saved countless slaves
From the grips of their masters.
It was made up of poor knaves
To congregational pastors.

When Harriet was young,
Nobody hung
Around her for her smarts.
She actually seemed quite dumb to most.

What it was, was that her host
Threw a weight one day,
And as close as one can say,
He broke her head right into parts.

He cracked her skull.
She never was the same.
She seemed kind of dull.
She seemed kind of lame.

But all the same, none of that was true.
In reality her mind was working overtime.
She was actually letting her mind brew
Tons of thoughts about freedom's chime.

That beautiful sound;
Always in tune,
When it comes and takes
A person on a roll.

One time there was a man named Joe
Who was worth 2000 dollars to his master.
He was one who was saved by Harriet, so
He got to the Promised Land faster

Than many of the slaves
Who had to wait 'till they died.
He went to the land that still had Indian braves.
He found that Canada was a good place to hide.

Because of the fugitive slave law,
Escapees weren't safe in the North.
It would have been like an old rickety seesaw,
Because what the slaves were worth

379

Made catching them a good way for a man to make a living,
And many were in fact brought back.
None were however, from Harriet's crew,
Who were made strong by the use of tact

In order to make themselves free.
Say, for instance with the use of carts
That were pulled by horses to avoid the melee
That would occur via the men with no hearts.

She gave a lot of thought to the Bible and God.
She saw herself living in Genesis.
Then Moses' spirit moved into her bod.
I couldn't sit and give you a list

Of all the names of all the people she saved.
One might wonder why it is that she behaved
In such a manner as she did.
But imagine that if the US is a melting pot, then slavery was a lid.

continued –>

Then, after all she had done,
Which included much government work,
The government refused what many thought was due.
Not a single government perk.

After all she had helped them
Being a spy, and a nurse, and a scout.
She helped them all over,
Repeatedly showing good routes

To get where they were going.
But then, she was showing
Such exemplary action that one reason for
Not giving her a pension or commendation is that never before

380

Had someone done the things she did
In her most exemplary style.
They had no mention in any of the books
That could help her. So, after a while,

She went back home to New York, where
The bank was foreclosing on her home!
But Jah/Jehovah stepped in even there,
And Harriet no longer had to roam

From place to place,
Looking for the grace
That would replace
The human unkindness done unto her race.

The pace that she set
Is one that we should never forget!

Let me not neglect to mention,
(I have a problem with memory retention.)
That Harriet was also an elegant speaker.
Some would say that she's of the weaker
When speaking of her sex.
But she showed it to be no hindrance.
Her strength was that of T-Rex.

She never let it get her down,
That is, being female.
It probably even helped her get around.
The stories that entail

The substance of her life,
The strife, the joys...

All the boys in "The Boy's Club" major
Would have a tough time with a wager
Whether they had done more or her.

The whir of it all
Makes her seem pretty tall
In the history of the world as we know it.

381

A Feat Accomplished

As the years passed are many,
And the time seems to've slipped away;
The seasons don't seem to last as long,
As they used to, back then, in the day.

And the children have grown up,
Gone on to have their own;
They'll try to teach their children respect
So that they won't be alone,

382

When the time comes around
That they find they need a hand,
And there's no one else to give them
The love their children can.

And you come to find out
That all the things you'd taught,
Most evident, the ones
About which they had fought

Are the things that they are trying
To teach unto their own.
It makes parents feel as though
They'd been put upon a throne

By the one's who must've listened,
However slight.
Apparently it's sunk in,
The words shared every night.

From the days way back when,
When they were back in school.
When you used to say what it was that was right,
And they used to say what was cool.

And now that they've lost that razor sharp edge,
And they're trying to teach what's the way;
You can look back and smile, and know in yourself,
That they'll be as happy someday.

383

Because You Forgot

So you walked out into the frigid early morning to the fog rolling in through town. Everyone around knew that there could be trouble before the day was out, but everyone knew that they were in the right, and that the battle needed to be won. The sun was just rising over the hill as the men carried signs – and sticks that were without placards as well. They knew who they were up against, and they had come prepared.

Reginald stood next to you, and you could count about sixty men there in the chilled street, walking toward the mill. He said he thought that there were some still to join y'all, so he let out a call that echoed through the company town's valley setting. You saw more men coming through front doors and around corners. You felt a sense of empowerment with so many men with you. You felt that maybe today would be the day where you could finish the work that had been started so long ago.

384

Reginald Dorsey and you had an appointment with the mill's management at noon, at which you would again present your, and the strikers', demands for an eight-hour day, overtime pay for people who earn it, and a reasonable base wage, so that all the folks who made their livelihood working there could lead decent lives. The strike had been incredibly long. Even though there had been longer ones; anybody on a strike that lasts any real amount of time feels the epic proportions of what he or she is involved in.

The strike had been on for 86 days. Thanks to the solidarity of the IWW, the families of the workers hadn't been starving. But there had been some serious situations. Bill Hanson had been killed by the Pinkerton officers that the mill bosses had hired, and Betsy… Well, when that happened, folks really steeled around the movement. At first, we only had about half the workers with us, but then with Betsy and Bill being attacked like that, the folks in town simply bonded beyond measure.

So the march was on. Only about a half a mile up the road was where all the main buildings for the mill were located. The offices were inside the second building on the left as you entered the complex. The guards kept the throngs of strikers out, but let you and Reginald in to go up to the offices. He looked at you and said, "Jean, I think that this day will be etched in our memory for a long time. Let's get this right." You could imagine that he was right, and you just prayed you could. You were still listening to the chanting outside as you ascended the steps to the offices of the management, who you knew were sitting up there smoking their cigars right then, just trying to figure how to convince you to step away from your demands.

Just as you figured they would be when you got there; there were about seven of them, all sitting and puffing away. They didn't offer you cigars, you wouldn't have taken one anyway. You weren't their friend. It wasn't a relaxing time for you. You were trying to figure out how to make the pompous greed-whores release the strangle-hold that they had on the profits of a business that, simply, meant everything to so many people that they could scarcely care less about. They had done no more than contract the installation of it – where your friends and neighbors had been sweating and laboring for years, making it actually viable – without a reasonable kickback of pay, or even the most basic human respect.

The two of you took the chairs that were sequestered at your own end of the long conference table, and you waited for the others to calm down. So then, Dwight Rexal, the owner of the mill, hastily and mockingly asked "Have you finally decided to come back to work for the fair, and even, rather generous wage that I've offered you for the last five years?" After which his management team laughed with a sarcastic, feigned stifle through their smoke at you.

Your old friend and partner in this deal, Reginald, slowly and cleanly replied, "Actually, we've decided to stay out of your buildings, off your lines, and at your doorstep, until you grant us not only a fair wage of our

continued –>

determining, but an eight-hour day, a forty-hour week, and overtime pay for those who choose to work longer than that."

You added, "We are not willing to go back to the pay that you have paid us for so many years, while you raise prices in your stores. We have not been able to pay for new clothes, much less pay back loans that we took out for our homes from your bank, or into savings for our children's future. What you are paying us is unconscionable and we simply, require an increase in our standard of living, through higher pay. Just look at you, smoking your cigars in your fine suits. You eat off silver, own jewels and expensive art. We make that money for you, and we live as paupers! There is no way of justifying the way you live. You will have to share the profits of this company with those who create it, or none will be made at all."

386   The managers weren't laughing at that point. The cigars all got still, and they looked at each other as if looking for the one who would volunteer his own luxurious lifestyle as the first on the chopping block. After a long silence, one of them looked to you as if he was trying to understand a foreign language and replied, "So you want to live in the streets?"

"Have you not been hearing a word I've been saying?" you asked. Another manager tersely remarked, "What I think you didn't hear there, was what Mr. Chappleton was saying; that we have no interest in paying you these inordinate amounts for your menial, and may I say, oftentimes, spotty labor. You have not proven that you are worth what you are asking, and as such, it will not be paid to you. You simply do not deserve it."

"Then we will shut you down," spoke Reginald. "How can you say these things!?" asked a manager. Adding to which, the owner continued, "We have ordered new workers. You and your men; I guess some of them have families, them too; must be out of our houses by the weekend so the new workers may move in with a minimum of difficulty." The managers seemed more at ease than earlier, snickering at this information. That was a twist of events. You and Reginald looked at each other with disbelief and pushed back your chairs. "This is not over," you said, and the both of you walked out.

As you went down those steps, you had an eerie feeling that things were going to get worse before they got better. You felt a chilling kind of emptiness; like a break in the connection with even the building that you were walking in. You had literally built that building with your own hands! You'd labored on the property for a lot of years, providing for your family (if even only just barely) because of this mill, and you had always felt a part of it; like it couldn't do without you as much as you couldn't do without it. As your hand slid down the smooth, cold railing during the descent of the stairs from the offices, it was the first time you could remember feeling so distant from that which you were touching with your own hands, that which had before, seemed so familiar,

Your despondence, however, found itself changing into embers of rage, as it was stirred by the sight of your brothers outside the chain link fence who were still holding their signs up with phrases on them that never should have been necessary to hoist into the air in the first place. You felt an almost cynical type of anger towards the owner and his men. And you could sense a wave of bristling hatred for the Pinkerton guards who were laughing at the two of you as you left. It was clear that they knew before you had gone up there what had been the news you'd received. You knew that you would be seeing each other again, but under very different circumstances when next you did.

387

You stoically walked in straight and determined steps towards the fence that your fellow strikers were standing beyond, only to be told as you got there that you were not allowed to exit through that gateway. The guards said they had been given orders to not open that gate under any circumstances, at all. You asked where you were supposed to leave through, and were told to go to the other end of the mill property, that that particular fence was not able to be opened, and that that would be the end of that.

You knew something was wrong with what you were hearing, and protested the point further; but the guard started getting aggressive, and you realized that a situation was at hand which needed to be played as cool as possible so that you didn't play into the hands of the conniving deviants any more than you apparently already had. As you started

continued –>

towards the office building, you were stopped by guards, again chiding, "You'd better leave before you're thrown out for trespassing!" You realized that they were having fun making things tough on you, so the two of you started towards the back gate which was down the main path, and on the side with the river, knowing that you were not going to be able to change their minds.

You yelled for some of your union brothers to meet you over at the back gate, and started walking over there. From where you turned the corner, you saw four guards standing at the back gate, waiting for you. They welcomed your approach to the opened gate with taunts about how you and Reginald were lucky that you hadn't been beaten for trespassing on company land yet. You held your tongue, knowing that they would love an excuse to do just that.

388

You could see your brothers from the line approaching and you waved to them. As you stepped through the gate's opening, you felt a thud of a sharp pain in your ribs. You realized that you had been struck, and could feel panic setting in. Turning around, you saw Reginald falling towards you. It looked as if he'd been struck in the head. His eyes were closed, and he was falling fast towards you and the opening in the fence. You reached to catch him and looked back to see your fellow strikers running towards you as the two of you fell.

As Reginald landed in your arms, you felt a strong push in the middle of your back with something large and heavy. You were being kicked out of the perimeter by one of the guards, literally. As you fell towards the ground under the heap of your friend, you understood that moment to be just a beginning of a new chapter in the saga that was unfolding in all of our lives. As the gate closed with a heavy, metallic clang after you, our friends finally made it to the scene; only to be able to help you up off the ground as the guards shut the gate behind you.

Reginald was becoming lightly conscious as you checked in on him again while two of the strikers with you started to yell through the fence at the offending guards. Things like, "I will remember you!" and, "Why don't you try and get somebody who's looking at you?" Taunting and angrily, the guards laughed and called back, "You should just leave now. There's no way you're going to get your jobs back now," and "You don't want to fight us, you don't have the strength. Just look at your leaders, in a crumpled ball…Who's going to talk for you now?" They turned to leave, laughing on their way.

The strikers continued to yell at them "We'll get you for this, I remember your face Pinkerton boy!" They turned to you and Reginald, who was coming out of his stupor with the help of the other striker who had stayed with you, holding Reginald's head with a piece of his shirt. The bleeding was slowing down, coming from his temple. He became more cognizant, but he seemed a lot angrier than before. More strikers were running in from around the corner. They had heard the fighting from afar and were joining you at the back of the mill yard. Some threw sticks and rocks over the fence. A sinking sensation came with the realization that things were going to get worse before they got better. The workers would not take the news of what had transpired well.

389

Feeling as if you'd maybe broken some ribs, you hobbled slowly, solemnly back to town among the familiar throng. Reginald was walking mostly under his own strength at that point, and the rest of the men were plain incensed. They were talking about battlements, fairness, scabs, the Pinkerton crew, and how they were going take the mill back for themselves. All sorts of thoughts that were simply inconceivable without violence and bloodshed. Inside you, there was a place that didn't want any of it. You wished you could just take your family far out West and hunt for a living, and have your wife take care of you and your youngins, not the bands of striking workers living in all those tents; to let them grow up and grow old, in peace.

You knew though, that you were too entrenched in this community to step away. The people needed a voice like yours, one that had stood for years as an articulate voice working as a translator between the old language and the management. There was no way you could walk away, too

continued –>

much depended on the solidarity that you provided. If the bosses won, hundreds of your fellow workers – friends – would be lost in the woods out there, and the hundreds of others – the new workers – would have to put up with the same treatment that you had been dealing with for too long. The bosses needed to be taught a lesson. And you, with the help of all these men, would have to be the ones to teach it.

Back in town, things were tense. People were stocking up on supplies and teeming in the streets, as if waiting for the mobilization to happen at any time. They all knew what would happen when the strikebreakers came; so everyone was gathering as much black powder and shot, lamp oil and canning jars, as they could manage. The town was going into war mode and you just felt sad. It was hard to feel good about the fact that it was all coming to a head the way it was. What you were asking of the bosses was not unreasonable. They were making so much money off the labor of others, and yet were completely unwilling to share that profit when the books were drawn up at the end of every month.

Maybe they had some sort of ingrained philosophy holding that, since they were the ones who'd initially invested all the primary capital, that they should be the primary receivers of all future income. As if it would be a bad thing if everyone in town were able to have full meals when they sat down to dinner at night with their families. As if it would be wrong for people to be able to afford enough soap to use it every time they washed their clothes. As if they had some sort of God-given right to all the luxuries that life had to offer, while everyone else had somehow been determined by God to be less deserving for some reason. Well, truly, it did have to stop, and if you were going to be the one that had to draw that line in the sand, as it looked you were about to do, then so be it.

Your determination steeled, looking around at the energy that your friends and neighbors were showing that day. It was easy to feel akin to your townsmen who were getting ready for the strange dawn which was about to rise. At home that night, you felt a calm sense of resolution that whatever would happen, would be for the best come morning.

There were many ideas about where to really draw the line though. Many people had decided that they would not leave their homes, and others had agreed to go with the union to the big clearing at the side of town to erect a tent city, so that the new residents, maybe wouldn't feel isolated immediately. There was a sense of hope that you would be able to sway them as well, to your side, co-opting the owner's goals of keeping them in his fold. You knew however, that would be a long shot, and that you would be lucky if they were anything less than violent towards you, in light of the fact that some would be denied homes by those of your collective who were refusing to leave their own.

You, Reginald, and most of the others who were fathers, had decided to take your families to the tent city, assuming that the earliest violence would be focused on the houses that the company still owned for the most part, even though many of you had been making payments on them 391 for many years. They were still not yours on paper; and as such, the management's thugs would be using all means available to them to assert their plan, and you wanted to have your children and wives out of the way when that happened. Many of the single men though, were ready and waiting for the Pinkerton boys who were headed their way. They were ready with shotguns and knives. They were ready with strong words, strong arms and strong hearts.

They had no intention of leaving their homes. You even knew of a few folks who had decided to rig their homes with booby traps for the Pinkerton crew; everything from harmless scare tactics to deadly, dangerous fire blazes that would start when doors opened or when tripwires were sprung. Those Pinkertons had no idea of what they were getting into.

If they hadn't been so cruel in the earlier months, you'd have felt bad for them. But they were the ones who had killed Bill, and they were the ones who had broken your ribs, Tim Lang, his legs, Betsy McConnah, the way she came home all bruised and crying one night. Everyone knew what had happened. It all had to stop. The lines had been drawn. There were now, so many lines, each with different surprises behind them. Now, all anybody could do was wait.

continued –>

The tent city had gone up with only a touch of difficulty. Some folks didn't want to dig trenches inside their tents, but the interstaters from the IWW had told us that if anything were to occur within the night, that we would need them. Some of our boys had been in The Great War, so they knew what was meant by "anything" and they tried to keep it as clean as possible for the women and children, but it needed to be said that midnight attacks could happen, and they needed to be defended against. It was a tough time and tough lines needed to be drawn.

The IWW was taking care of food and things, but they weren't allowed to import black powder. Some sort of annoying clause in their paperwork somewhere that would delegitimize their stance as a political organization if they were to provide arms to strikers. As if any other political organization in the world has ever acted without force.

Sunday night would be when the rubber hit the road. You could hear men hollering all night. The campfires were highest that night as well. You knew that the men who had decided to stay in their houses were going to have a showdown the following morning, and you and the rest had agreed to be in town to support them when it happened. The first train was scheduled to arrive at six o'clock in the morning, and when those new men got off those cars, that would start the day.

The Pinkerton boys all were carrying rifles and were walking with a fresh swagger for having been deputized by the sheriff over the weekend. They led the new workers down the middle of the main street in town to the homes that they were to live in. The first few were empty, but then they got to Joe Hampton's place; and he was there to greet them. Joe had always been a sucker for a good fight, and now he was able to put that into play with good reason. It was almost funny the way he just opened the door like there was a salesman at it or something, acting as if he had no idea what was going on!

That Pinkerton guard didn't know who he was looking at and tried to pull on Joe's arm. Good old Joe just grabbed that phony deputy and threw him right off his porch! He must have flown fifteen feet before he even hit the ground, and hit the ground he did! He must have slid another five or six feet before he stopped, but when he did, he got up (a bit slowly there), and looked so hot…

All of us were just standing there holding signs, to let the thoroughly confused new residents know what they were walking into. Some of them started to look worried. Some of them started to yell at Joe. He just looked at them and at the guard who was making his way back up the steps (this time with two more of his crew). Joe spat on the ground in front of them. He said "You better get off my porch." The mill deputy said "Oh yea?" and as soon as he did, Joe pushed a lever inside his doorway and the whole porch opened up into a vat of wet tar, which all three of them fell straight into! Boy, were they surprised. They were as stuck as they could be. All the sudden, some guard in the back let off a shot in the air. The fresh workers had been laughing, but they stopped right quick. You saw Joe pull out a cigarillo and light a match…

393

Dinner with Jello

As a child, I loved Rock and Roll.

I was sincerely pissed when Jane's Addiction released "Been Caught Stealing" off an album that had epic possibilities. If only "3 Days" had been chosen instead...

I was the kid with blow pops and gum packs in the hallway in third or sixth grade. It was how I supported my passion. My friends and I would go to town every day after school and surf through the vinyl, or the record bins as we called them back then, in the Music Staff, which was **the** real good record store in town at the time. We would look through them and pick one out, maybe buy a cassette while we were there while we were at it. I used to listen for hours to the music, simply contented to have the harmonies of the artists roll over me in the darkness as I got dreamy.

One thing that I noticed about music was that you could put an idea in it, in a setting that was somehow extra-physically correct. The containment of philosophical and sociological ideas within a musical context was liminal to the extreme. I had learned it from the Movement-era rock of the Beatles and Dylan. And in the early-mid eighties, there was the Dead Kennedys. A band that was aggressive in tone, and clear in expression. They held a weapon of style that really was rare in strength. They were led by a man known as Jello Biafra - naming himself after a nation in Africa that was only in existence for about a year and a half and was a proxy battle ground for major powers, leaving over a million dead in the wake of the turmoil – alluding to his political forwardness.

His lyrics left no question where he stood on an issue. And while he was youthful and bold, it was obvious that he was schooled in the topics he was writing about, and his thoughts, in relation to a subject, were bound to be well thought out, while straying into the comically satiric at times. His ability to pen strong work was unusually amplified by his application of cohesion through his rare ability of enunciation. One major problem with modern agro-rock is that the language is completely hidden by guitar licks that simply have too much prominence.

I enjoyed being able to hear Jello's words, and was inspired to become a writer in a similar style in no small part, because of his art. Earlier this year (2004/5?), he came to my school. When I heard he needed a ride to Seattle, I jumped at the opportunity. I was making the trip all the time anyway, and there was an opportunity to ride one of my heroes North on his road. I was stoked.

His spoken word performance was too long for me (but the chairs were bad, or maybe it was just badly lit), but it was chunky with thoughts that just needed to get out of him. He lamented about it whenever a review of the evening came up later. He asked me for ideas about what he should do to tighten it up. At first I was stunned – here I was with a guy who has been a super famous rock star for as long as I've been listening to music, asking me for help on his stage presence. I gave it some thought. I told him I couldn't tell him what to cut, but I could tell him what to keep.

395

So I talked about how I appreciated that he shared the forms of government that are present in other successful democracies in the world that allow for more voice from minority populations, as in the representative democracies of certain states of Europe where for example, if a party gets 15% of the vote – they get 15% of the representation. It is a step away from the two party system which lends itself to a collusion of monopolistic practices which are causing many problems today. So yea, it was definitely something else to say the least. I was real glad to have the randomness of the experience.

The night of the show, he was wearing a sweatshirt with the name of an old friend of his who's dead now, but was known for his street art and his bizarre musical designs. Wesley Willis was his name. One thing that he shared with some other folks that had joined us for beer and dinner at

continued –>

The Voyeur (man, they have good food there), was Wesley's method of greeting, which was to grab you by the head and to head butt you in the forehead. It was truly a sight, seeing this man grab a fan and rap him in the head with his own. Truly, truly a funny experience.

Finally, the waitress offered dessert, for Jello. "Would you like to see our bottle caps?" He started legitimizing the question to everyone, like he'd been caught doing something wrong. "I used to collect them when I was a kid," he said. "I don't really anymore, no really. Not unless, well, not unless they're really, really unusual." The waitress (who I may say was sporting her "Reading is Sexy" tee shirt memorably) had already left to get the bin that was kept by the establishment, for a man they surely had known was coming – to've known to offer it so.

396

It was funny, his eyes shined like a ten-year-old with baseball cards as he sifted through the small bin with a couple hundred unusual bottle caps. He found a good sized pile of random caps that he would add to his "surely non-existent collection," since he'd insisted that he doesn't really collect them anymore. It was fun, a truly enjoyable hour with one of Rock and Roll's legends. There were probably eight or nine other cats around who had come after the show sitting around with us, so the discussion was all over the place.

It was nice to reconnect with someone who I had considered part of my repertoire for so many years. He showed me a vision of perseverance and was able to embody the archetype of the external activist in his continued stage presence which he also still mixes with rock and roll when he performs with the Melvins like he did on New Year's in Seattle the same year.

He was a funny guy. Hopefully, he can pass on the idea of staying involved in social efforts, and keeping a sense of humor about life at the same time. If you ever get the chance to have dinner with Jello, I highly recommend it. Mixes well with Fish Tail Organic. You have been reading. Now you are sexy as well.

Lost Friends

Sometimes when I'm walking,
My friends begin their talking,
But I just hadn't wanted to be there then.

Some words could've stilled an insight
That a friend was right there having,
And me, I wasn't listening, and I spoke.
I'd see my friend there choke,
I try to apologize to the bloke,
And forget even what it was that I was sayin'.

Still I miss the friends I've lost
In dust, as I sped further,
'Cause there be heads around that I can't see.
En when I get enough time,
I send 'em a dose'a rhyme,
So they'll know that I ain't forgot'em.
But as it is...
I wish them bliss.

397

Revolution with Disassociation
or Subjugation to a Farce

Socrates once felt that "the only thing he should think about, when he acts, is whether it is the behavior of a good man or a bad man," referring to the directed man. That is, a person who is being controlled through a single, or a series of orders. When we are told to do something, we should automatically ask ourselves certain questions. We should look into who is telling us to act or think a certain way. We should decide whether or not the reasoning behind the direction is righteous or malicious. Ultimately, the instructed individual of which Socrates spoke must have a personal awareness as to the realism of his or her actions or thought process, and how it affects his or her self and those in association (Heidegger said that). I agree with them both.

In my opinion, at all times, "blind faith" is wrong. I think we should always attempt to see who or what we are following so that we are not led off a cliff. Jim Jones's followers were a clear enough example to me as far as that goes. We should always know where we are going, why we are going there, as well as what we're going there for. These ideas are just as important, if not more so, as how we can get there, and who will be there when we arrive.

We must have open eyes in this day and age, so that we don't fall prey to old prejudices and myths. Blindness handicaps. Faith, in contrast, can be good, if the believer is willing to be discerning in his or her actions. He or she must keep in mind that what was written, was written in the past; because what we have to deal with in society today is very different from what, for example, Jesus or Moses had to deal with in their days. So therefore, we must look for updated ideas for the sake of the new type of perspective made possible by living in the twenty-first century.

"The organized man has lost his capacity to disobey, he is not even aware of the fact that he obeys" (Erich Fromm). The dimension of this statement should not be downplayed. It implies that modern people (assuming that organization is a facet of modernization) are losing the innate capacity for critical thought; say for example, in the workplace, where modernization and organization are epitomized.

"At this point in history the capacity to doubt, to criticize and to disobey may be all that stands between a future for mankind and the end of civilization," he continues. If blind obedience is to be deemed a trigger to end enlightened society, and change is accepted as the only constant, we should understand that disobedience by the wise is a signal for institutional change. The question then should arise, "Who decides who is wise?" We must again discern as to how men or women will be chosen for ideologues.

For an example, we can consider the case of Henry David Thoreau's avoidance of the poll tax in the nineteenth century. We can discuss an instance of a decision made that went against the norm of the time; but now we see what he did as not only noble, but profoundly important. He was a man who was either before his time, or perfect for it.

It has been shown further, through now-infamous testing, that people under non-extenuating circumstances will, for the most part, agree to do just about anything that is asked of them by just about anyone for the simple fact that they are being asked to do it (Milgram). This is not good. We should learn to discern good from bad, and act accordingly. Unfortunately, it is hard to teach people to live critically and objectively, as opposed to from a singular perspective, or thoughtlessly.

Disobedience has not often been properly taught, correspondingly we have lessened the redress of change. For example, our government (USA) has found it necessary to stop and look into the recent past, to see

continued –>

just how bad it has gotten right here on our own turf, as in HR 891 (1995), a bill that establishes a commission to discuss the institution slavery as it stood in the United States. The codependence with rhetoric is amazing.

There are lines where we as a people should not allow ourselves to be pushed across. We should not allow ourselves to be oppressed, as people of color were made to be, or as a intuitive thinkers and others have been as well. We should also not allow police to dictate how we act. In the face of oppression, we should spit.

"Caught between my culture and the system. / Genocide! / Read my writing in the wall. / No one's here to catch me if I fall. / If ignorance is bliss / Then knock the smile off my face. / If we don't take action now, / We settle for nothing later. / We'll settle for nothing now, / And we'll settle for nothing later." (De la Rocha)

Everything we do is a reflection of our life's facets.

I've found that a reality of seeing ourselves as being a part of a group of sovereign individuals, rather than as being a part in a machine, can be formed as progression through existence occurs. All we do is represent how we feel in relation to stimuli.

We should accordingly, never deviate from our true beliefs (being that a few bombs can alter all that was and could have ever been), or standpoints that we proscribe to. Similarly, while an orator of direction can have reasoned his or her instructions to be sound, one must reason them out in the self. Then listen to one's own moral sense and act accordingly. It's called being true to, and trusting yourself; not some isolated individual whom you revere for some reason.

Rely on the self to lead, the self that has the information – the information that it needs to see the truth – thereby treating the mind like a center, not the masses with their numbers to get lost in. We can see anew every time our eyes are open. History may be written by the winners of the wars, but it will contain still, the actions of individuals producing the outcomes which define the present state of being, and the future.

The Philosophy is Coming to Dinner!

"The Philosophy is coming to dinner!"

"The what?"

"The Philosophy is coming to dinner!"

"The who?"

"The Philosophy! Yes, the Philosophy. The Philosophy is coming to dinner."

"Now, hold on. What do you mean?"

"Well, he's coming, and soon; so you better be ready. Come on!"

"What?"

"Follow me… First you need to brush your teeth and floss your hair and wash your face and hands well."

401

"But wait. Who is this person 'The Philosophy'?"

"He talks a lot – this you'll see. Now come quickly – here comes the Philosophy!"

"Hello, hello, hello. How are you today?" said a man who seemed okay.

"Fine, fine, fine," said the man who'd heard of him.

"Okay," said the other, a little surprised and hesitant.

"Well that's good to hear," said the man in the beard.

"I like being near confident people. All is easy while contented," he smiled.

"Yes, yes, yes," said the man who was anxious to hear spewed philosophy.

"But what is it you came to say?" he pressed.

"That was a good meal!" Mr. Philosophy said triumphantly.

The onlooker stifled a laugh.

"No, I mean your philosophies," said the man full of anticipation.

"Oh, them," said the man.

"Well, it's better to give than to receive – but it is still very nice to receive. Try not to run over anything while driving your car. We can be so bad about that."

continued –>

"No, no, no," said the eager one. "I want your philosophies like who God is, and why we're here. Where we're going – Stuff like that."

"Oh," he said softly and thoughtfully. "I think I see what you mean."

"Well, God is the guy that makes you smile or cry, or the mountain you want to climb, or have climbed, with all its vegetation and animal life on it for you to admire and enjoy, and…"

"No!" shouted the antsy one "I want more – how do you talk to God? … To get what you want, I mean?"

"Oh, I think I see," said he who was considering.

And "Hmm," said the third who had watched this whole thing from a nicely objective perspective.

402

"I think I see the problem," the third friend said.

"Huh?" said his friend.

"And what's that?" said the other.

"Here it is: You came for dinner with the two of us, or maybe just him," speaking of his friend, "and you want this man to spurt philosophy to you limitlessly," pointing back to Philosophy. "And you're both hoping that the other gives you what you came for."

"Yes!" said his friend, profoundly excited.

"Mmm hmmm," replied the other.

"Then why don't we sit at the table – that way we can do everything easier."

"I like him," said Philosophy.

"Makes sense," said his buddy.

So they all went over to the table to sit down.

When they were all seated, the philosopher decided he would try to get his dinner.

"What do you want?" he asked his host.

"I just want to hear you talk," he said quickly.

"Have you not been?" asked his friend.

"Yes, yes, yes, but…"

"Wait," said Philosophy. "I think I get it. You invited me over here to hear my philosophies and have been unable to."

"Well, I guess," he slowly replied.

"How's this then, I'll tell you how to *see* my philosophy: Watch what I do as well as what I say, and when I say something that has to do with anything, figure that that is my philosophy about that particular subject."

"Oh," was all that the man said as he turned to get the food that would ensure Philosophy's extended stay.

He then watched the two others converse on a wide array of topics over dinner. He found that his best bet was to stay out of the conversations to pull all he could out of them.

The other two found very good friends that day, and found themselves getting together on many occasions to converse on the topics of the world, and more or less.

Thanks

I'm thinking I got to be writing.

Thank you,
To people who have helped me
Get from place to place.

Thank you, to all of humanity.

404

So many of you, throughout
So many generations, have appreciated
Positive solutions along with the inconsistencies,
Even the destructive reduction, to achieve
Helpful and useful
Conclusions.

Glossary of Jimmish

Absolvement - n. Something that will absolve, or free someone, from something.

Achin' - adj. Shortened version of "aching."

Agro-rock - n. Rock and roll that is aggressive.

Ahh - excl. The sound of a voice as it is exclaiming.

Ain' - v. Also written as "ain't" sometimes. This is a slang version of "is not."

A.K.A. - Acronym; meaning "also known as."

All'a - adj. Contraction; shortened version of "all of."

Anslim - v. Action of a sort, to be defined by your imagination.

Aquification - n. When something has been made to be as liquid as water.

Astroplane - n. A place that is far beyond the atmosphere of our planet.

Authoristan - n. A person, as sovereign as a nation, due to creative authorship.

Aw - excl. The sound of appreciation or sadness.

Bali - n. A city in Indonesia; said to be one of the most lovely places on the Earth in consistent habitation.

Bebop - n. A type of music made famous by Louis Armstrong, Ella Fitzgerald, and others, it has continued through the music of Jazz throughout the years.

Bein' - v. Shortened version of "being."

Benzedrine - n. A form of amphetamine, A.K.A. bennies.

Blerk - n. To be defined by your imagination. Enjoy.

Blissing - v. Bringing bliss to something.

Bob Marley. b. Feb 6, 1945, d. May 11, 1981; Jamaican singer-songwriter and musician. The leading voice in the Rastafarian music canon.

He both gifted the world some of the greatest music of all time, and stood as a good example of a man who stood strong for what he believed in, never allowing people who would silence his voice get the upper hand.

His album Exodus was chosen by Time magazine as the greatest album of the 20th century.

Boomer'a - adj. Meaning lots, or many.

Bowloping - v. To be defined by your imagination. Heh heh.

Brahms, Johannes. b. May 7, 1833 d. April 3, 1897; German composer and pianist. Well known as a master of counterpoint, a rather complicated way of writing, which J.S. Bach also was big on.

- Was less known for having turned down an honorary doctorate in music from the University of Cambridge in 1877, though he did take one from The University of Breslau two years later.

Breathings - n. Similar in meaning to "breaths."

Breed'em - v./n. Contraction; shortened version of "breed them."

Bringin' - v. Shortened version of "bringing."

B-Tree. Living Pittsburgh hip-hop artist and poet - May have also been known as Luqmam Abdul-Salaam, but B-Tree for fluidity.

Build'em - v./n. Contraction; shortened version of "build them."

Bullshit - n. Common English expletive, sometimes shortened to "bull" or "B.S.," commonly used in connection with incorrect, misleading or false language statements.

First poetic usage was with T.S. Eliot's *"The Triumph of Bullshit"*

The first stanza being -

Ladies, on whom my attentions have waited
If you consider my merits are small
Etiolated, alembicated,
Orotund, tasteless, fantastical,
Monotonous, crotchety, constipated,
Impotent galamatias
Affected, possibly imitated,
For Christ's sake stick it up your ass.

Bumpin' - v. Shortened version of "bumping."

Bunch'a - n./pre. Contraction; shortened version of "bunch of."

Burnin' - **v.** Shortened version of "burning."

Bustin' - **v.** Shortened version of "busting."

Buzzin' - **v.** Shortened version of "buzzing."

Care'a - **v./pre.** Contraction; shortened version of "care of."

Carryin' - **v.** Shortened version of "carrying."

Catchin' - **v.** Shortened version of "catching."

C. - **adj.** Representing "circa" from the Latin, approximately meaning "near the year of."

'Cept - **prep.** Shortened version of "except."

Cha - **1. n.** Slang version of "you" and; **2. v./n.** Contraction; of "do you."

Chefin' - **v.** Shortened version of "chefing." That is: being a chef.

Chillin' - **v.** Shortened version of "chilling," but in this usage, "chilling" would be inappropriate, as it's specifically a slang term to mean relaxing, or taking it easy, it's always spelled like this.

Chlorines - **n.** Multiple of chlorine.

Chu - **v./n.** Contraction; slang version of "do you."

Chyour - **pron.** Slang version of "your," the posessive pronoun.

Clout - **n.** The amount of social pressure that a person can exude.

Comin' - **v.** Shortened version of "coming."

Conversate - **v.** To talk, the verb form of conversation.

Could'a - **adv.** Shortened version of "could have."

Criss cross - **v.** When something is crossed.

Crossin' - **v.** Shortened version of "crossing."

Crusin' - **v.** Shortened version of "crusing."

Cutie - n. A person who is cute.

Cuttin' - v. Shortened version of "cutting."

Dag - excl. Derived from "dang," a common, publicly acceptable, exclamation.

Dang - excl. Derived from "darn," as in: "Darn, that's big!"

Day-glo also: **Dayglo - adj.** Something that glows with a luminescence.

Delegitimize - v. To make illegitimate.

Demused - 1. n. A state of being without inspiration. also; 2. **v.** To remove the muse, or the inspiration.

Deserved'em - v./n. Contraction; shortened version of "deserved them."

De'vine - n. double entendre, (poetic device) meaning "the vine" and "divine" at the same time.

Diggin' - v. Meaning "liking," a shortened version of "digging."

Doin' - v. Shortened version of "doing."

Dolin' - v. Shortened version of "doling," or giving.

Don't'cha - adv./n. Contraction; shortened version of "don't you."

Dose'a - n./prep. Contraction; meaning "some of," it is a shortened version of "dose of."

Dreamin' - v. Shortened version of "dreaming."

Dreamscape - n. The territory where your dreams lay.

Dreeble - n. Yet another to be defined by *your* imagination.

Drinkin' - v. Shortened version of "drinking."

Drivin' - v. Shortened version of "driving."

Drop'a - n./prep. Contraction; shortened version of "drop of."

Dweeb - n. A person who is kind of silly, like a nerd.

Eatin' - v. Shortened version of "eating."

El Ni~no - n. A particular weather force; it is a periodic change in the atmosphere and ocean of the tropical Pacific region. It wrecks shit.

Elumphaliteration - 1. n. The state of being that a word can have for having too many letters. As in: "Your shit is stricken wit' some eluphaliteration." **2. v.** The action when someone is given too many books to read, but reads them anyway - consuming the material, but passing it out of the mind like the body passes fibrous food that is too strong for the intestinal tract to digest.

Enron - n. Corporation. An epic emblem of institutionalized, corporate, fraudulent behavior. It had been one of the world's leading energy providers. Listed by Fortune magazine for six years in a row as "America's Most Innovative Company" - worth 101 billion USD in 2001 - Also went bankrupt in 2001, and triggered a rupture to the world's economy.

En - art./con. Contraction; both representing "an" and "and."

Entitical - adj. Having to do with entities.

Expultionists - n. People who expel, or express.

Eyes'a - n./prep. Contraction; shortened version of "eyes of."

'Ey'll - pron./v. Contraction; shortened version of "they'll," or "they will."

Fave - adj. Shortened version of "favorite."

Feelin' - n. Shortened version of "feeling."

Fella - n. Slang form of "fellow."

Ferlinghetti, Lawrence. born: Mar. 24, 1919; Italian-American poet, publisher, artist and activist - well known for his book "A

Coney Island of the Mind" (1958), and being a member of the Beat Movement in poetry.

Ffffttsss - snd. The sound of high-velocity mist being sprayed.

Flamoblamamebo - excl. **I'll never tell.

Flomoxon - n. A mystical creature; rumored to be a cross between flame and oxen. It lives in water and can communicate with any species. When seen, it is usually wearing plaid.

Flowin' - v. Shortened version of "flowing;" sometimes meaning the act of water moving in a stream or river, sometimes meaning the act of a performer creating music improvisationally.

Flyin' - v. Shortened version of "flying."

Folks'll - n./v. Contraction; shortened version of "folks will."

Forgot'em - v./pron. Contraction; shortened version of "forgot them."

Formatic - adj. Having to do with being formal.

Fractalized - v. To have become a fractal.

Freakin' - adj. Shortened version of "freaking," meant in this text as a way to emphasize absurdity.

There is a long list of other meanings for this word. It can mean "dancing," "gosh darn it," or even "going crazy." It can be used as an expletive which is considered more socially acceptable than the word "fucking," if the situation requires no using that particular expletive. It can even mean the act of coitus.

Frickin' - adj. See "Freakin'." (though "frickin'" would be excluded from most of the additional meanings.)

Fromm, Erich. b. March 23, 1900, d. March 18, 1980; renowned thinker; helped create the Frankfurt School of critical theory.

Among other things, he considered love to be an interpersonal creative capacity, rather than an emotion.

Erich Fromm postulated five basic needs:

1. Relatedness - or relationships with others, care, respect, knowledge.

2. Transcendence - that is to say, creativity enough to develop a loving and interesting life.

3. Rootedness - or a feeling of belonging to people and place.

4. Sense of Identity - seeing ourselves as a unique person and part of a social group.

5. A frame of orientation - the need to understand the world and our place in it.

(He didn't include food or shelter there, but we'll let it slide, eh?)

Fuckin' - **adj.** Shortened version of "fucking," meant as a way to emphasize frustration at times, even pleasant amazement. Here, it is often meant to also emphasize absurdity. See also, "Freakin'."

Fuk - **excl.** Similar in meaning to "heck," though, not as widely acceptable socially.

Galaxial - **adj.** Having to do with galaxies.

Ganga - **n.** In this book it is a slang term for marijuana, a plant that is medically safe to ingest, but legally dangerous. The name is etymologically rooted in the name of the river Ganges, a sacred Hindu river that runs through India.

Gautch - **v.** To be defined by your imagination. (Isn't this fun?)

Geez - **excl.** Shortened version of "gee - whiz."

Getin' - **v.** Shortened version of "getting."

Gettin' - **v.** See: "getin'."

Gimmy - **v.** Slang term, meaning "give me..."

Givin' - **v.** Shortened version of "giving."

Glisteners - **n.** People who glisten, or shine.

Glitterized - **adj.** Having to do with having been glittered.

Goin' - **v.** Shortened version of "going."

Goodspace - **n.** Legendary traveling mystic family of the U.S.A, from the era of the 1960's, through the 1990's.

Got'em - **v./n.** Contraction; shortened version of "got them."

Goths - **n.** People who live with a ~darker~ outlook on life.

Groovin' - **1. adj.** Meaning: "good." **2. v.** Dancing.

GrossPointBlank - **n.** Movie; 1997 American comedy film, directed by George Armitage, starring John Cusack and Minnie Driver. It's awesome, you should see it.

Growin' - **v.** Shortened version of "growing."

G's'll - **n./v.** Contraction; shortened version of "gangsters will."

Hale-Bopp - **n.** A newly discovered comet in 1997, visible without visual aids for 569 days - a new record.

Halley - **n.** A periodic comet, occurring every 75-76 years. Last seen in 1986.

Hangin' - **v.** Shortened version of "hanging."

Havin' - **v.** Shortened version of "having."

Hearin' - **v.** Shortened version of "hearing."

He'd'a - **n./v.** Contraction; shortened version of "he would have."

Hedda - **n.** Slang term; shortened version of "header," meaning "one who uses his/her head."

He'd've - **n./v.** See "He'd'a."

Helldom - n. Place; representing the kingdom of Hell.

Helpin' - v. Shortened version of "helping."

Hmmm - snd. The sound of thought.

Hokus pokus - n. Having to do with magical things.

Holdin' - v. Shortened version of "holding."

Hopin' - v. Shortened version of "hoping."

Howloping - v. Please let *your* mind assign this definition.

HR - n. A legal document; known as a House Bill, these documents are part of the creation of law in the U.S.A.

Hyperblues - n. The blues (of jazz origin) when they are stronger than usual.

Inta - prep. Slang version of "into."

Intel-potions - n. Potions that are created for intelligence.

Interstaters - n. People who travel between states. An old term that was used derogatorily by people who were unhappy with newcomers.

Itemry - n. Another word for "items."

I Yie Yi - excl. General term of astonishment.

I yie yie - excl. See: "I yie yi."

Jah - n. Shortened version of "Jehovah." Used extensively, but not exclusively by the Rastafarian community.

Jammin' - v. Shortened version of "jamming," meaning making music in a creative way with others.

Jiss - adj. Slang version of "just," meaning: precisely, exactly, or only a moment ago.

Juss - adj. See: "jiss."

Karmically - adj. Adding an element of Karma to something.

Kats - n. Plural of a jazzer's term that means "people."

'Kause - con. Shortened version of "because."

Kenaf - n. A plant that is not yet widely known enough. See http://www.kenaf.com and http://www.visionfiber.com for more information.

Kicken' - 1. v. Shortened version of "kicking," also; **2. adj.** Good, or grooving, or really interesting or intriguing.

Killin' - v. Shortened version of "killing."

Kin - n. (typically) Family - however, can also mean "can" when spoken, or as is written here, in this book.

Kinda, also: **Kind'a - adj.** Shortened version of "kind of."

Kool-Aid - n. A tasty beverage, available in numerous flavors. Only occasionally spiked, sometimes with vodka, sometimes with LSD. My favorite is grape.

Leanin' - v. Shortened version of "leaning."

Learnin' - v. Shortened version of "learning."

Leavin' - v. Shortened version of "leaving."

Lemmy - v./n. Contraction; shortened version of "let me."

Liminal - adj. A way of describing the spiritual meniscus between the typically seen world, and the spiritual land; such as within the Celtic stories of The Mabinogion.

Livin' - v. Shortened version of "living."

Lobe'll - n./v. Depicting "lobe will;" here, "lobe" means "mind." So this term means "... mind will..."

Lookin' - v. Shortened version of "looking."

Lored - v. To be made into lore, or history - to be retold.

Lot'a - adj. Representing "a lot of."

Lots'a - adj. See: Lot'a.

Lovin' - v. Shortened version of "loving."

Lumony~gummony - n. Your turn! (Remember: it will gautch.)

Make'em - v./n. Shortened version of "make them."

Makin' - v. Shortened version of "making."

Manson's - n. (possessive) Referring to the musician Marilyn Manson.

Marblens - v. [wouldn't you like to know...]

Massagin' - v. Shortened version of "massaging."

Meditational - adj. Having to do with meditation.

Mel Torme. b. Sept 13, 1925, d. June 5, 1999; nicknamed The Velvet Fog, he was known for his freestyle jazz singing in the vein of Ella Fitzgerald, he was also featured on the sitcom Night Court in the 1980's.

Messin' - v. Shortened version of "messing," as in "making trouble for..."

Meth-heads - n. People who are addicted to the drug methamphetamine.

Might've - adv.-ph. Contraction; shortened version of "might have."

Milin' - v. Shortened version of "miling," as in, "making miles."

Misspeak - v. To speak with badly chosen words.

Mmm - adj. The sound of yummy.

Mon - n. A version of the word "man."

Movin' - v. Shortened version of "moving."

Mug's - n./v. Contraction; here, "mug" means "person." The contraction therefor represents "person has."

Must've - adv.-ph. Contraction; shortened version of "must have."

Nappy - adj. Having to do with tightly knotted hair.

Needin' - v. Shortened version of "needing."

None'a - adj./prep. Contraction; shortened version of "none of."

Nonpassivitiy - n. State of being where someone is not passive.

'Nother - adj. Shortened version of "another."

Nothin' - n. Shortened version of "nothing."

Nows - n. Plural state of "now."

Nuthin' - n. See: "nothin'."

Nutz - adj. Meaning "a little nutty," as in crazy, as in "off-the-rocker."

Off'a - adv./part. *In this case:* an adverbial particle, in conjunction with the use of a preposition. Meaning: in a direction away from the speaker or object. As in: "off of."

'Ol, also: **Ol' - adj.** Shortened version of "old."

One'a - adj./prep. Contraction; shortened version of "one of."

Others'll - n./v. Contraction; shortened version of "others will."

Out'a, also: **Outa' - n./prep.** Contraction; shortened version of "out of."

Out'ta - n./prep. Contraction; shortened version of "out to."

Owa - n. Jazzed out version of "hour."

Paintin' - v. Shortened version of "painting."

Patina'd - v. Having grown, or applied, a patina.

Payin' - **v.** Shortened version of "paying."

Penage - **n.** Having to do with pens.

Perihelion - **n.** The point in the orbit of a planet, asteroid or comet where it is nearest to the sun.

Phat - **adj.** modern vernacular term with the meaning of excellent, sexy, prominent, or rich in texture.

Phuched also: **Phucked** - **v.** Slang term meaning "fucked," as in "not in a good way."

Pinkertons - **n.** Private security firm; used extensively, but not exclusively, by companies in the late 19th and early 20th century in the U.S.A., in order to "keep their employees in line." At one point it employed more people than the US Army. Much like a Blackwater of their age, they were well known for being brutal and criminal, while being so well connected that their agents were virtually untouchable by any laws, excepting Ohio, where the agency was illegal for fears that it could be used as a private army.

Pissed, also written as: **Pissed off** - **n.** The state of being angry.

Pisses you off - **v.-ph.** Makes you angry.

Pleasin's - **n.** Shortened version of "pleasings."

Plenty'a - **adj./prep.** Contraction; shortened version of "plenty of."

Pome - **n.** A phonetic spelling of "poem."

Poon - **n.** A slang term for the woman's genitalia.

Positivities - **n.** Plural of positivity.

Post-Frisco - **n.** The time which followed the San Francisco explosion of psychedelic revolution and social upheaval that pushed the 1960's of the U.S.A. into a uniquely interesting time.

Powloping - **v.** Much like eowloping, but with more punch.

Preventally - adv. Having to do with prevention.

Prismed - n. The state of having made a prism out of something.

Pristinely - adv. Having to do with a pristine state.

Protectivism - n. Defensiveness.

Prrrfect - adj. Another way of spelling "perfect."

Puget Sound - n. The body of water, which is East of the Olympic Peninsula, and West of Seattle, Washington.

Pushin' - v. Shortened version of "pushing."

Rappin' - v. Shortened version of "rapping," as in "making music."

Reelings - n. Plural of "reeling." Typically a verb; here it is to be considered a noun for the purpose of imagining a time when one is reeling.

419

Revoltee - n. One who revolts.

Ribbit - n. A noise that a frog makes.

Rollin' - v. Shortened version of "rolling."

Rosnim - n. An indicator, which tells a fisherman where to fish. It is based on electropulses and is designed for two dimensional extraterrestrials who have no sense of a 3rd dimensional plane - in order to help them on relaxing weekends at the lake.

Runnin' - v. Shortened version of "running."

Sake'a - n./prep. Contraction; shortened version of "sake of."

Salinas - n. A city in California (or so they say...).

Sawl - n./v./n. Contraction; a shortened version of "it is all."

Sayin' - v. Shortened version of "saying."

Schemin' - v. Shortened version of "scheming."

Screamin' - v. Shortened version of "screaming."

Seein' - v. Shortened version of "seeing."

Seethin' - v. Shortened version of "seething," so as to say, when one seethes.

Sellin' - v. Shortened version of "selling."

Shinin' - v. Shortened version of "shining."

Show'em - v./n. Contraction; shortened version of "show them."

Showloping - v. (pronounced Shou-low-ping) The movements that the great master Shou Lo Ping used to teach.

Sittin' - v. Shortened version of "sitting."

Skat - n. Type of music, much like bebop, made popular by Cab Calloway, Louis Armstrong, and many others of their age. Rhythmic, yet improvisational in style and fluid in motion; it is still kept as a form of art that is as typically unpennable by most literati, I however, enjoy to.

Slancing - v. What you do to a dreeble in order to make a lummony~gummony gautch.

Sleepin' - v. Shortened version of "sleeping."

Slinkyness - n. The nature of being slinky-like.

Slow-mo - n. Shortened version of "slow motion."

Smellin' - v. Shortened version of "smelling."

Smilin' - v. Shortened version of "smiling."

Soakin' - v. Shortened version of "soaking."

Some'll - n./v. Contraction; shortened version of "some will."

Somethin' - n. Shortened version of "something."

Songing - n. The act of making a song.

Sorta - n./prep. Contraction; shortened version of "sort of."

Sorts'a - n./prep. Contraction; shortened version of "sorts of."

Spankles - v. What a blerk does, especially when dirty.

Speakin' - v. Shortened version of "speaking."

Sprayin' - v. Shortened version of "spraying."

Stalkin' - v. Shortened version of "stalking."

Starin' - v. Shortened version of "staring."

Stead'a - prep.-ph. Contraction; shortened version of "instead of."

Steerin' - v. Shortened version of "steering."

Stripgum - n. A type of bubble gum that comes on a roll.

St. - n. Shortened version of "saint," and "street."

Suh - con. Slang version of "so."

Sunbeat - adj. Having been in the sun for a long time, and having been effected by that fact.

Superspace - n. The space beyond space...

Surfin' - v. Shortened version of "surfing."

Sux - v. Shortened version of "sucks," as in "is not good."

Swimmin' - v. Shortened version of "swimming."

Symptomaticization - n. If I tell you, you'll never wonder about it.

Ta - prep. Slang version of "to."

Takin' - v. Shortened version of "taking."

Talkin' - v. Shortened version of "talking."

Tang - n. double entrendre, 1. Sexual activity. 2. Sharp flavor - like a citrus, low on the sweet.

Tappin' - **v.** Shortened version of "tapping."

Technicals - **n.** Plural of something that requires technical knowledge.

Tell'em - **v./n.** Contraction; shortened version of "tell them."

Tellin' - **v.** Shortened version of "telling."

Tha - **art.** Slang version of "the."

That'cha - **adj./n.** Contraction; shortened version of "that you."

That'd - **n./adv.** Contraction; shortened version of "that would."

That'll - **n./v.** Contraction; shortened version of "that will."

That've - **n./v.** Contraction; shortened version of "that have."

They'll've - **n./v.** Contraction; shortened version of "they will have."

Things'll - **n./v.** Contraction; shortened version of "things will."

Tickly - **adj.** Something that tickles.

Tisk tisk - **excl.** Words spoken as a chide.

Told'em - **v./n.** Contraction; shortened version of "told them."

Toke - **n.** A puff of marijuana.

To've - **v.** Contraction; shortened version of "to have."

Transitionary - **adj.** Having to do with transitions.

Trippy - **adj.** As if to say that something is interesting, in a psychedelic kind of way.

Trowloping - **v.** * \ Can't you just feel it?!? / *

Trup-ble - **n.** Another way to pronounce "trouble."

Tryin' - **v.** Shortened version of "trying."

'Twould - n./adv. Contraction; shortened version of "it would."

Um - excl. A sound of thinking.

Unassurity - n. A state of not being sure.

Underwhelmed - n. The opposite state of being from "overwhelmed."

Unstuck'll - n./v. Contraction; shortened version of [being] "unstuck will."

Use'em - v./n. Contraction; shortened version of "use them."

Utop-AM - v. double entrendre, Created to double the idea of having utopia in the morning, while making the sound of "opium" at the same time.

423

U. - n. Shortened version of "university."

Waitin' - v. Shortened version of "waiting."

Walkin' - v. Shortened version of "walking."

Wanna - v. /prep. Contraction; shortened version of "want to."

Wantin' - v. Shortened version of "wanting."

Wastin' - v. Shortened version of "wasting."

Watchin' - v. Shortened version of "watching."

Wearin' - v. Shortened version of "wearing."

Webelos - n. The younger level of Boy Scouts in the U.S.A.

What'll - n./v. Contraction; shortened version of "what will."

Whoou - excl. This term is more of a sound than a word.

Whored - v. To have been, or been made to be, a whore.

Who've - n./v. Contraction; shortened version of "who have."

Why'd - n./v. Contraction; shortened version of "why did."

Wikky Wikky Wac - adj. Slang term; as if to say "crazy," as in "a crazy thing to do." Often used in musical situations.

Winnie the Pooh - n. Historical figure within children's stories.

Wishin' - v. Shortened version of "wishing."

With'em - adj./n. Contraction; shortened version of "with them."

Woh - excl. As if to say "wow."

Womandom - n. The realm of women.

Writin' - v. Shortened version of "writing."

Wunder - v. A slang spelling of the word "wonder."

424 **Wundrin' - v.** Shortened version of a slang spelling of the word "wondering."

Wunna - v./prep. contraction. Shortened version of "want to."

Xowloping -> v. That's for you to know, and for me to find out.

Y'all - n. Shortened version of "you all," meaning a group of people.

Ya're - n./v. Contraction; shortened version of "you are."

Yield'em - v./n. Contraction; shortened version of "yield them."

Yi - n. Shortened version of "you."

You'a - pron. Possessive pronoun, phonetic version of "you're."

Youngins - n. Children.

Yup - adv. A word used to show agreement.

Zippin' - v. Going fast.

Z'wat - v./n. Shortened version of "is what."

Acknowledgements

As mentioned in the introduction, the visual art that is inside this book was largely made by others for this text, specifically. Most of the art was created by friends from my home of Seattle, Washington.

The photos were already shot, but my dear friend Ann McCormick went through her collection; reviewed and edited, then narrowed down the set we eventually used. We then processed them further and reviewed them again. The results were a pleasant surprise.

The filigree that Brandis Svendson (also well-known for her sculpture in the art world) created was so great to work with! I gave her poems on paper, and she drew right onto the page itself, allowing the poem to inspire the lines. So, what I did with that was to scan the work into a computer, and digitally rebuilt them in the many variations of ways you see throughout the book. Her work actually led me to learn new ways to deal with images, and I was able to do a huge amount of experimentation in the world of graphics manipulation as a result. Truly, thousands of hours were spent moving the pixels around with Brandis's designs. What a bliss that was.

425

With Daniel Young's work, I changed nothing. His work is so stark and crisp, I even only repeated an image one time. His work has a solidity that couldn't allow for the fluid application of the filigree. They balance well that way, methinks.

Each chapter's title-page except one use portions of oil paintings created by the Portuguese artist Santiago Ribeiro. He graciously allowed me to use his images after being introduced to me by a mutual friend. His fantastic creations here in this book are but a glimpse of the surrealism that his brush strokes emit. I am honored by his enjoyment for being included in this book of dreams.

While I was living in Korea (where I stayed for two incredible years, in order to have the time to complete the refinement and production of *Rainshine*), I was helped with photo manipulation by 백정임 (Baek Jeong Im). She is the mother of a student named Bran, who I am pleased to have been able to keep in touch with. They had become friends during my stay in Korea, and I can easily say that they added quite a lot more than digital knowledge to my time spent there. They added a vast wealth of experience while in Korea, taking me and my partner to botanical gardens, temples, museums, and on fantastic hiking trips. I am extremely grateful for all that was shared. The image that is the chapter heading for the chapter titled "Love," was created with her help. She also assisted in most of the photo alterations that happened throughout the book with Ann McCormick's images.

The people mentioned here so far have lent material assistance, and yet I know the list could continue even further. Two years of Korean reality lean a strong impression into a person. I want to thank the people who kept it real for those brief glimpses of life among kimchi. Catie, Sean, Juliette, Laura, Lizzy, Alexander, Molly, Colleen, Justin, Brandon, Rusty, Zaid, Priya, Whit, Lindsay, Lucy, Chris, Young Min, Daniel, Hye Jin, Crow, Jeff, Brad, Wil, and the rest of you: Anyeong haseyo, and kamsamnida.

In the process of making this book, so many people helped out, it's hard to list them all without needing to use an entire chapter to do so. Karen and Steve, Catie, Jenn and Jim, Katja, Craig, Mary and Jamie, Steve and Juicy, Bevin and Morgan, Krista, Michael, Cari, Eli, Sara, Lee and Alexandra, all who opened their homes to me while I was traveling for weeks and months, allowing me to focus on shifting gears with the process of creation. To them, I send great warmth and gratitude. There were certainly others who I can't remember due to the fluidity of the time, and the distance from then to now.

You folks not only helped me by sharing what was yours, you also repeatedly reminded me that friends and family really do make the world a nicer place. You not only fabulously helped me along my trail, but more abstractly, you showed sincere trust in another person and deserve to be recognized. Thank you.

I want to thank those who were distinct inspiration for writings in just one group comment. I have had to change your names for almost all of the poems. And it should be said that my emotions shared in this book do not stand as current sensations, for the time that produced them is gone. But I have one thing rooted deeply in my way, and that is that love never dies. It just goes somewhere else sometimes. Sometimes it is gradual, sometimes it's abrupt. But it is always there, somewhere, waiting to be uncovered and allowed to glow. And so, for the emotions that you elicited, I thank you, even the ones that really sucked.

I want to also thank Luara Moore for her design on the back of the lenticular/hologram that is the cover. And also, my first publisher, Beth Yockey-Jones of Abecedary Press, who's line "I think this thing has legs" one day over lunch at the Georgetown Liquor Company, encouraged my progress and echoed along the way. That is a singular phrase that I think every writer from age 6 is looking to hear a publisher say. You have added a level of professionalism and many intricate librarian-assuaging elements to Rainshine that I sincerely appreciate. You showed me how it was done.

Looking out from the lens that I have on my view, I see quite a few more people who are deserving of appreciation whom I will name by naming the organization, or collective that we participated together because of. The Stronghold Collective, Marmalade, The Machine Crew, Fire Pod, Tahoma Music, Burners Without Borders, Ignition Northwest, Blue House, Burning Man, Goodspace Family, Eugene Circus Kids, Kesey Productions, Love Labs Productions, Utilikilts, The Specialist Clan, AIRFLO, Orange, DPW, Freemont Fine Arts Foundry, F2M, Art of Resistance, The Rachel Corrie Foundation, and Rung Studios. You've served as inspiration, been materially helpful, or simply showed me some love that I could only hope to relate back and out around.

Thank you for that,

Jimmer~ February 15, 2010

Again, thanks.

In relation to the 2025 release, I would add a new page of thanks, for having re-read what was written above - I would add recognition to my helpful guides at Ingram Spark, the distributors and production folk who see my work on the way to the printers. They have been kind enough to offer technical advice and have helped me produce better and grow as a designer in the process. And to my family who are inspiration for me to create books every five years, as I plan to make it to the reunions with new tales to tell. While this book is a reprint, I have created another for them this year that this is being reproduced in parallel with. That book, *Takin' the Long Road*, will be available from July, 2025 at Oblectation.com.

428

This reproduction wouldn't have a purpose if it weren't for the people in my life. Re-reading the pages that preceded this one remind me that there are many people in my life now who have been here for a very long time. I am still regularly associated with more than half of the people and organizations named above, and those that have dispersed into the ether otherwise have done so with grace at a percentage that is respectable. I even sit on the board of directors for one of the organizations named above, which was materially supportive all those years ago, as my gift back in return. I am honored by that and invite anyone in the Seattle area to look up Ignition Northwest for what they may be able to offer you, if you are a producing artist or event designer of sorts.

Without further ado, I will release this collection into the future, in hopes that it serves others in ways that I can not imagine. May your season be healthy, and if it is not, may it be with less pain, and if that is not possible, may the trial not traumatize you beyond healing, and if that is not possible, may you express your frustrations in ways that reduce the pain to where you can still manage. For this world turns the most beautiful flowers into dirt that then feeds new plants. The legend of the lotus is one for us all. We are all part of the cycle. May you be vibrant in your ways.

~ Jimmer Shine, February 6, 2025